Chinese Finance Policy for a New Era

Editors
Dexu He
Institute of Finance and Banking
Chinese Academy of Social Sciences
Beijing, China

Zhixiong Du
Chinese Academy of Social Sciences
Beijing, China

Jiechang Xia
Chinese Academy of Social Sciences
Beijing, China

Translated by
Ms. Han Jie and Ms. Ke Liejuan

Edited by
Ms. Zhu Wenjun

Sponsored by B&R Book Program

ISBN 978-981-33-4053-4 ISBN 978-981-33-4054-1 (eBook)
https://doi.org/10.1007/978-981-33-4054-1

Jointly published with Social Sciences Academic Press
The print edition is not for sale in China Mainland. Customers from China Mainland please order the print book from: Social Sciences Academic Press.
ISBN of the China Mainland edition: 978-7-5201-2959-6

This Palgrave Macmillan imprint is published by the registered company Springer Nature Singapore Pte Ltd.
The registered company address is: 152 Beach Road, #21-01/04 Gateway East, Singapore 189721, Singapore

Preface

The 19th National Congress of the Communist Party of China (the CPC) has made it clear that, "the principal tension facing Chinese society is now between uneven and under development and people's aspiration for a better life". It is of utmost importance for both researchers and practitioners to fully embrace such a change, what it entails, and clearly identify and understand major strategic issues in finance and economy concerning the nation's goals and strategies of building a moderately prosperous society in all respects, a great modern socialist country, and a modern economic system. Xi Jinping Thought on Socialism with Chinese Characteristics for a New Era, which builds on profound insight and effective theoretical framework, enriches the Marxist philosophy, and presents a new notion of development that put the interest of the people front and center. As the political declaration and action plan for the new era, it unveils a new chapter in the theory of Socialism with Chinese Characteristics.

The National Academy of Economic Strategy of the Chinese Academy of Social Sciences, a national academic institution and think tank, is mainly engaged in theory and policy research in the fields of finance and economy. Given its imperative duty to explore how should China develop its financial and economic strategy that fully embodies the spirit of the 19th National Congress of the CPC and Xi Jinping Thought on Socialism with Chinese Characteristics for a New Era, it set up a research team for this purpose shortly after the 19th Congress.

This book consists of fifteen chapters and looks into both the theoretical and practical questions concerning China's development strategy for economy and finance in the new era. Below is a summary of each chapter.

Chapter 1, "Upholding and Improving China's Basic Economic and Distribution System". This chapter reviews how the basic economic and distribution systems have evolved in the ages of the planned economy, the transition economy, and the socialist market economy, and describes the distinctive features of each stage. As the basis upon which our economy is built, these basic systems determine the nature of our society and superstructure and produce an impact on productive forces, according to what Marxism says about the interactions between productivity and relations of production, and between economic base and superstructure.

Chapter 2, "Understanding the Principal Sources of Tension in Chinese Society in the New Era". Understanding the evolution of the principal tension in Chinese society and its new requirements is key to the understanding of the guidelines in the report to the 19th CPC National Congress and the major tasks in the new era. The new era calls for strategic actions to address imbalance and underdevelopment in the nation's economic, political, cultural, social, and ecological progress, with the aim to achieve all-round, balanced, and adequate growth and meet people's needs for a better life in all dimensions.

Chapter 3, "From a Moderately Prosperous Society in All Respects to a Great Modern Socialist Country". By 2020, China is to secure a decisive victory in building a moderately prosperous society in all respects. From 2020 to 2035, socialist modernization will be basically realized. From 2035 to the middle of the twenty-first century, efforts will be made to make China a great modern socialist country that is prosperous, strong, democratic, culturally advanced, harmonious, and beautiful.

Chapter 4, "The Innovation-Driven Development and Nation-building Strategy". China still has a long way to go in its transition toward an innovation-driven development model. A full understanding of risk preference, time preferences, and other cultural characteristics of the society, as well as the opening-up and competition policies is required to implement the innovation-driven development strategy and make China a country of innovators.

Chapter 5, "Expediting the Creation of a Modern Public Finance System: Goals and Strategies". In his report delivered to the 19th National Congress of the CPC, General Secretary Xi Jinping said, "We will expedite the creation of a modern public finance system, and establish a fiscal relationship between the central and local governments built upon clearly defined powers and responsibilities, appropriate financial resource allocation, and greater balance between regions. We will put in place a comprehensive, procedure-based, transparent budget system that uses well-conceived standards and imposes effective constraints; and we will implement performance-based management nationwide. We will deepen reform of the tax system, and improve the local tax system". Built on remarkable achievements in its fiscal and tax reform, China needs to expedite the creation of a modern public finance system that can well accommodate the needs of building a great modern socialist country. This requires us to clearly identify the reform goals and priorities.

Chapter 6, "Deepening Reform of the Tax System and Improving the Local Tax System". The report to the 19th National Congress of the CPC has made it clear from a global and strategic perspective that we will expedite the creation of a modern finance system, "deepen reform of the tax system and improve the local tax system". The local tax system should be based on a framework that matches expenditure responsibility and actual expenditure with fiscal power and fiscal revenue. Using the full budget and under an optimized structure of local government fiscal revenue, we can determine local tax revenue by linking local government expenditures with revenues for special purposes, and generated by assets and debts.

Chapter 7, "Building a Transparent, Standardized, Scientifically-Sound and Binding Budget System". The budget system in the new era must be put in place under the guidance of the Thought on Socialism with Chinese characteristics for a new era and the basic policies stated in the report to the 19th National Congress of the CPC, and must reflect full confidence in the path, theory, system, and culture of socialism with Chinese characteristics. We should draw upon past experience, draft standardized procedures, laws and regulations, identify problems, and improve institutions. We will put in place a comprehensive, procedure-based, transparent budget system that uses well-conceived standards and imposes effective constraints; and we will implement performance-based management nationwide.

Chapter 8, "Priorities of Financial Reform in the New Era". Advancing reform in the financial sector and making China a major player in the global financial market has strategic importance in our endeavor to secure the success of socialism with Chinese characteristics for a new era. Without a strong financial sector, we cannot build a comprehensive industrial system with coordinated development of real economy, technological innovation, modern finance, and human resources. As the principal tension facing Chinese society has evolved, the financial sector should meet people's ever-growing needs for financial services. Also, the problem of uneven and under development across the country should be addressed.

Chapter 9, "Deepening Pricing System Reform and Managing Price Expectations". China is undergoing critical transition to further promote the price reform and innovation in the price mechanism. We should fully understand the distinct features of different growth stages in China, implement the new development concept, and achieve the goals of our economic system reform. Under this new context, while prices should be determined by the market, the government will play a better part in the economy. We will promote the price reform and stabilize price expectations by tighter price supervision, improved price regulation, and better quality in the supply chain, with an aim to optimize resource allocation and increase economic efficiency.

Chapter 10, "Consumption: Mainstay of the Economy and Key Driver of Growth". The report to the 19th National Congress of the CPC has made it clear that "leverage the fundamental role of consumption in promoting economic growth". Insufficient supply, bad environment, and poor infrastructure currently hinder growth in consumption. We will carry out various measures in different areas and strengthen supervision, with a view to promote consumption as the economic "stabilizer" and "ballast" in the new era of socialism with Chinese characteristics.

Chapter 11, "Creating More and Better Jobs". Employment is pivotal to people's well-being. China's labor market has seen significant changes. While modern service industries and new technologies have been creating new jobs, it also poses a serious challenge to the workforce. Thus, employment policies should be tailored to maintain healthy and stable economic growth.

Chapter 12, "Facilitating Rural Rejuvenation by Addressing Key Sources of Tension". The report to the 19th National Congress of the CPC has stated "Pursuing a rural vitalization strategy". Yet agricultural modernization is still the weakest link of the Four Modernizations. National modernization will not be achieved without the modernization of agriculture and rural areas. The Central Committee of the Communist Party of China has given priority to agriculture and rural work. Addressing issues relating to agriculture, rural areas, and rural people has a central place on the work agenda of the Party. According to the report to the 19th National Congress of the CPC and the central rural work conference, the modernization process of agriculture and rural areas must be synchronized with national modernization. The rural revitalization strategy should serve as a guide to action in agriculture and rural work both for now and for a future period.

Chapter 13, "Openness as the Cornerstone of the New Economic System". We will focus on trade, investment, and finance, explore both domestic and overseas markets, ensure support and security, and speed up building new institutions of the open economy. New strategies, new ideas, and new measures will be put in place to build new institutions of the open economy and expand opening-up in the new era of socialism with Chinese characteristics.

Chapter 14, "Digital Trade: Strategic Significance and Policy Recommendations". Digital trade plays an important part both in meeting people's growing needs and in shifting China's economy from high-speed growth to higher-quality development. We should promote digital trade as a major approach to develop new models and new forms of trade and turn China into a trader of quality. Efforts should be made to give priority to the digital economy, improve the digital infrastructure, nurture and foster market players, strengthen legislation and supervision, launch digital trade free trade zones, expand presence in the global market, develop market leaders, and leverage the influence of the Belt and Road Initiative to promote digital trade.

Chapter 15, "Tourism in China: Fresh Aspirations in a New Era". Tourism contributes heavily to addressing basic social tensions, building a moderately prosperous society in all respects, and realizing socialist modernization. It also has a unique role in establishing a new type of international relations, participating in the global governance system, and working to build a community with a shared future for humanity. Hence, tourism in China will assume new functions and become a major contributor to quality life, an instrument for social integration, a breakthrough in deepening reform, the frontier for opening-up, a driver of regional development, an innovator in modern economy, a leader in ecological civilization, a reflector of modern governance, an integral part of the community with a shared future for humanity.

This book is the result of joint efforts of researchers from the School of Finance and Economics. As the team leader, I worked with research fellows Du Zhixiong and Xia Jiechang to review and revise the draft of all chapters and complete the final version. We are still at an early stage in the research on China's economic and financial development strategy in the new era and errors are inevitable. We would greatly appreciate comments and suggestions from experts, scholars, and readers, which we are certain will help us improve our future work.

Beijing, China Dexu He
May 2018

Contents

1 **Upholding and Improving China's Basic Economic and Distribution System** 1
Shuyi Yu
1.1 Why Are These Systems Important 2
1.2 Evolution of the Systems 3
1.3 Primary Tasks 16
1.4 Conclusions and Policy Recommendations 33
References 37

2 **Understanding the Principal Sources of Tension in Chinese Society in the New Era** 39
Shuangshuang Li
2.1 Understanding the Principal Sources of Tension in the New Era 40
2.2 Understanding the New Requirements Imposed 50
References 57

3 **From a Moderately Prosperous Society in All Respects to a Great Modern Socialist Country** 59
Muzi Li
3.1 The Historical Context of the New Goal 60
3.2 Understanding "a Powerful Socialist Modern Country" 66

3.3 *Challenges in Building a Great Modern Socialist Country* 74
3.4 *Construction of a Great Modern Socialist Country at Full Steam Ahead* 79
Reference 82

4 **The Innovation-Driven Development and Nation-Building Strategy** 83
Chunping Zhong
4.1 *Understanding the Strategy* 83
4.2 *How Far Does China Still Have to Go?* 88
4.3 *How to Drive Economic Growth with Innovation?* 90
4.4 *Building a Country of Innovators: Optimal Policy Mix and Institutional Guarantee* 95
Reference 97

5 **Expediting the Creation of a Modern Public Finance System: Goals and Strategies** 99
Zhiyong Yang
5.1 *Significance* 100
5.2 *Goals* 101
5.3 *Strategies* 107
References 117

6 **Deepening Reform of the Tax System and Improving Local Tax Systems** 119
Zhang Bin
6.1 *Socialism with Chinese Characteristics in a New Era Calls for Furthering Taxation Reform* 120
6.2 *Changing Status of Tax Codes: Replacing Rules and Regulations with Legislation* 121
6.3 *Improving Tax Structure and Building a Fairer Tax System* 125
6.4 *Establishing a Modern Multiple Tax System Serving Different Objectives* 130
6.5 *Improving Local Tax Systems and Central-Local Fiscal Coordination* 134

6.6 *Establishing a Modern Tax Collection and Management System* 136

7 **Building a Transparent, Standardized, Scientifically Sound and Binding Budget System** 139
Dehua Wang and Zaozao Zhao
7.1 *A Modern Budget System: Cornerstone of a Modern Public Finance System* 140
7.2 *Making Budgets and Final Accounts More Standardized and Transparent* 141
7.3 *Approaches to Preparing Scientifically Sound Budgets* 145
7.4 *Strengthening Budgetary Constraint on Government Investment and Other Expenditure* 147
7.5 *Implementing Performance-Based Budget Management Nationwide* 149
References 154

8 **Priorities of Financial Reform in the New Era** 155
Dexu He and Chaoyang Wang
8.1 *The Financial Sector Must Serve the Interest of the Real Economy* 156
8.2 *Improving Financial Regulation to Reduce Systemic Risks* 160
8.3 *Deeping Comprehensive Financial Reform and Pursuing Greater Openness* 167

9 **Deeping Pricing System Reform and Managing Price Expectations** 173
Qunqun Zhang, Zhenxia Wang, Di Sheng, and Yongsheng Feng
9.1 *Challenges of Pricing System Reform* 174
9.2 *Explorations and Innovations in Pricing Regulation* 178
9.3 *Deepening Pricing System Reform in Resource and Energy Sectors to Promote Green Development* 182
9.4 *Pricing Reform for Key Commodities and Stabilizing CPI* 190

10 **Consumption: Mainstay of the Economy and Key Driver of Growth** 199
Shaohua Yi and Guiyang Xu
10.1 Changing Role of Consumption in Economic Growth 200
10.2 Main Features of China's Consumer Market 204
10.3 Main Issues in Consumption Growth in China 211
10.4 Policy Recommendations 216

11 **Creating More and Better Jobs** 227
Binbin Zhang
11.1 Employment as the Bedrock of Survival and Living Standard 227
11.2 Optimizing Match Between Labor Supply and Demand and Improving Quality of Employment 229
11.3 New Employment Trends 242
11.4 New Employment Challenges 245
11.5 Policy Recommendations 247
References 250

12 **Facilitating Rural Rejuvenation by Addressing Key Sources of Tension** 251
Zhixiong Du
12.1 Problems and Challenges in Agricultural and Rural Development in the New Era 252
12.2 Rural Development: A Matter of National Interest 257
12.3 Ten Relationships Crucial to Rural Development 261

13 **Openness as the Cornerstone of the New Economic System** 271
Jin Zhao, Xianliang Xia, and Ning Zhang
13.1 Framework and Approaches 271
13.2 Pathway and Achievements 275
13.3 Future Directions and Reform Measures 280

14 Digital Trade: Strategic Significance and Policy Recommendations 297
Jiechang Xia
14.1 If Not Now, When? 298
14.2 Problems and Challenges 303
14.3 Experiences of Other Major Economies 305
14.4 Conclusions and Development Strategies 309
Reference 313

15 Tourism in China: Fresh Aspiration in a New Era 315
Rui Song
15.1 A New Historical Phase 316
15.2 Two Basic Principles 319
15.3 Maxmizing the Contribution of Tourism Toward National Development and Socialist Modernization 321

List of Contributors

Zhang Bin Chinese Academy of Social Sciences, National Academy of Economic Strategy, Beijing, China

Zhixiong Du Chinese Academy of Social Sciences, National Academy of Economic Strategy, Beijing, China

Yongsheng Feng National Academy of Economic Strategy, Chinese Academy of Social Sciences, Beijing, China

Dexu He National Academy of Economic Strategy, Chinese Academy of Social Sciences, Beijing, China

Muzi Li National Academy of Economic Strategy, Chinese Academy of Social Sciences, Beijing, China

Shuangshuang Li National Academy of Economic Strategy, Chinese Academy of Social Sciences, Beijing, China

Di Sheng National Academy of Economic Strategy, Chinese Academy of Social Sciences, Beijing, China

Rui Song Chinese Academy of Social Sciences, National Academy of Economic Strategy, Beijing, China

Chaoyang Wang National Academy of Economic Strategy, Chinese Academy of Social Sciences, Beijing, China

Dehua Wang National Academy of Economic Strategy, Chinese Academy of Social Sciences, Beijing, China

Zhenxia Wang National Academy of Economic Strategy, Chinese Academy of Social Sciences, Beijing, China

Jiechang Xia National Academy of Economic Strategy, Chinese Academy of Social Sciences, Beijing, China

Xianliang Xia National Academy of Economic Strategy, Chinese Academy of Social Sciences, Beijing, China

Guiyang Xu National Academy of Economic Strategy, Chinese Academy of Social Sciences, Beijing, China

Zhiyong Yang Chinese Academy of Social Sciences, National Academy of Economic Strategy, Beijing, China

Shaohua Yi National Academy of Economic Strategy, Chinese Academy of Social Sciences, Beijing, China

Shuyi Yu National Academy of Economic Strategy, Chinese Academy of Social Sciences, Beijing, China

Binbin Zhang National Academy of Economic Strategy, Chinese Academy of Social Sciences, Beijing, China

Ning Zhang National Academy of Economic Strategy, Chinese Academy of Social Sciences, Beijing, China

Qunqun Zhang National Academy of Economic Strategy, Chinese Academy of Social Sciences, Beijing, China

Jin Zhao National Academy of Economic Strategy, Chinese Academy of Social Sciences, Beijing, China

Zaozao Zhao National Academy of Economic Strategy, Chinese Academy of Social Sciences, Beijing, China

Chunping Zhong National Academy of Economic Strategy, Chinese Academy of Social Sciences, Beijing, China

List of Figures

Fig. 1.1	Formation and development of the basic economic system and distribution system	15
Fig. 1.2	Proportions of the number of enterprises by type of ownership in 2010–2016 (*Source* Calculations based on data from *China Statistical Yearbook* of years concerned)	23
Fig. 1.3	Proportions of assets of industrial enterprises by type of ownership in 2007–2016 (*Source* Calculations based on data from *China Statistical Yearbook* of years concerned)	24
Fig. 1.4	Proportion of assets of enterprises above designated size in wholesale and retail trades by type of ownership in 2007–2016 (*Source* Calculations based on data from *China Statistical Yearbook* of years concerned)	26
Fig. 1.5	Proportions of fixed-asset investment of enterprises by type of ownership in 2007–2016 (*Source* Calculations based on data from *China Statistical Yearbook* of years concerned)	27

Fig. 1.6	Proportions of number of employees in urban units by type of ownership in 2007–2016 (*Note* Due to limitations of statistical data, the indicator value is not the proportion in the total number of employees in urban units, but the proportion in the total number of employees in urban units of each type of ownership. Analysis is available only for urban employment due to incomplete statistics of the number of employees in rural areas. *Source* Calculations based on data from *China Statistical Yearbook* of years concerned)	28
Fig. 1.7	Gini coefficient of national per capita disposable income in 2003–2016 (*Source* Website of National Bureau of Statistics, http://www.stats.gov.cn/ztjc/zdtjgz/yblh/zysj/201710/t20171010_1540710.html)	29
Fig. 1.8	Development trend of China's labor productivity in 1978–2016 (*Source* Wind)	30
Fig. 2.1	China's real estate inventory situation and destocking cycle (*Note* The destocking cycle is calculated by dividing the area for sale by the average area sold over the past three years. *Source* Website of National Bureau of Statistics)	46
Fig. 2.2	Prime operating cost rate of enterprises in China (*Source* Wind, the National Bureau of Statistics)	47
Fig. 2.3	Gini coefficient of China (*Source* National Bureau of Statistics)	50
Fig. 11.1	Daily job postings of some industries (*Source* Data from 51job.com)	236
Fig. 11.2	Daily job postings of some industries (*Source* Data from 51job.com)	236
Fig. 11.3	Demand and supply of China's labor market by quarter (*Source* Data from China Human Resources Market Information Monitoring Center's monitoring data collected from about 100 Chinese public employment service agencies)	239
Fig. 11.4	Education of the urban-registered unemployed (*Source* Data from *China Labor Statistical Yearbook* and *China Population* and *Employment Statistics Yearbook*)	241
Fig. 11.5	Trends in worker composition of each industry (*Source* Data from *China Statistical Yearbook*)	242
Fig. 15.1	Tourism—the propeller for building a moderately prosperous society in all respects and for achieving socialist modernization	324

List of Tables

Table 1.1	Key statements on the basic economic system and distribution system in Xi Jinping thought on socialism with Chinese characteristics for a new era	4
Table 1.2	Asset structure by type of ownership in selected years (construction enterprises) (Unit: RMB 100 million, percent)	25
Table 1.3	Growth rates of labor productivity of the world and some economies (Unit: percent)	31
Table 2.1	Indicators of the material and cultural living standards of the Chinese people	42
Table 2.2	Capacity utilization rate in some sectors since 2009 (Unit: percent)	45
Table 2.3	International comparison of quality of life indicators	48
Table 2.4	Income gap between urban and rural areas in China	48
Table 2.5	Regional income gap in China	49
Table 3.1	Statements on socialist modernization of the previous national congresses of CPC	67
Table 3.2	China's GNI per capita In USD	70
Table 3.3	PM2.5 in air Unit: Mg/m^3	78
Table 11.1	Urban job creation in China from 2011 to 2016 (Unit: 10,000 people, RMB100 million)	228
Table 11.2	Education level composition of employed people of China (Unit: percent)	233

CHAPTER 1

Upholding and Improving China's Basic Economic and Distribution System

Shuyi Yu

The report to the 19th National Congress of the Communist Party of China (the CPC) said that, socialism with Chinese characteristics has crossed the threshold into a new era, which unfolds a new chapter in Chinese history. Strategies, guidelines, regulations, and polices of the country's governance system will be reformed or adjusted under the new context. Xi Jinpings Thought on Socialism with Chinese Characteristics for a New Era is the most important achievement of the 19th National Congress of the CPC. It is "a guide to action for all our members and all the Chinese people as we strive to achieve national rejuvenation". With 14 basic policies, it provides an answer that is a systematic combination of theory and practice and addresses "what kind of socialism with Chinese characteristics the new era requires us to uphold and develop and how we should go about doing it".

S. Yu (✉)
National Academy of Economic Strategy, Chinese Academy of Social Sciences, Beijing, China

D. He et al. (eds.), *Chinese Finance Policy for a New Era*,
https://doi.org/10.1007/978-981-33-4054-1_1

1.1 Why Are These Systems Important

According to the above analysis, the top priority in development is to establish sound systems. Why only the basic economic system and distribution system are highlighted? Article 6 of Chapter I General Principle in the Constitution stipulates that, "During the primary stage of socialism, the State adheres to the basic economic system with the public ownership remaining dominant and diverse sectors of the economy developing side by side, and to the distribution system with the distribution according to work remaining dominant and the coexistence of a variety of modes of distribution". The basic economic system and distribution system are the basis of the socialist system with Chinese characteristics and play a decisive role in the development of other systems.

The importance of the basic economic system and distribution system in a nation's institutional system can be well explained by the basic principles of Marxism on productivity and relations of production, and on economic base and superstructure. Marx wrote in the Preface to *A Contribution to the Critique of Political Economy* that the basic tension of all social forms is the tension between productivity and relations of production and the tension between economic base and superstructure.[1] Productivity determines relations of production, which in turn impacts on productivity. Economic base determines superstructure, which in turn impacts on the economic base. The sum total of all production relations constitutes the economic base, and the sum total of social ideology and corresponding legal and political institutions constitutes the superstructure. When there is a conflict, the superstructure will be transformed through revolution or reform to correspond to the economic base. Despite the fact that social advancement is driven by changes in basic social tensions, the economic base is the real basis among the two pairs of basic social tensions.

China's basic economic system and distribution system, which by nature are the economic base, determine the superstructure and impact on the development of productive forces. The economic base consists of the ownership of the means of production, the relationship between people in production, and the distribution relationship. Among these

[1] Karl Marx (1995). Preface to *A Contribution to the Critique of Political Economy*. *Selected Works of Marx and Engels*, vol. 2. People's Publishing House, p. 32.

three factors, the ownership of the means of production and the distribution relationship constitute the basic economic system and distribution system, which by nature are China's economic base. Hence, the basic economic system and distribution system are the base of the economy in the new era and the corresponding guiding ideology.

Xi Jinping Thought on Socialism with Chinese Characteristics for a New Era represents the latest innovative achievement in adapting Marxism to the Chinese context since the 18th National Congress of the CPC. In the development of this theory, the importance and role of the basic economic system and distribution system have been stated and reaffirmed in a number of discussions (see Table 1.1). It is imperative to adapt China's basic economic system and distribution system to socialism with Chinese characteristics in the new era and enrich the implications of Xi Jinping Thought on Socialism with Chinese Characteristics for a New Era.

1.2 Evolution of the Systems

After forty years of reform and opening up, China has become the world's second largest economy by 2018, rising from the 15th place. China has witnessed tremendous economic growth and created the China miracle. General Secretary Xi Jinping said that, "In a couple of decades, China has completed the growth process which developed countries took hundreds of years to achieve. This fully shows that the Chinese people are on the right path".[2] We are now firmly on the right path of socialism with Chinese characteristics, in which the basic economic system and distribution system play a decisive role. These two systems are socialist by nature and in development direction, as the public ownership and the distribution according to one's work remain dominant. Diverse sectors of the economy developing side by side and the coexistence of a variety of modes of distribution demonstrate the Chinese characteristics. The basic economic system and distribution system have been evolving and developing with distinct features in different periods, which reflect changes in the tension between productivity and the relations of production. Under the context of the new era, we will accordingly redefine the implications and extension of the basic economic system and distribution system.

[2] Xi Jinping delivered a keynote speech entitled "Promoting Openness, Inclusion and Peaceful Development" at the City Hall of the City of London on October 21, 2015.

Table 1.1 Key statements on the basic economic system and distribution system in Xi Jinping thought on socialism with Chinese characteristics for a new era

Statements	*Source*	*Significance*
We must adhere to the "two unswervinglies" in order to uphold and improve the basic economic system. The decision proposes reform measures on multiple levels to encourage, support, and guide the development of the non-public sectors of the economy, and to stimulate its vigor and creativity	Explanatory Notes for the *Decision of the Central Committee of the Communist Party of China on Some Major Issues Concerning Comprehensively Deepening the Reform* delivered by Xi Jinping to the Third Plenary Session of the Eighteenth Central Commission of the CPC (November 9, 2013)	It was clear that we must "uphold and improve" the basic economic system: to uphold "two unswervinglies" and to improve by encouraging, supporting, and guiding the development of the non-public sectors of the economy
The decision proposes to vigorously develop a mixed economy. It stresses that a mixed economy with cross-shareholding by and blending of state-owned capital, collective capital, and non-public capital is an important way to materialize the basic economic system of China. It helps to improve the functions of state-owned capital, increase its value, and raise its competitiveness	Explanatory Notes for the *Decision of the Central Committee of the Communist Party of China on Some Major Issues Concerning Comprehensively Deepening the Reform* delivered by Xi Jinping to the Third Plenary Session of the Eighteenth Central Committee of the CPC (November 9, 2013)	It was clear that we must adhere to the dominant role of the public economy and improve the vitality, control, and influence of the state-owned sector in the new circumstances, and create new ways to materialize the basic economic system
We shall introduce flexible micro-economic policies. We must uphold and improve the basic economic system, optimize the market environment, enhance business vitality and potential in consumption. We shall develop positive policies and mechanisms to create open market and investment opportunities and facilitate free movement of goods and fair trade	Speech delivered by Xi Jinping at the Eleventh Meeting of the Central Leading Group for Financial and Economic Affairs (November 10, 2015)	It emphasized the importance of the basic economic system and market environment in micro-economic decision-making

(continued)

Table 1.1 (continued)

Statements	*Source*	*Significance*
China's basic economic system is an important pillar of the socialist system with Chinese characteristics and the foundation of the socialist market economic system. We must unswervingly adhere to the basic economic system with public ownership remaining dominant and the state-owned sector remaining the leading force in the economy. It lays a solid foundation to ensure people of all ethnic groups can share development benefit, and to consolidate the Party's capacity to govern and lead, and to adhere to the socialist system	Speech delivered by Xi Jinping at the 28th group study session of members of the Political Bureau of the Eighteenth Central Committee of the CPC (November 23, 2015)	It reaffirmed the importance and role of the basic economic system and emphasized the basic economic system with public ownership remaining dominant and the state-owned sector remaining the leading force in the economy
We must adhere to China's socialist basic economic system and distribution system. We must work to make income distribution fairer by a redistribution mechanism that leverages taxes, social security, and government transfers. We must safeguard fairness, justice, and equality in the society and narrow income gap to see that the gains of reform and development benefit all our people in a fair way	Speech delivered by Xi Jinping to the special seminar of provincial and ministerial-level officials on grasping and implementing the guiding principles of the Fifth Plenary Session of the Eighteenth Central Committee of the CPC (January 18, 2016)	It explored the basic economic system and distribution system from the perspective of distribution

(continued)

Table 1.1 (continued)

Statements	*Source*	*Significance*
The Party has made it clear that we must adhere to the basic economic system. On this point, we remain unswervingly firm and we are strengthening efforts. It is clearly stated in the Constitution of the Communist Party of China. This will not change, and must not change	Speech delivered by Xi Jinping at a panel discussion with political advisors from the China Democratic National Construction Association and the All-China Federation of Industry and Commerce on the Fourth Meeting during the Twelfth Chinese People's Political Consultative Conference (CPPCC) (March 4, 2016)	It reaffirmed that we must adhere to China's basic economic system: unswervingly adhere to the basic economic system and promote healthy development of economic entities of diverse ownership

1.2.1 The Ownership of the Means of Production and the Distribution System in the Planned Economy Period (1949–1977)

During this period, the ownership of the means of production evolved from diverse sectors of the economy developing side by side to a single socialist public ownership, and the distribution system from exploitation to the practice of "everybody has a share in eating from the same big communal pot".

In the economic recovery period after the founding of the People's Republic of China, five sectors existed in the economy, namely, "state ownership, cooperative economy, individual ownership of peasants and craftsmen, private capitalist economy, and national capitalist economy".[3] In 1952, the Party's general line of the interim period was laid out

[3]The Common Program was adopted by the First Plenary Session of the Chinese People's Political Consultative Conference on September 29, 1949, which acted as an interim constitution. It stipulated that, "The People's Republic of China shall weigh and balance the state ownership, the cooperative economy, the individual ownership of peasants and craftsmen, private capitalist economy, and national capitalist economy in terms of business scope, raw material supply, sales market, work conditions, technology and equipment, fiscal and financial policies. The state ownership shall be the leading force and other sectors shall collaborate and contribute to the development of the entire society and economy".

and the socialist transformation in agriculture, handicraft trade, and capitalist industry and commerce was launched. When the transformation of three sectors was completed in 1956, the individual ownership of peasants changed to the socialist collective organizations and the individual ownership of craftsmen to the handicraft cooperatives. Capitalist industry and commerce first developed into national capitalist public–private partnerships in the whole industry, and later became state-owned enterprises after the government valued their capital and bought out all private holdings. By then, a single (or pure) socialist public ownership of the means of production was formally established in China. With the demise of the exploiting classes, egalitarianism in distribution gradually became mainstream. When the planned economy was finally practiced in China, the egalitarian practice of "everybody has a share of eating from the same big communal pot" became dominant in the distribution system in this period.

1.2.2 *The Ownership of the Means of Production and Distribution System in the Transition Period (1978–2001)*

During this period, the Party acknowledged that, "A socialist society does not necessarily mean a pure form of socialism or absolute equality".[4] Non-public economies recovered and egalitarianism in the distribution system was abandoned. The basic economic system and distribution system in the primary stage of socialism was put in place.

Reform and opening up have transformed China from a socialist planned economy to a socialist market economy. The Third Plenary Session of the Eleventh Central Committee of the CPC marks both the starting point of China's reform and opening up and the end of the planned economy in China. The period from then until China's entry into the World Trade Organization (WTO) in 2001 can be called the transition period. The Protocol on the Accession of the People's Republic of China to the WTO required other WTO members in 15 years to determine

[4] The report to the 13th National Congress of the CPC in 1987, entitled "March on the Path of Socialism with Chinese Characteristics", pointed out that, "In terms of ownership and distribution, the socialist society does not necessarily mean a pure form of socialism or absolute equality. During the primary stage of socialism, we shall develop non-public sectors of the economy with the public ownership remaining dominant, and adopt a variety of modes of distribution with the distribution according to work remaining dominant. We shall encourage some people to get rich first through hard work and integrity in business for the purpose of common prosperity".

whether to recognize China as a market economy, which would reduce trade partners' ability to curb goods sold below cost. In such cases, they could use the price or cost in the Chinese market as evidence in lawsuits against government subsidies and dumping, otherwise a third-party price or cost would be used. Since New Zealand gave China market economy status in 2004, a total of 81 countries have announced that they would regard China as a market economy by the end of 2016. Facts show that China has transformed from a planned economy to a market economy and joined WTO under commitment to a fully open market economy. We can safely take China's entry into the WTO as the end of the transition period. Although China failed to fully embrace the open market-oriented policies at that time, China has endeavored to meet the WTO rules by speeding up and deepening market reforms. Thus China's joining the WTO can also be seen as the starting point of the socialist market economy period.

In light of the basic economic system and distribution system, during the transition period, reform and opening up have broken down the single public ownership of means of production under the planned economy and allowed non-public sectors to be gradually accepted and recovered. They have also dismantled the egalitarian practice of "everybody has a share of eating from the same big communal pot" in the distribution system and set "distribution according to work" as the basic principle of distribution, while other modes of distribution were gradually recognized and accepted.

Non-public sectors of the economy were recognized and legitimated in succession, with first the individual ownership, then the foreign capital economy, and later the private ownership. In the 11th National Congress of the CPC, it was first mentioned that, "We shall encourage the individual ownership of urban and rural working people, as a necessary and useful complement to the socialist public economy, to operate within the limits approved by the State and develop under the industry and commerce supervision". The Fifth Plenary Session of the Fifth National People's Congress in 1982 adopted *the Constitution of the People's Republic of China*, in which the individual ownership was written.[5] The Third Plenary Session of the Twelfth Central Committee of the CPC in

[5] The Fifth Plenary Session of the Fifth National People's Congress in 1982 adopted *the Constitution of the People's Republic of China*. It stipulated that, "The individual ownership of urban and rural working people, operated within the limits prescribed by law, is a complement to the socialist public economy. The state protects the lawful rights

1984 adopted the *Decision of the Central Committee of the Communist Party of China on the Reform of the Economic System*, in which it stated that, "We shall introduce foreign capital, attract foreign investment to set up equity joint ventures, co-operative joint ventures and wholly-owned foreign enterprises in China. They are necessary and useful supplements to China's socialist economy". The foreign investment economy was thus recognized. In the 13th National Congress of the CPC, private ownership was recognized. It pointed out that, "The development of the private ownership to some extent will promote production, increase market activities, enhance employment, and meet people's needs for better life. It is a necessary and useful supplement to the public economy". Also for the first time, public ownership was recognized as dominant in the economy. It stated that, "The public ownership must remain dominant in the primary stage of socialism" and "we shall continue to develop other sectors of the economy with the public ownership remaining dominant". The First Session of the Seventh National People's Congress in 1988 adopted the Amendment to the Constitution of the People's Republic of China, in which the private ownership was written.[6] An ownership framework of "public economy as the mainstay with non-public economy as the supplement" began to shape in China.

The wording of "diverse sectors of the economy developing side by side" first appeared in the report to the 14th National Congress of the CPC. Then the *Several Decisions of the Central Committee of the Communist Party of China on Establishing a Socialist Market Economy System* adopted by the Third Plenary Session of the Fourteenth Central Committee of the CPC said that, to achieve the goal of putting in place the socialist market economic system, "we must adhere to the principle of the public ownership remaining dominant and diverse sectors of the economy developing side by side". The 15th National Congress of the CPC stressed four "upholds and improves" for building

and interests of the individual ownership. The state guides, helps and supervises the individual ownership by exercising administrative control".

[6]The First Session of the Seventh National People's Congress in 1988 adopted the Amendment to the Constitution of the People's Republic of China. It stated that, "The State permits the private sector of the economy to exist and develop within the limits prescribed by law. The private sector of the economy is a complement to the socialist public economy. The State protects the lawful rights and interests of the private sector of the economy, and exercises guidance, supervision and control over the private sector of the economy".

a socialist economy with Chinese characteristics. Among them, "uphold and improve the basic economic system with the socialist public ownership remaining dominant and diverse sectors of economy developing side by side" was given top priority. It also said that, the basic economic system "is determined by the nature of socialism and China's conditions in the primary stage", which means it bears distinctive features of the primary stage of socialism. The basic economic system was written in the Constitution[7] in 1999 when the Amendment to the Constitution of the People's Republic of China was adopted on the Second Session of the Ninth National People's Congress. Thus the basic economic system in the primary stage of socialism was formally established in China.

The distribution system in the transition period also underwent a series of institutional changes with the reform of the ownership of the means of production. Specific provisions on distribution were first written in the second Constitution of the People's Republic of China adopted by the First Session of the Fourth National People's Congress in 1975. It was clear in different versions of the Constitution that the socialist distribution principle was the principle of "from each according to his ability, to each according to his work". However, it was put in different ways: "He who does not work, neither shall he eat" and "from each according to his ability, to each according to his work" in the Constitutions of 1975 and 1978; "The system of socialist public ownership supersedes the system of exploitation of man by man; and it applies the principle of 'from each according to his ability, to each according to his work'" in the *Constitution* of 1982. The 13th National Congress of the CPC set the basic principle as "the distribution according to work" under the context of the primary stage of socialism and revised it to "the distribution according to work remaining dominant and other modes of distribution as supplement". Efficiency and fairness in the distribution were also stressed. The 14th National Congress of the CPC reiterated such principle of distribution and made it clearer about efficiency and fairness in the distribution: "We shall encourage outstanding performance, boost efficiency, allow moderate growth of the income gap while at the same time guarding against polarization and working toward shared prosperity". The 15th National Congress of the CPC redefined the distribution system at the

[7] In 1999 the Second Session of the Ninth National People's Congress adopted The Amendment to the Constitution. It stipulated that, "During the primary stage of socialism, the State adheres to the basic economic system with the public ownership remaining dominant and diverse sectors of the economy developing side by side".

institutional level and changed the role of "other modes of distribution" from "supplement" to "coexistence". Specifically, it said that, we must "adhere to the distribution system with the distribution according to work remaining dominant and the coexistence of a variety of modes of distribution", and "adhere to distribution according to work and according to factors of production and give priority to efficiency with due consideration to fairness". In Article 6 of the Amendment to the Constitution of the People's Republic of China adopted by the Second Session of the Ninth National People's Congress in 1999, it added the clause on the basic economic system in the primary stage of socialism and the provision of "adhere to the distribution system with the distribution according to work remaining dominant and the coexistence of a variety of modes of distribution". By then, China's distribution system in the primary stage of socialism has been formally established.

1.2.3 Basic Economic System and Distribution System in the Socialist Market Economy Period (2002 to Present)

During this period, the implications of the basic economic system and distribution system in the primary stage of socialism have been continuously enriched, and more distinct features can be seen.

In the socialist market economy period, it is critical to properly handle the relationship between the government and the market. The government should create a supportive environment that gives full play to the market and enables all market participants to grow well. This will accelerate development of the socialist market economy and do full justice to the strengths of China's socialist system. The basic economic system should therefore be the first and foremost institution that the government will put in place.

The 16th National Congress of the CPC further explored how to uphold and improve the basic economic system and put forward the principle of "unwaveringly consolidate and develop the public sector of the economy, unswervingly encourage, support and guide the development of the non-public sector". It also explained the relationship between adhering to the public ownership remaining dominant and promoting the development of the non-public sectors, and stated that these two elements are "integral components in the socialist modernization and should not be considered contradictory. Diverse sectors of the economy are mutually reinforcing and can tap into their strengths in the market competition for common growth". This principle enriches the implications of the basic economic system and determines the basic direction to uphold and improve the basic economic system in the socialist market economy period. With a clear direction ahead, the basic economic system displays more distinct features of the era.

First, in terms of the creation of a fair market environment. The 17th National Congress of the CPC reiterated the principle of "Two Unswervinglies" and put forward that "We need to ensure equal protection of property rights, and create a new situation in which all economic sectors compete on an equal footing and reinforce each other". The 18th National Congress of the CPC changed it to "ensure that economic entities under all forms of ownership have equal access to factors of production in accordance with the law, compete on a level playing field and are protected by the law as equals". The Third Plenary Session of the Eighteenth Central Committee of the CPC further summarized it as "equal rights, equal opportunities and fair rules". It also proposed that both the public sector and the non-public sectors "are integral components of the socialist market economy", and they "are the basis of China's economic and social development". In the protection of property rights, it stated that, "the property rights of the public economy are inviolable, as are the property rights of the non-public economy". In the protection of the rule of law, the Fourth Plenary Session of the Eighteenth Central Committee of the CPC stated that, "the socialist market economy is one under rule of law by nature", "we shall improve the legal system of the socialist market economy", and "consolidate property rights protection systems with fairness at the core, strengthen protection of the property rights of economic organizations of all kinds of ownership systems and individuals". The Fifth Plenary Session of the Eighteenth Central Committee of the CPC stressed "the protection of the rights and interests of various sectors of the economy according to law", and stated that, "we encourage the private enterprises to enter more industries according to law, introduce the non-state capital in the reform of state-owned enterprises (SOEs), and to stimulate vigor and creativity of the non-public sectors". During this period, the growth path of the basic economic system focused more on creating institutional conditions for the development of the non-public sectors of the economy, which means creating a fair market environment in terms of institutions to meet the needs of the development of the socialist market economy. Due to path dependence in the process of market reform, the non-public sectors of the economy faced many hidden barriers that should be removed in the basic system.

It responds to the call of the times to protect the legal status and the role of the non-public sectors in the market economy and push them as a new driving force for economic growth.

Second, in terms of the realization form. Early in the transition period, China has started to work on the realization form of public ownership[8] and made some achievements in the era of socialist market economy period. Firstly, we made clear that the shareholding system is the main realization form of public ownership. Secondly, we made clear that the mixed-ownership economy is the main realization form of the basic economic system. The report to the 16th National Congress of the CPC stated that, "we shall actively promote the shareholding system and develop a mixed ownership economy". The Third Plenary Session of the Sixteenth Central Committee of the CPC discussed various forms of the public ownership and made clear that, "the shareholding system shall be the main realization form of the public ownership" and "vigorously develop a mixed ownership economy that state-owned capital, collective capital, non-public capital and other cross-holdings are crossed-shared and integrated". The 17th National Congress of the CPC proposed that, "We shall develop a mixed-ownership economy based on the modern property rights system". The Third Plenary Session of the Eighteenth Central Committee of the CPC made it clear that the mixed-ownership economy is the main realization form of the basic economic system, and the state-owned sector and other non-public sectors of the economy are allowed to develop into a mixed-ownership economy. The implications of the basic economic system have thus been enriched in that, both the public ownership and the non-public economies can be realized under the mixed-ownership economy, various ownership economies can be cross-shared, and employee shareholding in mixed-ownership enterprises will benefit both capital owners and workers.

[8] The report to the 13th National Congress of the CPC noted the shareholding system and horizontal economic union in the reform and recognized their role. The report to the 14th National Congress of the CPC put forward that "various economic entities can form economic union at their own will" and suggested the piloting of the shareholding system. The report to the 15th National Congress of the CPC made it clear that "the public ownership should have diverse forms of realization", and changed the definition of the shareholding system from "an organizational form of socialist enterprise property" in the 13th National Congress of the CPC to "an organizational form of capital of modern enterprises". It also stated that the state-owned component and the collective component of the mixed ownership economy should also be included in the public ownership economy.

During the socialist market economy period, the distribution system has continuously been enriched. The 16th National Congress of the CPC deepened the understanding of distribution according to factors and set it as the distribution principle, saying that "...establish the principle of distribution according to contribution of factors of production including labor, capital, technology, and management". With a deeper understanding of efficiency and fairness in distribution, the report said that, efficiency should be the key consideration in primary distribution by means of market tools and fairness in secondary distribution by means of government measures. The 17th National Congress of the CPC integrated the distribution according to factors into the distribution system, and further stressed efficiency and fairness in distribution by saying that, "A proper balance should be struck between efficiency and fairness in both primary and secondary distribution, with particular emphasis on fairness in secondary distribution". The share of individual income in the distribution of national income and the share of work remuneration in primary distribution should be raised, and property income should be recognized and encouraged. The 18th National Congress of the CPC further expanded the tasks of the distribution system reform in that, "we must increase individual income in step with economic development and work remuneration in step with improvement in labor productivity", and proposed to improve the mechanism of primary distribution and the regulatory mechanism of secondary distribution.

The 19th National Congress of the CPC made a major judgment that socialism with Chinese characteristics has crossed the threshold into a new era, which renders the basic economic system and distribution system with distinct features of the new era. We have seen productivity further develop and the principal tension facing Chinese society evolve in the new era. The basic economic system and distribution system which represent the production relations should be further reformed to accommodate the development of the productive forces and to address the principal tension. Meanwhile, it must be clear that the basic dimension of the Chinese context and biggest reality in the new era is that our country is still in the primary stage of socialism, another major judgment made in the report of the 19th National Congress of the CPC. We must therefore uphold and improve the basic economic system and distribution system in the new era. This is a foremost historic mission after forty years of reform and opening up, and is determined by the status and role of the economic basis in social development (Fig 1.1).

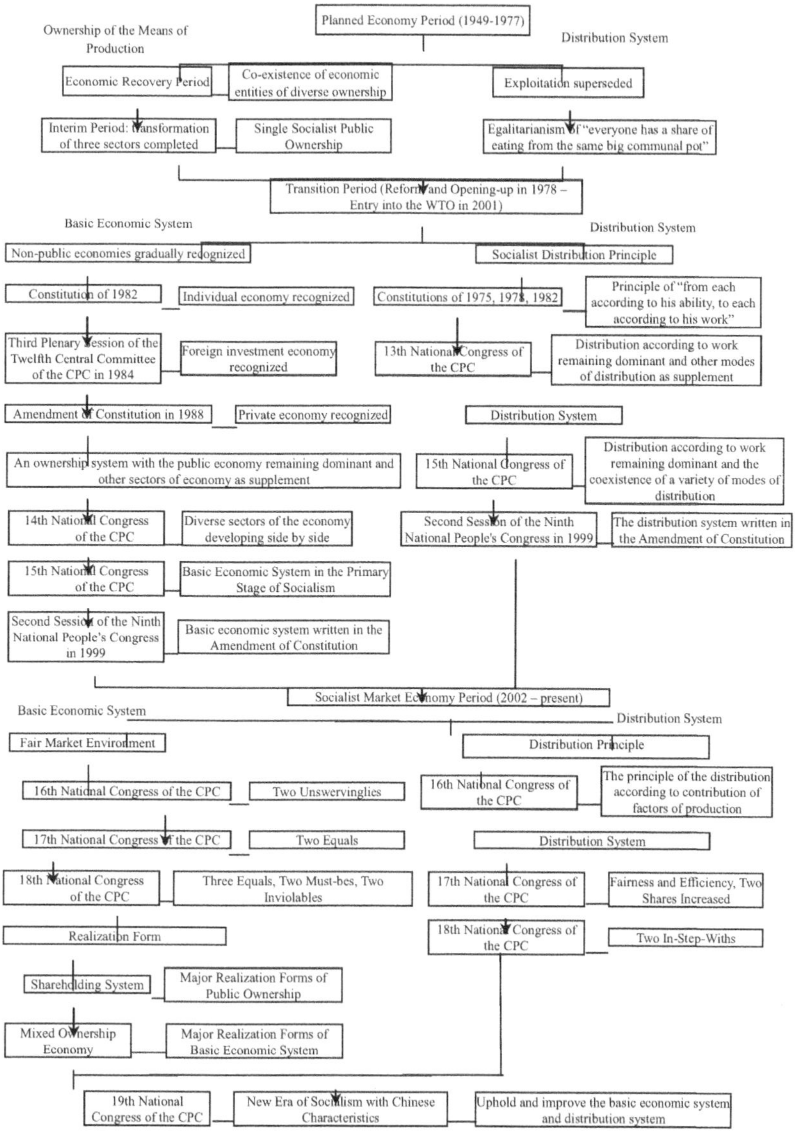

Fig. 1.1 Formation and development of the basic economic system and distribution system

1.3 Primary Tasks

In a historical context, the basic economic system and the distribution system have been formed and developed along two paths, one in socialism and the other in market economy. As China's social nature and economic system have not changed, the basic economic system and distribution system must follow such two growth paths and consolidate further in the new era. Under these premises, we must properly view the opposition unity of the two paths. While they achieve unity in the dimension of the socialist market economy, the two diverge in terms of efficiency and fairness, quantity and quality, and growth and stability. At present, many trends of thought rise out of these divergences. Since the economic basis is of great importance to national governance, we must be clear that the primary task of socialism with Chinese characteristics in the new era is to adhere to and improve the basic economic and distribution system, and grasp and internalize the tension between and within them by reaching consensus in theory and creating synergies in practice.

1.3.1 Reaching Consensus in Theory

The unity of the two paths, which is easy to understand, means that they converge in the process of the establishment and development of the socialist market economy. Both have advanced the establishment and improvement of the basic economic system and distribution system as times change. Then how shall we understand the opposition between them? On the one hand, China's socialist nature requires the public ownership and distribution according to work remain dominant. On the other hand, the improvement of the market economic system requires that economic entities of diverse ownership have equal market status and all factors participate in the distribution equally.

Why does the socialist nature require that the public ownership and distribution according to work remain dominant? This can be demonstrated by the Marxist philosophy on the relationship between productive forces and production relations. Marxism believes that the basic nature and development direction of a society is determined by the dominant ownership of the means of production. The "decisive difference" between a socialist society and a capitalist society "is whether it organizes production...on the basis of the public ownership of all means of production",[9] because the production relations must adapt to the development of productive forces. It is the common law of all kinds of society. In the capitalist society, the means of production are privately owned by capitalists, while the productive forces bear a social nature. As productive forces constantly grow and display stronger social attributes, the production relations with the capitalist private ownership as dominant in the economy hinder the development of productive forces. To resolve this tension, the relations of production must be changed to replace the private ownership with the public ownership of the means of production, thereby capitalism with socialism.

The conclusion will be even clearer when the distribution relationship is introduced. Since the ownership system of the means of production determines the distribution system, China's basic economic system and distribution system must match in pair, that is, the public ownership remaining dominant and distribution according to work, diverse sectors of the economy developing side by side and the coexistence of a variety of modes of distribution. Under the socialist public ownership, members of society have equal ownership over the means of production, and workers are capital owners. Distribution according to work is then formed on such basis, which can inspire workers and eliminate the loss of efficiency caused by unequal labor status. To achieve common prosperity is an essential requirement of socialism, and a goal that the CPC has worked tirelessly to achieve by mid twenty-first century, as proposed on the 19th National Congress of the CPC, as well as a distinctive feature of the new era. Common prosperity gives special emphasis to fairness in distribution. Marx's labor theory of value holds that the value of a commodity derives from the amount of labor necessary to produce that commodity. Distribution according to work, which is based on the quantity and quality of labor, can fully ensure fairness in distribution and hence is an important condition to achieve common prosperity. To include factors other than labor in the distribution process is to allow differences and lead to the division of rich and poor, which is contrary to the goal of common prosperity.

Therefore, to sustain the socialist nature of the Chinese society, we must adhere to the public ownership and distribution according to work

[9] *Selected Works of Marx and Engels*, vol. 4. People's Publishing House, 2012, p. 693.

remaining dominant. This, on one hand, matches the social attributes of productive forces, and on the other hand, achieves both fairness and efficiency and further drives the growth of productive forces. If the public ownership and distribution according to work no longer remain dominant in the economy, the social nature of socialism is otherwise rejected, and the production relations no longer match with productive forces. The basis for further development of productive forces will no longer exist.

Why does the market economic system require that economic entities of all ownership have equal market status and that all factors participate in the distribution equally? The market economy, as such a vehicle of economic operation, must jointly work with the social system to promote economic growth and social progress. By far, both socialist and capitalist countries have chosen the market economy, for the market economy has been recognized as the most efficient and dynamic economic operation model. It is conducive to liberating and developing the productive forces, as determined by the characteristics of the market economy.

Regarding the characteristics of the market economy, there are many conclusions drawn from different perspectives. Li Zhenhuan and Quan Heng (1993) summarized ten characteristics of the market economy: autonomy, equality, competitiveness, efficiency, serviceability, openness, risk, legal principle, macrocontrol, and innovation.[10] Xiang Kaibiao and Huang Li (2017) believed that economic freedom is the premises of the market economy, property rights protection is the foundation of the market economy, and entrepreneurship is the soul of the market economy, and analyzed that the Chinese economy has such basic characteristics as economic freedom, property rights protection, and entrepreneurship and is an important type of modern market economy.[11] The characteristics of the market economy in the textbook of political economy are summarized as market allocation of resources, clear definition of rights, responsibilities, and profits of economic entities, market competition as the basis of economic operation, implementation of necessary and effective macrocontrol, and the internationalization of economic relations.[12]

[10] Li Zhenhuan and Quan Heng, Characteristics of Market Economy, *Journal of Social Sciences*, No. 4, 1993.

[11] Xiang Kaibiao and Huang Li, The Chinese Economy Is an Important Type of Modern Market Economy, *People's Daily*, March 16, 2017.

[12] Song Tao, *Political Economy*, 10th Edition, China Renmin University Press, 2013.

Despite differences in these conclusions, it is unanimously agreed that all economic entities in the market economy must be treated equally, for the market economy follows the law of value, the law of supply and demand, and the law of competition. A fair and just environment in the market economy is required for these laws to work. Specifically, the market economy requires that all economic entities have equal status in production, exchange, consumption, and distribution. And they have equal access in acquisition and provision of the factors of production, enjoy equal opportunities for market access and discretion in decision and operation, have their due share of income in distribution according to their respective contribution made by the factors of production they provide, bear tax and other burdens on equal basis, receive equal protection of the law, and compete in fair play. Otherwise, if economic entities of different types of ownership have different economic status and cannot have their due share in distribution according to the contribution of various factors of production, we are not following the path of market economy.

What impact will the differences between the two growth paths taken by the basic economic system and the distribution system have in theory? Divergence of the two paths occurs mainly on the dominant component in the economy. Socialism emphasizes public ownership as the mainstay of the economy, while market economy emphasizes equal treatment. Such difference gives rise to a numnber of different positions, which have a direct impact on China's reform. As the ownership of the means of production determines the distribution system, these trends of thought focus mainly on the basic economic system.

First, support for privatization. It regards the development of the market economy as the core, and believes that the public ownership is inefficient and cannot be compatible with the market economy. A true market economy can only be established by privatization. The theoretical basis of this trend of thought is neoliberalism or market fundamentalism in western countries, supported by theories on human selfishness, eternal nature of private ownership, and universal market. They want to lead the reform of state-owned enterprises to privatization, on the grounds that state-owned enterprises are inefficient and their existence undermines the order of the market economy, which results in "the state advances, the private sector retreats" in market competition. The core of this view is to modify China's basic economic system and even subvert the socialist system.

Second, rejection of the dominance of the state ownership. Also guided by neoliberalism, one view holds that state-owned enterprises are state-monopolized, where regulation of the market competition mechanism does not work. They should leave the free competition market not competing with other market entities, and enter into markets that other market entities are unable or unwilling to enter, and provide public goods in market failure. Another view is neoliberalism disguised as "Marxism". It holds that the state ownership is "bureaucratic monopoly capital" and should no longer be dominant in the economy, while the individual ownership and private ownership should apply to the "**people**" for their collective benefit and be given the main role in the economy.

Third, a misinterpretation of Marxism on this view, economic development is what is important. As long as the economy grows, it matters little whether state ownership remains dominant, and no special emphasis should be given. Something new here is that it denies the scientific nature of Marxism or considers Marxism out-of-date. It advocates abandoning or amending Marxism in the process of improving the theoretical system of socialism with Chinese characteristics. For instance, it denies that the ownership of the means of production determines the nature of a society, on the grounds that the non-public sectors exist and grow rapidly. It denies that the elimination of exploitation is the essence of socialism, on the grounds that wage labor still exists and grows, and even denies the theory of surplus value. It regards the work to encourage, support, and guide the development of the non-public sectors as the practice to develop the capitalist economy, a capitalist economy under socialism and the dictatorship of the proletariat. It even considers the socialist economy with Chinese characteristics as a mixed economy, with the dual nature of socialism and capitalism.

Fourth, support for orthodox Marxism. One view is that we must strictly follow the basic principles of Marxism in the development of socialism. It calls for efforts to expand and enhance the socialist public ownership, eliminate private ownership and exploitation as soon as possible, and establish a single socialist public ownership. Another view holds that the practice of socialism with Chinese characteristics is at odds with the basic principles of Marxism, for it not only fails to eliminate private ownership and exploitation, but also encourages and supports their development, and thus undermines socialism with Chinese characteristics.

With respect to the growth path of the basic economic system and that of the distribution system, we find out that these positions stem from the problematic notion that since socialism and the market economy exist in isolation from each other, so must public ownership and other sectors of the economy. The interaction between productive forces and relations of production is also ignored. General Secretary Xi Jinping pointed out that, "Whether the public-owned economy or the non-public sectors, both have encountered tensions and problems and are facing difficulties and challenges in their course of development. We must work together to find a solution. But, do not let a leaf before the eye shut out Mount Tai. Do not seize upon one point and lose sight of the whole picture. Any views that deny either the public economy or the non-public sectors are all wrong, for they are against the fundamental interests of the overwhelming majority of the Chinese people, and against China's reform and development needs".[13] Therefore, the primary task to promote the development of China's basic economic system and distribution system in the new era is to achieve unity in thinking and eliminate cognitive differences.

1.3.2 Synergies in Practice

To apply theoretical consensus in practice, we must collect information on the development level and the share of the factors of production in distribution of different types of economies in China, and consolidate them to create synergies in the relations of production and promote productivity at a higher starting point.

According to the explanation of indicators statistics by the National Bureau of Statistics, enterprises are classified into three categories, namely domestic-funded enterprises, enterprises with investment from Hong Kong, Macau, and Taiwan, and enterprises with foreign investment, in the light of the registration status of an enterprise in industrial and commercial administration agencies. Domestic-funded enterprises include state-owned enterprises, collective-owned enterprises, cooperative enterprises, joint-stock ownership enterprises, limited liability corporations,

[13] Speech delivered by General Secretary Xi Jinping at a panel discussion with political advisors from the China Democratic National Construction Association and the All-China Federation of Industry and Commerce on the Fourth Meeting during the 12th Chinese People's Political Consultative Conference (CPPCC) on March 4, 2016.

share-holding corporations limited, private enterprises, and other enterprises. By the nature of the ownership of the means of production, state-owned enterprises, collective-owned enterprises, joint-stock cooperative enterprises[14] are classified as the public economy; private enterprises, enterprises with investment from Hong Kong, Macau, and Taiwan, and enterprises with foreign investment are classified as the non-public sectors; and joint ownership enterprises, limited liability companies, share-holding corporations limited and other enterprises are classified as the mixed economy with both public and non-public components of the economy. Due to limitations of statistics, data of different economic components in the mixed economy are not collected separately. In the absence of such detailed statistics, we can only include them in a broad category of the mixed economy. Under this classification standard, we can use statistics to conduct quantitative studies on the development of the public-owned economy, the non-public sectors, and the mixed economy in China as well as the structural relationship between them.

1.3.2.1 First, Analysis of Corporate Structure

Currently, data on "Number of Enterprises by Registration Status of Enterprises" published by the National Bureau of Statistics start from 2010. Calculated by classification, the percentage of the number of enterprises in the public economy in China has remained low, with a peak value of only 6.41 percent in 2010 and falling ever since to 2.34 percent in 2016. The percentage of the number of enterprises in the non-public sectors has been much higher with 75.2 percent the highest and 70.62 percent the lowest. The percentage of the number of enterprises in the mixed economy had been increasing from 18.39 to 26.62 percent before 2015, and then declined to 24.19 percent in 2016 (see Fig. 1.2).

Analysis of the raw data published shows that percentages of the number of state-owned enterprises, collective-owned enterprises, joint-stock cooperative enterprises, joint ownership enterprises, limited liability corporations, share-holding corporations Limited, private enterprises,

[14] Joint-stock cooperative enterprise is a collective economic organization that is based on the cooperative system in which all employees make contributions and hold shares of the firm, together with a certain proportion of social capital. It has discretion in management and operations, bears profits and losses, allows joint labor and democracy in administration, and implements distribution according to work and pays dividends according to shares.

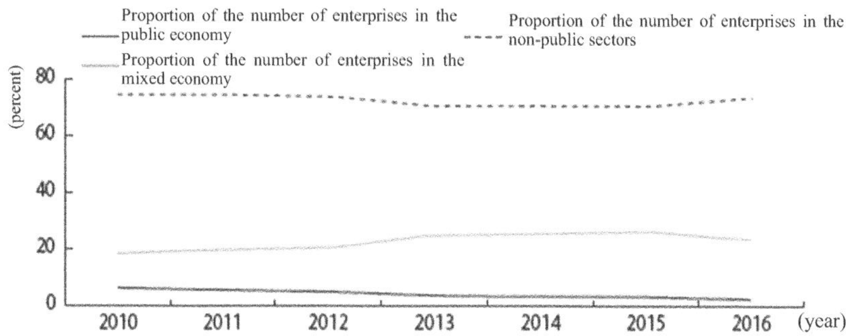

Fig. 1.2 Proportions of the number of enterprises by type of ownership in 2010–2016 (*Source* Calculations based on data from *China Statistical Yearbook* of years concerned)

enterprises with investment from Hong Kong, Macau, and Taiwan, enterprises with foreign investment and other enterprises in China in 2016 were 0.91 percent, 0.97 percent, 0.46 percent, 0.14 percent, 17.32 percent, 1.20 percent, 71.83 percent, 0.81 percent, 0.84 percent, and 5.53 percent, respectively. The proportion of private enterprises is the largest, over 70 percent, while the ones of state-owned enterprises, collective-owned enterprises, and joint-stock cooperative enterprises are less than 1 percent, respectively.

1.3.2.2 Next, Analysis of Asset Structure

As data on assets by type of registration are only available for industry, construction, wholesale and retail trades, percentage contribution of these three sectors are 33.3 percent, 6.7 percent, and 9.6 percent, respectively, and 49.6 percent in total in the GDP increase, in light of the industry-by-industry value-added breakdown of GDP in 2016. Although statistics can not fully cover the situation, the analysis of these industries can be representative. Due to different statistical dimensions used in collecting data on assets of the three industries, we analyzed them separately. As shown in Fig. 1.3, in a decade from 2007 to 2016, the percentage of assets of industrial enterprises with public ownership in the economy dropped from 26.77 to 15.12 percent, or more than one percentage point each year. The percentage of assets of industrial enterprises in the non-public sectors remained stable at around 43 percent. The percentage of assets

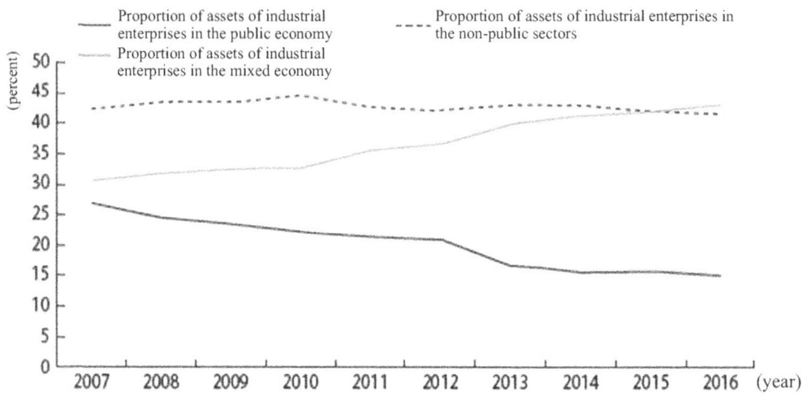

Fig. 1.3 Proportions of assets of industrial enterprises by type of ownership in 2007–2016 (*Source* Calculations based on data from *China Statistical Yearbook* of years concerned)

of industrial enterprises in the mixed economy rose from 30.83 to 43.22 percent, ranking first among the three in 2016.

Looking back at 2000, the proportions of assets of industrial enterprises in the public economy, in the non-public sectors, and in the mixed economy were 56.87 percent, 23.44 percent, and 19.69 percent, respectively.[15] With the change of the times, the ownership structure of industrial enterprises has undergone fundamental changes. Assets of the public economy have seen a change from absolute dominance to the lowest proportion, while assets of the mixed economy have seen just the opposite.

Due to incomplete and discontinuous statistics of the construction industry, comparison is made only for selected years. As shown in Table 1.2, the proportion of assets of state-owned construction enterprises continued to decline from 53.07 percent in 1998 to 26.36 percent in 2007, and then to 17.1 percent in 2016. The proportion of assets of collective-owned construction enterprises fell even faster, from 31.17 percent in 1998 to 5.43 percent in 2007, and then to 1.47 percent in 2016.

[15] *China Statistical Yearbook* (2001), http://www.stats.gov.cn/tjsj/ndsj/2001c/mulu_m.htm.

Table 1.2 Asset structure by type of ownership in selected years (construction enterprises) (Unit: RMB 100 million, percent)

Indicators	*2016*		*2007*		*1998*	
	Assets	*Percentage*	*Assets*	*Percentage*	*Assets*	*Percentage*
Construction Enterprises	182,482.07		43,029.27		11,870.42	
State-owned Construction Enterprises	31,197.09	17.10	11,344	26.36	6300	53.07
Collective-owned Construction Enterprises	2685.3	1.47	2335.05	5.43	3700	31.17
Construction Enterprises with Investment from Hong Kong, Macau, and Taiwan	1191.72	0.65	264.39	0.61	125.69	1.06
Construction Enterprises with Foreign Investment	905.79	0.50	370.16	0.86	84.31	0.71

Source Calculations based on data from *China Statistical Yearbook* of years concerned

Enterprises above designated size in wholesale and retail trades have also seen structural changes in asset ownership. In a decade from 2007 to 2016, the proportion of assets of enterprises in the public-owned economy kept decreasing, with that of enterprises of wholesale trade from 30.35 to 6.45 percent, and that of enterprises in retail trade from 10.97 to 1.89 percent. The proportion of assets of enterprises in the non-public sectors increased substantially, with that of enterprises of wholesale trade from 28.38 to 39.08 percent, and that of enterprises in retail trade from 37.65 to 40.99 percent. The proportion of assets of enterprises in the mixed economy remained high and went up rapidly, with that of enterprises of wholesale trade from 41.27 to 54.47 percent and that of enterprises in retail trade from 51.39 to 57.12 percent (see Fig. 1.4).

Looking back at 1999, the proportions of assets of enterprises of wholesale trade in the public economy, in the non-public sectors, and in the mixed economy were 85.38 percent, 1.17 percent, and 13.44 percent,

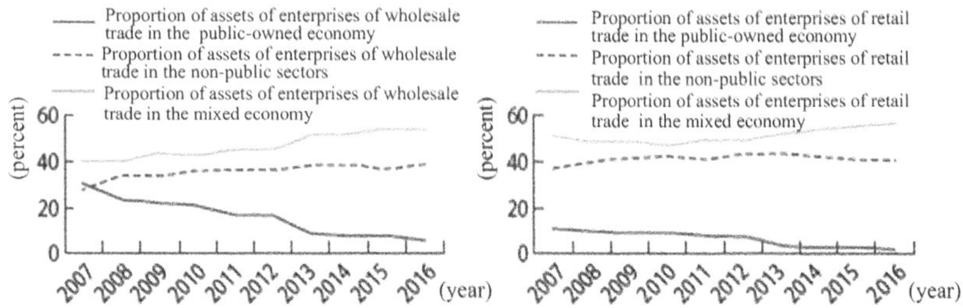

Fig. 1.4 Proportion of assets of enterprises above designated size in wholesale and retail trades by type of ownership in 2007–2016 (*Source* Calculations based on data from *China Statistical Yearbook* of years concerned)

respectively. The proportions of assets of enterprises of retail trade in the public economy, in the non-public sectors, and in the mixed economy were 54.07 percent, 9.77 percent, and 36.16 percent, respectively.[16] With the change of the times, assets of enterprises in the non-public sectors and the mixed economy have multiplied significantly, while the proportion of assets of enterprises in the public economy shrunk.

1.3.2.3 Then, Analysis of Investment Structure

In a decade from 2007 to 2016, the proportion of fixed-asset investment of enterprises in the public economy decreased from 32.20 to 22.93 percent, with an average annual rate of 1 percentage point. The proportion of fixed-asset investment of enterprises in the non-public sectors increased from 33.84 to 37.17 percent, and the proportion of fixed-asset investment of enterprises in the mixed economy increased from 33.96 to 39.90 percent (see Fig. 1.5).[17] Both kept increasing, with the latter growing faster.

Looking back at 1998, the proportions of fixed-asset investment of enterprises in the public economy, in the non-public sectors, and in the mixed economy were 68.86 percent, 23.65 percent, and 7.49 percent, respectively.[18] With the change of the times, the investment structure

[16] *China Statistical Yearbook* (2000), http://www.stats.gov.cn/tjsj/ndsj/zgnj/mulup.html.

[17] *China Statistical Yearbook* (2017), China Statistics Press, 2016.

[18] *China Statistical Yearbook* (1999), http://www.stats.gov.cn/yearbook/indexC.htm.

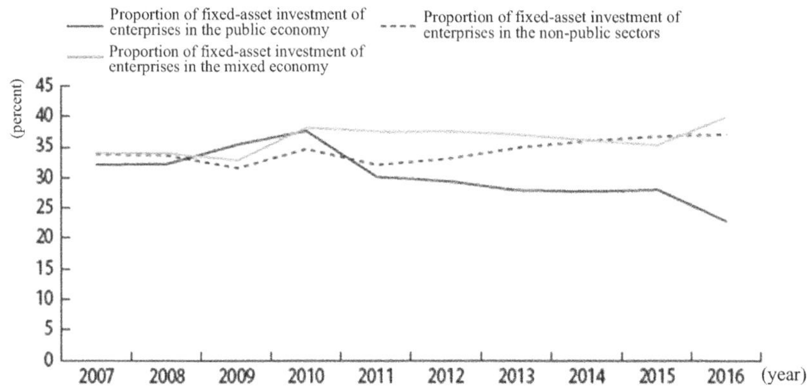

Fig. 1.5 Proportions of fixed-asset investment of enterprises by type of ownership in 2007–2016 (*Source* Calculations based on data from *China Statistical Yearbook* of years concerned)

changed a lot, from the public economy as the majority to a balanced structure, and later to the mixed economy outperforming.

1.3.2.4 Finally, Analysis of Urban Employment Structure

In the ten years between 2007 and 2016, the percentage of employees in various types of publicly owned businesses, including state-owned enterprises, collective-owned enterprises, and joint-stock cooperative enterprises, decreased from 37.13 to 17.51 percent, with an average annual drop of 2 percentage points. The share of the number of employees in enterprises of the non-public sectors, including private enterprises, enterprises with investment from Hong Kong, Macau, and Taiwan, and enterprises with foreign investment, rose from 48.11 to 61.02 percent, and kept increasing since 2013 after an adjustment. The share of the number of employees in enterprises of the mixed economy, including joint ownership enterprises, limited liability companies, shareholding corporations limited, and other enterprises, increased from 14.76 to 21.47 percent. A turning point occurred in 2013, when it started to go downward after having increased for years, both at a moderate pace (see Fig. 1.6). The adjustment in 2013 was given particular emphasis because the new classification standard was adopted in 2013. There were major revisions to the number of employees in units of some types of economy

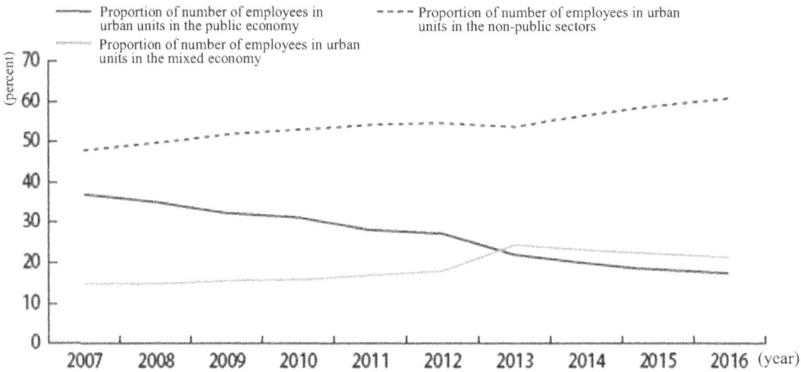

Fig. 1.6 Proportions of number of employees in urban units by type of ownership in 2007–2016 (*Note* Due to limitations of statistical data, the indicator value is not the proportion in the total number of employees in urban units, but the proportion in the total number of employees in urban units of each type of ownership. Analysis is available only for urban employment due to incomplete statistics of the number of employees in rural areas. *Source* Calculations based on data from *China Statistical Yearbook* of years concerned)

and some sectors, though they had little impact on the conclusion of the trend analysis.

Looking back at 1998, the percentage of employees in urban units in the public economy, in the non-public sectors, and in the mixed economy were 70.09 percent, 23.99 percent, and 5.92 percent, respectively.[19] With the change of the times, various economies had seen changes in the employment structure. The share of employment in the public economy turned from an absolute majority to an absolute minority. The share of employment in the non-public sectors rose from 25 to 50 percent, an absolute majority. The share of employment in the mixed economy surged from 5 to 25 percent.

In terms of the distribution of household income resulted from changes in the distribution system, China's Gini coefficient decreased for seven consecutive years since 2008 with a narrowing wealth gap, though still exceeded the international warning line of 0.4. In 2016 the index rose to 0.465 from 0.462 in 2015 (see Fig. 1.7). While China has seen

[19] *China Statistical Yearbook* (1999), http://www.stats.gov.cn/yearbook/indexC.htm.

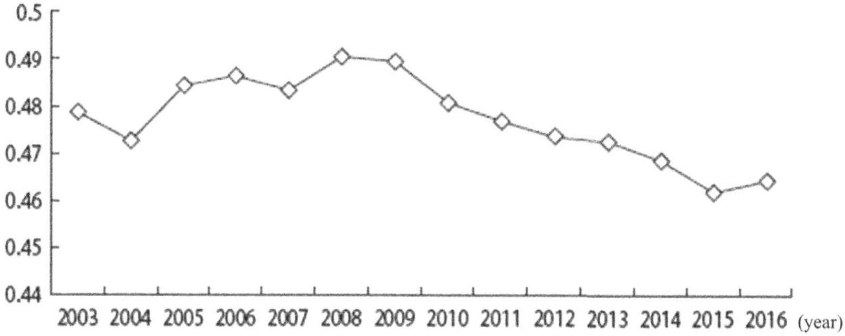

Fig. 1.7 Gini coefficient of national per capita disposable income in 2003–2016 (*Source* Website of National Bureau of Statistics, http://www.stats.gov.cn/ztjc/zdtjgz/yblh/zysj/201710/t20171010_1540710.html)

a remarkable increase in household income, income inequality still exists and is growing. The National Bureau of Statistics started to collect data on income and consumption expenditure and basic conditions of urban and rural households in 2013. Statistics show that per capita disposable income of the richest 20 percent households was 10.78 times, 10.73 times, 10.44 times, and 10.72 times that of the poorest 20 percent households in China in 2013 to 2016, respectively. Such indicator values of urban households were 5.84 times, 5.49 times, 5.32 times, and 5.41 times, respectively. Such indicator values of rural households were 7.41 times, 8.65 times, 8.43 times, and 9.46 times, respectively. It appears that the income inequality in China had been improving, but rose in 2016. Urban areas displayed similar growth pattern with nationwide, while the income gap in rural areas was widening with fluctuations. Moreover, the income gap between urban and rural areas was large and the wealth gap in rural area was more serious.

By far, we have made a quantitative description of the development process and results of the relations of production in China. Let us have a look at the development of the productive forces using quantitative methods. As shown in Fig. 1.8, China's labor productivity (or unit labor output) had been growing rapidly since the reform and opening up. The indicator increased about 17-fold in forty years from RMB916.19 per person in 1978 to RMB15,310.10 per person in 2016, with an average annual growth rate of 7.58 percent. China achieved double-digit growth

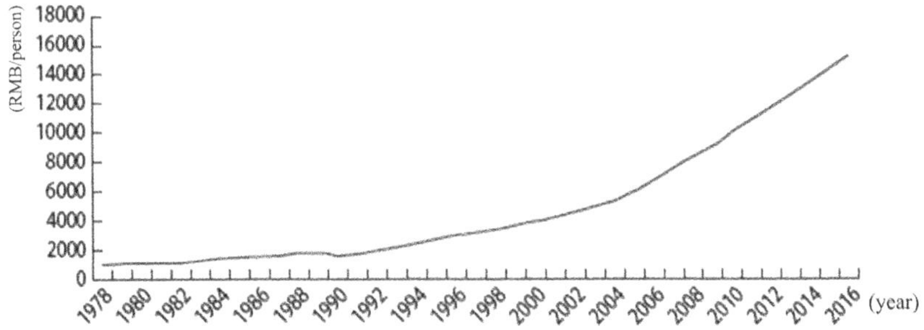

Fig. 1.8 Development trend of China's labor productivity in 1978–2016 (*Source* Wind)

in labor productivity from 2005 to 2007 before the international financial crisis.

Cross-sectional analysis of major countries in the world finds that, China's annualized average labor productivity growth rate was 8.6 percent in the past 20 years, about 7 percentage points higher than the world's average, and greater than that of the US, the European Union (EU), Japan, and India (7.0 percentage points, 7.9 percentage points, 7.7 percentage points, and 3.3 percentage points, respectively, see Table 1.3). At the absolute level, however, China's performance is still far behind that of some major economies. In 2015, China's labor productivity was USD7318 per person, or only 40 percent of the world's average (USD18,487 per person), 7 percent of that of the US (USD98,990 per person), 10 percent of the Eurozone's average (USD76,068 per person), and 11 percent of that of Japan (USD68,631 per person), although higher than that of India (USD3,559 per person).[20]

A better measure of productivity growth is the total factor productivity (TFP).[21] The report to the 19th National Congress of the CPC made it clear that we need to "raise total factor productivity". However,

[20] International Statistical Information Center of National Bureau of Statistics, International Comparison Shows Rapid Growth of China's Labor Productivity, website of National Bureau of Statistics, http://www.stats.gov.cn/tjsj/sjjd/201609/t20160901_1395572.html, September 1, 2016.

[21] Total factor productivity (TFP) represents growth in real output which is in excess of the growth in inputs such as labor and capital. Or, it represents the increase in total production which is in excess of the increase that results from increase in inputs and

Table 1.3 Growth rates of labor productivity of the world and some economies (Unit: percent)

Year	*World*	*US*	*Eurozone*	*Japan*	*India*	*China*
1996	1.6	2	1	2.3	5.5	8.9
1997	2.3	2.6	1.7	0.8	2.4	7.6
1998	1	1.9	1.1	−1.7	3.9	7.3
1999	1.6	2.8	1	1	6.9	6.4
2000	2.8	2.9	1.5	2.8	2.1	7
2001	0	0.9	0.9	0.3	1.2	7.6
2002	0.7	2.3	0.2	1.7	1.6	8.1
2003	1	2.3	0.2	1.8	4.4	9.1
2004	2.4	2.8	1.5	2	4.9	9.4
2005	1.6	1.5	0.6	0.9	6.9	10.3
2006	2.5	0.5	1.4	1.3	8.9	12
2007	2.4	1.4	1.1	1.3	8.8	13.1
2008	0.3	−0.6	−0.4	-0.7	4.3	9.6
2009	−2.3	1.4	-2.7	-4.3	8.2	9
2010	2.9	2.7	2.6	4.5	9.1	10.1
2011	1.5	0.7	1.5	0.6	6.5	8.6
2012	1	0.4	-0.4	1.9	4	7.2
2013	1.3	1.8	0.4	0.6	5.4	7.2
2014	1	0.4	0.3	−0.8	5.7	6.9
2015	1.1	0.9	0.6	0.9	5.6	6.6
Average growth rate	1.34	1.58	0.71	0.86	5.32	8.6

Source International Statistical Information Center of National Bureau of Statistics. International Comparison Shows Rapid Growth of China's Labor Productivity. Website of National Bureau of Statistics. http://www.stats.gov.cn/tjsj/sjjd/201609/t20160901_1395572.html, September 1, 2016

the report of the National Bureau of Statistics said that it was difficult to calculate the total factor productivity in China at the moment. The method adopted by the International Labor Organization, which is internationally comparable, was then applied to measure China's labor productivity. It measures the labor productivity by the employed population (the ratio of constant price GDP to the employed population).[22]

is attributable to knowledge, education, technological training, scale of economy, and organizational improvement.

[22] International Statistical Information Center of National Bureau of Statistics, International Comparison Shows Rapid Growth of China's Labor Productivity, website of National Bureau of Statistics, http://www.stats.gov.cn/tjsj/sjjd/201609/t20160901_1395572.html, September 1, 2016.

While academic studies on China's total factor productivity was underway, the National Information Center calculated it in a report. It showed that "the average growth of TFP in China during the period 2001–2013 was 2.03 percent, and contributed 22.25 percent to GDP growth, while factor inputs contributed 77.75 percent annually to GDP growth. China's economic growth remains heavily dependent on the growth in inputs".[23] Despite different results of calculations, it was unanimously agreed that TFP growth has been declining in recent years. Cai Fang (2016) estimated that the average annual TFP growth in China during the period 1995–2009 was 3.9 percent, fell to 3.1 percent during the period 2011–2015, and would further drop to 2.7 percent during the period 2016–2020.[24] According to Liu Mingkang and Chen Yongwei (2016), China's TFP growth declined rapidly after the international financial crisis. Except for a short rebound in 2011, the TFP growth decreased every year. It plunged to only 0.1 percent in 2013, and −0.1 percent in 2014.[25] Studies by Lu Yang (2016) concluded that China's TFP growth has shown a downward trend after 2008, from 7.24 percent in 2007 to less than 3 percent in 2008, and further to 1.68 percent in 2011, and later to less than 0.5 percent in recent years.[26] The International Monetary Fund also examined the total factor productivity in China and found that TFP growth in China during the period 2002–2007 was 5–6 percent and declined to 2–3 percent during the period 2008–2013.[27]

To sum up, there are still a number of problems in China's basic economic system and distribution system, either in a static state or in a dynamic process. While various ownership structures are changing over time, there was little synergy between the public ownership as the leading force of the economy and the more creative non-public sectors for the

[23] Wu Qiong, Measurement and Decomposition of Total Factor Productivity in China, Economic Forecasting Department of National Economic Information Center, http://www.sic.gov.cn/News/455/6841.htm, September 2, 2016.

[24] Cai Fang, Total Factor Productivity in China May Drop to 2.7 percent in the 13th Five-Year Plan Period, China News Network, http://www.chinanews.com/cj/2016/01-10/7709752.shtml, January 10, 2016.

[25] Liu Mingkang and Chen Yongwei, Total Factor Productivity in China: Current Conditions, Problems, and Policy Solutions, *Comparison*, No. 3, 2016.

[26] Lu Yang, Total Factor Productivity Growth in China, *China Finance*, No. 20, 2016.

[27] The First Centenary Sprint: CPC Draws Blueprint for a New Five-Year Economic and Social Planning, Xinhuanet.com, http://www.xinhuanet.com/fortune/2015-10/29/c_1116983841.htm, October 29, 2015.

development of productive forces. In the new era, China needs to reform the relations of production and improve the basic economic system and distribution system so as to further emancipate and develop productivity. In order to give full play to the positive impact of the relations of production on the productive forces, it is crucial to address the "forces" in the relations of production by grouping forces and taming "contradictory forces" in pair.

1.4 Conclusions and Policy Recommendations

This paper examines the basic economic system and distribution system in China under historical context both in theory and in practice, and draws the following conclusions.

First, in light of the development process, China's basic economic system and distribution system have evolved through the planned economy period, the transition period, and the socialist market economy period. They bear distinct characteristics of the times and contain rich implications and specific tasks in each period. Along two development paths of socialism and the market economy, China has developed from the single ownership and distribution principle to the rich and diversified basic economic system and distribution system, which have become the basic institutional guarantee for sustainable and healthy economic growth.

Second, in light of the theoretical basis, the basic principles of Marxism, including the theory of the productive forces and the relations of production, the basic philosophy of scientific socialism and the labor theory of value, guide the formation and development of China's basic economic system and distribution system. At the same time, China has also been working on adapting Marxism to the Chinese context in the reform, which, in turn, promotes the development of the Marxist theory. The basic economic system and distribution system will thus be able to see their implications and tasks to advance with the times, respond to the call of our era, and are dynamic with vitality. As the new era creates more growth potential for such systems, we need to give them new implications and tasks on a theoretical basis. We shall take note of the opposition unity between the two paths of socialism and the market economy and view them as interactive and ever-growing, avoiding erroneous trends of thought caused by isolating the two.

Third, in light of operation in reality, pure public ownership economy has no longer being the leading force of the economy, in terms of the number of enterprises, assets, investment, and the number of employees in the current basic economic system, with a continuously declining share. The non-public sectors and the mixed economy, on the contrary, have seen remarkable growth and are gaining momentum in the above-mentioned important dimensions. The reason behind this is the rapid development of the market economy, the inclusiveness of the socialist system with Chinese characteristics, and the basic conditions of China in the primary stage of socialism. Under the current distribution system, although the wealth gap in China continues to narrow, it still exceeds the international warning line and is widening recently, for income inequality is much worse in rural areas due to the low-income level of rural households. Under such relations of production, the productive force in China has been growing fast, yet still at a low level. While the unit labor output is growing fast, it is still far below the international average. The TFP growth keeps declining, which means that China's economic growth is still heavily dependent on factor inputs, and the contribution of technological progress is small and dwindling.

What shall we do to adhere to and improve China's basic economic system and distribution system?

First, we must follow the guidance of Marxism. Since it develops in a dynamic context and moves with the times, Marxism can provide a scientific worldview and methodology. Under the guidance of Marxism, China has stood up and grown rich in the past, and is becoming strong in the new era. We must follow the guidance of Marxism, enrich and develop it under the Chinese context and with the characteristics of the era. Our current task is to uphold and develop Xi Jinping Thought on Socialism with Chinese Characteristics for a new era and to realize a new leap in adapting Marxism to the Chinese context.

Second, we must link the two growth paths. Firstly, we must adhere to the socialist system. It is a common practice in today's world that various ownership and diverse distribution methods co-exist, and the single ownership system and distribution method cannot be found in any other country. China adheres to socialism with Chinese characteristics, and we must unswervingly adhere to the basic economic system and distribution system with the public ownership and the distribution according to work remaining dominant. Since key indicators show that the public economy has been shrinking, we must take actions to strengthen the basis of the socialist system to prevent the public economy from further declining in terms of asset, employment, and investment structure and ensure that the public economy will achieve quality growth to maintain competitiveness. We must increase the controlling share of state ownership in key industries and areas that determine the national security and the economic lifeline of a country to serve the national strategic goals. We must ensure that state ownership plays its role in promoting sustainable, stable, and coordinated development of the national economy by providing public services, increasing employment, improving people's living standards and building ecological civilization. Secondly, we must adhere to the direction of developing the market economy. As China has chosen the path of the market economy, we must follow and observe the principles and laws of the market economy in market operation, and unswervingly adhere to the principles that economic entities of diverse ownership develop side by side, all economic entities have equal status in the market, and all factors of production have due share in distribution according to their contribution. The State must provide a fair and just market environment so that the laws of the market economy can fully function. On one hand, while the law of value and the law of supply and demand work well, the government exerts macro-economic regulation to solve market failures, aiming for optimized allocation of resources. On the other hand, while the law of competition works well, the government implements the secondary distribution policy to narrow the income gap, spur workers' initiative and vigor, and improve efficiency through innovation in technology and management to effectively increase total factor productivity. Thirdly, we must tap the potential of the mixed economy to "turn opposition into unity". In fact, one most important strategy to eliminate differences and create synergies for the basic economic system and distribution system is to put the economic components of different ownership and the suppliers of different factors in the "smallest economic unit" and form a community of shared interest. To do this, it would be best to take effective measures to foster enterprises in the mixed economy. Market entities of different ownership invest to jointly set up mixed-ownership enterprises, or transform into mixed-ownership enterprises by cross share-holding and blending, which is a sign of a mature market. In other words, market players in a mature market economy will follow a natural path that a mixed economy exists and grows. At present, China encourages state-owned capital to invest in non-state-owned enterprises in various ways, encourages all types of capital to participate in the mixed-ownership reform of state-owned enterprises, and performs pilots of employee ownership in mixed enterprises. These measures can help enhance the control of the public economy in that the state-owned capital can exert a greater influence without a controlling share. They can also help increase the vitality of the non-public sectors in that, with the shareholding of the public sector, the mixed economy has a much higher credit rating than the non-public sectors. It will have a much lower growth risk and hidden barriers such as difficulty in obtaining bank loans will be automatically removed. Moreover, they can help invigorate the enthusiasm and creativity of all factor suppliers, because the mixed-ownership system allows employee ownership, in which investors, workers, and managers all become stakeholders with shared interest, turning trade-offs into synergies and jointly promoting the development of the productive forces.

Third, we must step up efforts in the relations of production to improve total factor productivity in China. According to the Marxist theory, the relations of production can have an impact on the productive forces and institutional arrangements should be put in place to make the impact positive. Since our country will long remain in the primary stage of socialism with low productivity and imbalanced and under development, the basic direction for improving the basic economic system and distribution system in the new era must be to emancipate and develop productivity. To maximize the positive impact of the relations of production on productivity, we must focus on increasing total factor productivity. Measures are taken to give play to the guiding role of the public economy in transforming the production methods and the industrial structure, deepening the reform of state-owned enterprises, and disposing of zombie enterprises. Non-public sectors are encouraged to leverage their adaptability and flexibility in the supply-side structural reform, improve the supply quality, and increase effective supply. The mixed-ownership economy will develop at a high starting point with improved efficiency in technological progress and play a greater role in the innovation-driven development strategy. Efforts are made to promote new urbanization and accelerate labor transfer, increase public transfers in education, technology and culture, and focus on the role of taxation in the redistribution of income, thereby increasing the speed and intensity of human capital accumulation.

References

Cai Fang (2016). Total Factor Productivity in China May Drop to 2.7 percent in the Thirteenth Five-Year Plan Period. China News Network. http://www.chinanews.com/cj/2016/01-10/7709752.shtml, January 10, 2016.

The First Centenary Sprint: CPC Draws Blueprint for a New Five-Year Economic and Social Planning. Xinhuanet.com. http://www.xinhuanet.com/fortune/2015-10/29/c_1116983841.htm, October 29, 2015.

International Statistical Information Center of National Bureau of Statistics (2016). International Comparison Shows Rapid Growth of China's Labor Productivity. Website of National Bureau of Statistics. http://www.stats.gov.cn/tjsj/sjjd/201609/t20160901_1395572.html, September 1.

Li Zhenhuan and Quan Heng (1993). Characteristics of Market Economy. *Journal of Social Sciences,* No. 4.

Liu Mingkang and Chen Yongwei (2016). Total Factor Productivity in China: Current Conditions, Problems, and Policy Solutions. *Comparison,* No. 3.

Lu Yang (2016). Total Factor Productivity Growth in China. *China Finance,* No. 20.

Marx (1995). Preface to *A Contribution to the Critique of Political Economy. Selected Works of Marx and Engels*, vol. 2. People's Publishing House.

Reports to the National Congress of the Communist Party of China in different years.

Selected Works of Marx and Engels, vol. 4. People's Publishing House, 2012.

Song Tao (2013). *Political Economy*, 10th Edition. China Renmin University Press.

Wu Qiong (2016). Measurement and Decomposition of Total Factor Productivity in China. Economic Forecasting Department of National Economic Information Center. http://www.sic.gov.cn/News/455/6841.html, September 2.

Xiang Kaibiao and Huang Li (2017). The Chinese Economy Is an Important Type of Modern Market Economy. *People's Daily*, March 16.

CHAPTER 2

Understanding the Principal Sources of Tension in Chinese Society in the New Era

Shuangshuang Li

In accordance with the report to the 19th National Congress of the Communist Party of China (the CPC), the principal tension in Chinese society has changed from "the tension between the ever-growing material and cultural needs of the people and backward social production" to "the tension between uneven and under development and the people's ever-growing needs for a better life", marking China's entry into a new era of socialism with Chinese characteristics. Given the new principal tension, the report provided, in a targeted way, new requirements with overall, systematic, focused, and distinctive features. An accurate understanding of the change of principal tension and its new requirements in the new era is not only the key to mastering the core of the report to the 19th National Congress of the CPC, but also the key to doing a good job in the major work required in the new era.

S. Li (✉)
National Academy of Economic Strategy, Chinese Academy of Social Sciences, Beijing, China

D. He et al. (eds.), *Chinese Finance Policy for a New Era*,
https://doi.org/10.1007/978-981-33-4054-1_2

2.1 Understanding the Principal Sources of Tension in the New Era

2.1.1 Sources of Social Tension in China in an Earlier Era Are Largely Eliminated

In the early 1980s, the supply of material and cultural products in China was extremely scarce. "The tension between the ever-growing material and cultural needs of the people and backward social production" was true of the shortage economy at that time. Thanks to the reform and opening up policy, especially since China's entry into the WTO at the turn of the new century and its gradual integration into the process of economic globalization, the economic growth of China is stronger than expected, and its economic aggregates constantly broke through previously forecasts. While creating economic miracles, China made it possible to solve the problem of material and cultural scarcity in advance. The judgment made in the report to the 19th National Congress of the CPC on the transformation of principal tension in Chinese society in the new era demonstrates the possibility has come true.

Judging by the indicators of an all-round well-off society, the principal tension between "the ever-growing material and cultural needs of the people and backward social production" determined in the early 1980s has been basically resolved. The competent authorities worked out ten standards for building a moderately prosperous society in an all-round way in accordance with international indicators of modernization and China's national conditions.[1] These indicators broadly reflect the material and cultural needs of the people. Given the report to the 19th National Congress of the CPC proposed to achieve the goal of getting rid of

[1] The basic criteria of a moderately prosperous society in all aspects include: (1) the per-capita GDP exceeds USD3000, which is the fundamental sign of having built a moderately prosperous society in an all-round way; (2) the per capita disposable income of urban residents reaches RMB18,000; (3) the per capita net income of rural households reaches RMB8000; (4) the Engel coefficient is less than 40 percent; (5) the per capita residential floor area in urban area reaches 30 square meters; (6) the urbanization rate reaches 50 percent; (7) the household computer penetration rate reaches 20 percent; (8) the college enrollment rate reaches 20 percent; (9) the number of doctors per thousand people is 2.8;. and (10) the minimum living security rate of urban residents is more than 95 percent.

[2] In the report to the 16th National Congress of the CPC held in 2002, China set the economic goal of "striving to quadruple the GDP of the year 2000 by 2020" in the part concerning building a moderately prosperous society in an all-round way.

poverty completely by 2020, when China would have built a moderately prosperous society in an all-round way, this paper uses the incidence of rural poverty to replace the minimum living security rate of urban residents in its calculations. Based on the indicator put forward by the 16th National Congress of the CPC that the GDP quadruples, this paper lists 11 indicators, which broadly reflect the improvement of the Chinese people's material and cultural living standards through their changes (see Table 2.1).

Table 2.1 shows that China greatly exceeded the pre-established standards in advance in 2016 (or 2015) in the indicators, except the "Doctors Per Thousand People" and "Poverty Incidence Rate in Rural Area". It performed quite well in the "GDP", "GDP Per Capita", "Household Computer Penetration Rate", and "College Enrollment Rate", exceeding by 80 percent, 1.7 times, 1.8 times, and 1.1 times, respectively, which indicated that China's social productivity had met the people's basic material and cultural needs, and the principal tension in early 1980s had been basically resolved.

2.1.2 *Growing Prominence of Principal Social Tension in China in the New Era*

2.1.2.1 *Increasing Urgency of Poeople's Demand for Democracy and Rule of Law*

According to Maslow's hierarchy of needs, human needs can be divided into five tiers from low to high: physiological needs, safety needs, belongingness and love needs, esteem needs, and self-actualization. Needs lower down in the hierarchy must be satisfied before individuals can attend to needs higher up, which will become the main incentive then. In China, people's basic material and cultural needs, which are physiological needs, have been basically satisfied. The needs in security focusing on democracy, rule of law, fairness, justice, security, environment, and so on become increasingly urgent. Baidu Index,[2] a big data tool, provides better real data support for this trend. In recent years, the search volume of the words "rule of law", "justice", "food safety law", "environmental protection law", "air pollution prevention law", "smog", and "justice" has been

[2] Baidu Index is also known as Baidu Search Index, which based on Baidu's massive netizen behavior data, shows the search volume of a keyword in Baidu and its trend changes over a period of time.

Table 2.1 Indicators of the material and cultural living standards of the Chinese people

Indicator	*1980*	*1990*	*2000*	*2010*	*2016*	*Target value*	*Performance*
GDP (RMB100 million)	4588	18,873	100,280	413,030	744,127	401,120	Over standard 343,007
Per Capita GDP (USD)	314	348	959	4561	8130	Exceeding USD3000	Over standard 5130
Per Capita Disposable Income of Urban Residents (RMB)	478	1510	6280	19,109.4	33,616	18,000	Over standard 15,616
Per Capita Net Income of Rural Households (RMB)	191	686	2253	5919.0	12,363	8000	Over standard 4363
Engel Coefficient	–	–	–	–	30.1	40	Over standard 9.9
Per Capita Residential Floor Area of Urban Residents (m)	7.18	13.65	20.25	31.6	36.6	30	Over-standard 6.6
Urbanization Rate (percent)	19.39	26.41	36.22	49.95	57.35	50	Over standard 7.35
Household Computer Penetration Rate (percent)	–	–	4.2	25.2	55.5[2]	20	Over standard 35.5
College Enrollment Rate (percent)	2.22	3.45	7.95	26.5	42.7	20	Over standard 22.7
Doctors Per Thousand People	–	–	1.68	1.42	2.2	2.8	Below standard –0.6

Indicator	*1980*	*1990*	*2000*	*2010*	*2016*	*Target value*	*Performance*
Poverty Incidence Rate in Rural Area (percent)	96.2	73.5	49.8	17.2	4.5	0	Below standard −4.5

Source Data on the GDP, Per Capita GDP, Disposable Income of Urban Residents, Per Capita Net Income of Rural Households, Per Capita Residential Floor Area of Urban Residents, and Poverty Incidence Rate in Rural Area of 1980, 1990, 2000, and 2010 comes from *China Statistical Yearbook*. The above indicators come from the National Bureau of Statistics; the data on Engel Coefficient and Urbanization Rate comes from the National Bureau of Statistics; the Household Computer Penetration Rate of 2015 is from *China Statistical Yearbook* of 2016, and the Rates of 2000 and 2010 are calculated by the author on the basis of the data on the number of households and the computers per hundred households in urban and rural areas; the data on College Enrollment Rate comes from ***International Statistical Yearbook*** and the statistical communiqué on national education development; the data on Doctors Per Thousand People comes from the National Bureau of Statistics on the rise. In particular, the search volume of "justice" and "air pollution prevention law" began to present a "plateau-style" steep increase in 2013 and 2015, respectively, and the attention paid to them continued unabated. It reflects they are of great concern to Chinese people and the relevant needs of people are increasing.

2.1.2.2 *Uneven and Under Development as Serious Issues*

The report to the 19th National Congress of the CPC summarizes the uneven and under development with about 200 Chinese characters as follows: "Development quality and efficiency remain wanting. China's innovation ability needs to be stronger, the real economy awaits improvement, and we have a long way to go in protecting the environment. In people's livelihood, there are many areas where we fall short; and poverty alleviation remains a formidable task. There is large gap between the development of and income distribution in rural and urban areas; and Chinese people face many difficulties in employment, education, healthcare, housing and old-age care. The level of civilization needs to improve. Social tensions and problems are intertwined. Much remains to be done to fully advance law-based governance, and to strengthen China's system of and capacity for governance. The struggle in ideological sphere is still complicated, and we face new incidents in national security. Some reform plans and major policies and measures need to be further implemented. Many dimensions of the building of the CPC remain weak". This concise and comprehensive description reflects that the uneven and under development covers the imbalance and deficiency of the development of real economy, people's livelihood, rule of law, ideology, the building of the CPC. This part specifically looks into the uneven and underdevelopment of China's real economy and people's livelihood on the basis of necessary data.

Uneven and Inadequate Development of Real Economy

The uneven and underdevelopment of China's real economy is mainly manifested in serious structural economic problems, including overcapacity, excess inventory in real estate, too high leverage ratio and costs of enterprises, and inadequate innovation, infrastructure, and public services, which are the targets of the five priority tasks of cutting overcapacity, reducing excess inventory, deleveraging, lowering costs, and strengthening points of weakness, and are obstacles to the sustained and stable growth of China's economy.

Table 2.2 Capacity utilization rate in some sectors since 2009 (Unit: percent)

Sector	*2009*	*2010*	*2011*	*2012*	*2013*	*2015*
Electrolytic aluminium	61.2	59.6	58.6	71.9	73.5	78
Photovoltaic	–	–	–	<60	–	–
Shipbuilding	–	–	–	About 60	65.7	About 60
Calcium carbide	67	82.6	61.6	–	–	–
Cement	67.1	65.2	64.5	67.1	75.7	73.8
Coke	72.6	70.4	69.4	–	–	–
Plate glass	69.2	71.4	77.6	73.1	73.5	68
Crude steel	81.1	82	79.2	72	72	67
Coal	91.8	89.3	87.2	74.9–75.5	–	64.9
Automobile	85.7	105	94.4	88	–	76

Source Data from the National Development and Reform Commission, Ministry of Industry and Information Technology, and the National Bureau of Statistics

First of all, overcapacity, the old structural problem of economy recurred. According to the internationally accepted standard, the capacity utilization rate over 90 percent means insufficient capacity, of 79–90 percent is normal level, lower than 79 percent means overcapacity, and lower than 75 percent indicates serious overcapacity. According to this standard, the problem of overcapacity occurred in China in the 1990s, and reappeared after the economic stimulus policies adopted in 2009. What is different is that the overcapacity in the 1990s mainly occurred in the light industry dominated by textiles, while the one at present mainly concentrates on the heavy industry, with cement, crude steel, plate glass, coal, and shipbuilding facing serious overcapacity (see Table 2.2). Although it is not a new problem, it is more difficult to solve this time. One of the important reasons is that, compared with the light industry dominated by textiles, which has a relatively small share of fixed cost, the heavy industry dominated by iron and steel has a significant proportion of fixed cost and a high operating leverage. Enforcing production cuts or stopping production by administrative means will incur a high cost and encounter big obstacles, which will slow down the effectiveness.

Excessive real estate inventory is another serious structural problem of China's national economy. In the narrow sense of inventory (the area for sale), China's inventory of residential commercial housing in 2016 was 720 million square meters, which seems not high because it could be digested in about six months. However, in the broad sense of inventory

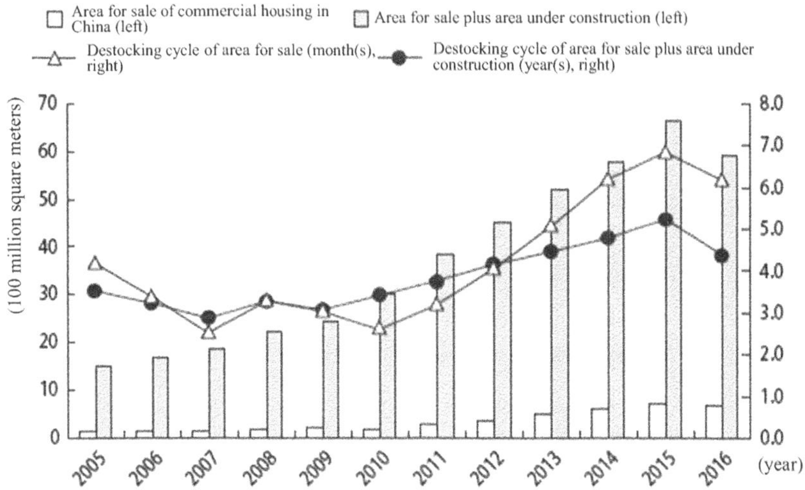

Fig. 2.1 China's real estate inventory situation and destocking cycle (*Note* The destocking cycle is calculated by dividing the area for sale by the average area sold over the past three years. *Source* Website of National Bureau of Statistics)

(the area for sale and under construction), the inventory stood at 6.62 billion square meters, which needs 4.4 years to digest (see Fig. 2.1).

Excessive leverage is a third structural economic problem. The leverage ratio mainly measures the debt level of the sector of government, household, or enterprise. In recent years, China's leverage ratio has been rising, with the ratio of overall outstanding debt to GDP increasing from 158 percent in 2007 to 282 percent in 2014. From the perspective of the structure of sector, high leverage of the enterprises is a prominent feature of China's debt structure. According to *China's National Balance Sheet 2015*, after the global financial crisis of 2008, the ratio of debt to GDP rose from 42 percent in 2007 to about 55 percent in 2014 for the government sector; from 20 percent to about 38 percent for the household sector; and from 72 to 125 percent for the non-financial enterprise sector.

Reducing cost is one of the five major tasks of the supply-side reform in China. Chinese enterprises have long faced high costs, which are now at a record high. In 2015, operating costs of their main businesses for Chinese enterprises accounted for 85.68 percent of revenue, nearly 5 percentage points higher than in 2000 (see Fig. 2.2). Such high cost directly caused

Fig. 2.2 Prime operating cost rate of enterprises in China (*Source* Wind, the National Bureau of Statistics)

the industrial enterprises to experience a rapid decline in profit growth and even a negative profit growth for the first time in 2015.

In the 40 years of reform and opening up, China has made remarkable achievements in economy. However, it is undeniable that the market economy is far from perfect and there are still many weaknesses. At present, the main weaknesses include lack of innovation ability and shortage of public products and infrastructure. According to the 2015 Global Innovation Index, China ranked the 29th in the world, which was not commensurate with its position as the world's second largest economy. At present, in terms of per capita public goods, capital stock of infrastructure, and material and technological equipment, the values of China is only a third of the ones of western Europe and a quarter of the ones of North America. In 2015, China only ranked 39th in the comprehensive ranking of global infrastructure. In addition, China needs to address the problems such as low investment in scientific and technological research and development, low conversion rate of scientific and technological achievements, and insufficient building of talents.

Uneven and Inadequate Development of People's Livelihood

To eradicate poverty, to enable people to enjoy better healthcare, education and environment, and to narrow the income gap between the rich and poor are the top priorities for a better life. However, the development

Table 2.3 International comparison of quality of life indicators

Indicator	*China*	*World average*	*Middle-income countries*	*High-income countries*
Average Years of Schooling (year(s))	7.2	7.9	8.2	11.8
Proportion of medical expenditure in GDP (percent, 2014)	5.6	10	5.8	12.3
Medical Expenditure Per Capita (USD, 2014)	419.7	1061	289.4	5251.2
PM2.5 (microgram/m)	58.4	44	50.3	16.6

Source The data on PM2.5 comes from World Bank, *World Development Indicators* (September, 2017), the other data comes from *International Statistical Yearbook* (2016)

Table 2.4 Income gap between urban and rural areas in China

Year	*Per capita disposable income of urban residents (RMB)*	*Per capita net income of rural households (RMB)*	*Absolute income gap between urban and rural areas (RMB)*	*Difference between urban and rural income (times)*
1980	478	191	287	2.50
1990	1510	686	824	2.20
2000	6280	2253	4027	2.79
2010	19,109	5919	13,190	3.23
2016	33,616	12,363	21,253	2.72

Source National Bureau of Statistics

of the abovementioned aspects which are critical for people's livelihood in the new era is uneven, or inadequate, or uneven and inadequate.

Table 2.3 shows the comparison of indicators in education, healthcare, and environment between China and the other parts of the world, and Tables 2.4 and 2.5 show the income gap between urban and rural areas and between regions, respectively. As shown in Table 2.1, China still has a heavy task to shoulder in thoroughly eradicating poverty and achieving the goal of 2.8 doctors per thousand people. Table 2.3 shows that China still lags behind the high-income countries or even some middle-income countries in education, healthcare, and environment. China's average

Table 2.5 Regional income gap in China

Region	*2005*		*2010*		*2015*	
	Per capita disposable income (RMB)	*Income difference with the Eastern Region (times)*	*Per capita disposable income (RMB)*	*Income difference with the Eastern Region (times)*	*Per capita disposable income (RMB)*	*Income difference with the Eastern Region (times)*
Eastern	13,374.88		23,272.83		28,223.3	
Central	8808.52	1.52	15,962.02	1.46	18,442.1	1.53
Western	8783.17	1.52	15,806.49	1.47	16,868.1	1.67
Northeastern	8729.96	1.53	15,940.99	1.46		1.34

Source National Bureau of Statistics

years of schooling is only 7.2 years, which is lower than the average of middle-income countries (8.2 years) and the average of high-income countries (11.8 years), and even lower than the global average (7.9 years). China also fails to meet the nine-year compulsory education standard set by itself. In terms of medical expenditure, the proportion of medical expenditure in GDP in China[3] is lower than the world average, the ones of middle-income and high-income countries, while the per capita medical expenditure burden is higher than that of middle-income countries. This indicates China's public medical expenditure is insufficient, and the medical expenses borne by individuals are higher. In addition, China is confronted with a relatively high pressure in environmental protection, with the PM2.5 concentration in the air being much higher than the level of high-income countries, and higher than the level of middle-income countries and the world average.

According to the data on urban–rural income gap, regional income gap and the Gini coefficient, China's income gap shows a trend of widening, which reverses the previous trend of narrowing. The absolute income gap between urban and rural areas has been expanding since the 1980s. The relative income gap continued to expand at first. In recent years, with the rapid growth of income in rural areas, it began to close. But it is still higher than the level of the 1980s. From the perspective of regional

[3] Medical expenditure comprises government health expenditure, social health expenditure and personal health expenditure.

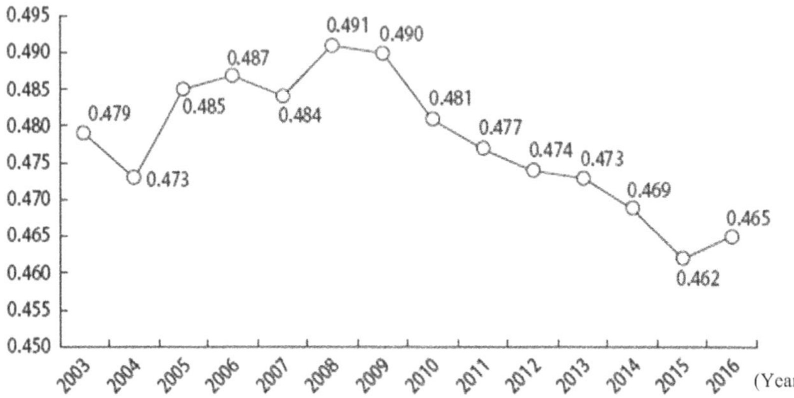

Fig. 2.3 Gini coefficient of China (*Source* National Bureau of Statistics)

income gap, the income gap between the northeast and the east has been narrowing, but the income gap between the central and western regions and the eastern region decreased initially followed by an increase, and currently has exceeded the level more than ten years ago (as shown in Tables 2.4 and 2.5). Measured by the Gini coefficient, China's income gap declined year by year after the economic crisis of 2008; however, in 2016, it rebounded (as shown in Fig. 2.3).

2.2 Understanding the New Requirements Imposed

After making a judgment on the change of the principal tension in Chinese society in the new era, the report to the 19th National Congress of the CPC immediately put forward new requirements on how to deal with the new principal tension. First of all, the report summarized the new requirements: "We must recognize that the evolution of the principal tension facing Chinese society represents a historic shift that affects the whole landscape and that creates many new demands for the work of the Party and the country. Building on continued efforts to sustain development, we must devote great energy to addressing development's imbalances and inadequacies, and push hard to improve the quality and effect of development. With this, we will be better placed to meet the ever-growing economic, political, cultural, social, and ecological needs of our people, and to promote well-rounded 4human development and all-round social progress". The fifth to ninth parts of the report elaborated in detail the new requirements concerning the economic, political, cultural, social, ecological, and other aspects, respectively, showing that the requirements of the new era refer to arrangements made to address imbalances and inadequate provision in the five-sphere integrated plan for realizing all-round balanced and full development, and comprehensively meet the people's needs for a better life.

The new requirements correspond to the new principal tension and differ from the old requirements. In particular, the new requirements addressed social and ecological aspects. Before the 17th National Congress of the CPC, the reports basically covered three aspects of economy, politics, and culture. The report to the 17th National Congress of the CPC added requirements in social work, and the report to the 18th National Congress of the CPC incorporated ecological requirements, showing the profound insights and understanding of the CPC and the state of changes of tensions in Chinese society, as well as the timely adjustment of work requirements by the Party and the state.

The work requirements in the report to the 19th National Congress of the CPC involve all aspects. Scientific understanding of the requirements in the new era cannot be achieved by "trying to attend to everything at once irrespective of priority". It needs to be recognized that the work requirements in the report to the 19th National Congress of the CPC are not all new requirements. There is an emphasis on the original work deployment in the report. Only by grasping the content that is really first mentioned, first advocated or highlighted in a different way from the past can we scientifically understand the new requirements in the new era.

2.2.1 New Economic Requirements

The report to the 19th National Congress of the CPC proposed, for the first time, to build a modernized economic system, and established furthering supply-side structural reform as the first specific requirement in this regard. In addition, it is also clearly proposed to promote the formation of a new pattern of comprehensive opening up. This marks the furthering of China's reform and opening up process as it enters a higher stage.

In order to gain an accurate understanding of this new economic requirement, we must accurately understand the modernized economic system. The core word is "system", which means the goal is to build a complete economic system. According to the description of modernized economy in the report to the 19th National Congress of the CPC, the core elements include improved socialist market economic system ("an economy with more effective market mechanisms, dynamic micro-entities, and sound macro-regulation" in the report), modern agriculture, industry (advanced manufacturing), and services ("an industrial system that promotes coordinated development of the real economy with technological innovation, modern finance, and human resources"), regional coordination, and comprehensive opening up, while achieving the domestic core goal of putting quality first and giving priority to performance, and the international core goal of strengthening the innovation capacity and competitiveness. Such a system needs to be realized through three major changes of quality, efficiency, and power. Specifically, this means deepening supply-side structural reform, accelerating building of a country of innovators, pursuing the rural vitalization strategy, implementing the coordinated regional development strategy, accelerating the improvement of the socialist market economic system, and promoting formation of a new pattern of all-round opening up. Establishing the modernized economic system means we have given up the development mode of pursuing speed alone, but turned the focus to the improvement of product quality. It also means that China's economic construction will be more market-oriented, more open, and more coordinated.

2.2.2 *New Political Requirements*

The new political requirements in the report to the 19th National Congress of the CPC are characterized by a special emphasis on seeing that the people run the country. The sixth part of the report elaborates on the new political requirements. The heading of this part ("Improving the System of Institutions through Which the People Run the Country and Developing Socialist Democracy") and the first two secondary headings ("Upholding the unity of Party leadership, the running of the country by the people, and law-based governance", "Strengthening institutional guarantees to ensure the people run the country") all focus on running of the country by the people, reflecting the fact that the CPC and the state are giving special attention to satisfying the people's political needs in the new era.

The fundamental reason why the CPC can lead the Chinese people to win in the New Democratic Revolution and produce remarkable achievements is that China has succeeded in exploring and implementing the mass line of relying on and doing everything for the masses. The Chinese people, which have grown from 400 million when the PRC was founded in 1949 to 1.3 billion today, have always been supporting the CPC's leadership, primarily because the CPC led them to fight against and topple the "three mountains" of imperialism, feudalism, and bureaucrat-capitalism, and made it possible for them to become masters of the country. In times of peace, some cadres in the Party divorced themselves from the masses or even placed themselves above the masses, resulting in negative impact on the credibility of the government. The Party and state leaders identified and worked to solve the problems in a timely manner. While "taking out tigers and swatting flies", they are making efforts to promote the mass line by learning what the masses were thinking and providing the masses with what they need; and emphasizing to strengthen the institutional guarantee for the people to be the masters of the country and improve the system of the people to be the masters of the country by the integration of the Party's leadership, running of the country by the people and rule of law, thus achieving the political goal of socialist democracy.

2.2.3 New Cultural Requirements

Culturally, the report to the 19th National Congress of the CPC gave special emphasis to the confidence in culture and ideological work. The former is put forward against a background that China's economic "hard power" has been significantly enhanced, while its cultural "soft power" is relatively weak. Today, when China pursues the Belt and Road Initiative, its vast savings, investment, and infrastructure capacity have attracted many countries to participate in it. However, due to the lack of cultural "soft power", some countries, which want to obtain support from China's resources, have doubts about China's intentions, resulting in misunderstandings and misinterpretations such as "new colonialism" and "new tributary system". In addition, China is already the second largest economy in the world in terms of economic aggregates, but remains relatively backward in cultural construction. Cultural works and academic research have made gains in terms of quantity, but the quality is not high enough. There is a lack of highly skilled works in various disciplines, and there is considerable underachievement in terms of the country's international influence. At the same time, with the increase of western learning and the decline of studies of Chinese ancient civilization, the dominance of Chinese culture has waned.

In terms of new requirements in cultural construction, the report to the 19th National Congress of the CPC attached special importance to the ideological work. On the one hand, "ideology determines the direction a culture should take and the path it should follow as it develops", and on the other hand, there are problems such as excessive western influence and marginalization of Marxism in the field of ideology in China. The basic principles of Marxism are important guidelines for the CPC, but Marxism is increasingly being marginalized in the society. The universities show little interest in offering courses on Marxism, and the students lack interest in learning. In the field of economics, western economic theories dominate, while Marxist political economics becomes an unpopular major. Hostile forces, which exist in the real world or network environment, and netizens, who are confused, tend to greatly appreciate the western ideology while despising or even belittling the basic principles of Marxism. If the problem of ideology is not solved and the guiding ideology is not made clear, the CPC's actions will fall into confusion, and there will even be doubts about the CPC's history, and the determined direction of the road will not be as firm as it needs to be. Given this, the special importance of ideological work in the new era lies in responding and cleaning up the open and covert attacks in the ideological field, truly clarifying the guiding ideology of action in the new era, strengthening the consciousness and determination of the whole Party and the whole people, to form a united and patriotic national united front and lay an ideological foundation for the great rejuvenation of the Chinese nation.

2.2.4 New Social Requirements

In terms of social work requirements, the report to the 19th National Congress of the CPC added two aspects of "the battle against poverty" and "national security", which are important in the new era. Attaching importance to the battle against poverty, because lifting the poor out of poverty is one of the tasks yet accomplished for construction of a moderately prosperous society. A well-off society where there is a poverty-stricken population cannot be seen as being well-off in an all-round way, and the development which does not eradicate poverty is not a balanced and sufficient one. As is shown in Table 2.1, against the rural poverty line of RMB2300 per person per year, the rural poverty rate in China is 4.5 percent. The 13th Five-Year Plan in 2015 set the goal of lifting 70 million poor people out of poverty by 2020. The report to the 19th National Congress of the CPC once again emphasized that "ensure that by the year 2020, all rural residents living below the current poverty line have been lifted out of poverty, and poverty is eliminated in all poor counties and regions", which means that the task of poverty eradication must be completed in one go in the remaining three years.

The 19th National Congress of the CPC attached high importance to national security out of consideration of the current complex situation at home and abroad. World peace is still the mainstream, and there is no possibility of major unrest at home and abroad. However, in the new era, the content of national security has greatly expanded, not only including traditional concepts such as political security and homeland security, but also containing new elements such as network security and ecological security. We should not relax our vigilance against potential threats in all aspects. For example, in terms of political security, western hostile forces have never given up their subversive activities against China, trying to implement a Western political system in our country; and religious infiltration has never stopped, aiming to intervene in the religious affairs of China so as to carry out the activities of ethnic separatist and secessionist activities. In terms of homeland security, the US built military bases jointly with Japan and with South Korea respectively to form a military encirclement in China's northeast border areas and eastern coastal areas; the conflict between China and India, which has dragged on and reached a deadlock, is difficult to resolve; Vietnam, the Philippines, and other Southeast Asian countries are fighting over the southern seas and islands of China with a view to plundering China's marine resources. Network security issues also pose a threat to political security. With the global opening up of the Internet, disorderly, malicious, and even hostile network political participation has brought new challenges to political security. In terms of ecological security, China is also facing a severe situation. Air pollution, land degradation, ecological imbalance, destruction of vegetation, sharp decline and accelerated deterioration of biodiversity, and sudden environmental pollution accidents have entered a peak season.

2.2.5 New Ecological Requirements

The report to the 18th National Congress of the CPC began to deploy China's ecological work. Different from the report to the 18th National Congress of the CPC, however, the report to the 19th National Congress of the CPC shifted from simply giving importance to ecological protection and construction to stressing the ecological system reform. The report called for "reforming the environmental regulation system. We will strengthen overall planning, organization, and leadership for building an ecological civilization. We will establish regulatory agencies to manage state-owned natural resource assets and monitor natural ecosystems, and improve environmental management systems. These agencies will, in a unified way, perform the duties of the owner of public-owned natural resource assets, the duties of regulating the use of all territorial space and protecting and restoring ecosystems, and the duties of monitoring the discharge of all pollutants in urban and rural areas and conducting administrative law enforcement. We will establish systems for developing and protecting territorial space, improve supporting policies on functional zones, and develop a nature reserves system composed mainly of national parks. We will take tough steps to stop and punish all activities that damage the environment".

In the past, China had been advocating not to follow the way of "treatment after pollution", but local governments, to win in the "GDP championship", had always been pursuing economic growth as the core element of the work at the expense of the ecological environment, leaving the environmental protection and ecological construction empty talk. Although the economic aggregates continued to grow and people's income continued to increase, breathing clean air and enjoying clear water and blue sky became extravagant hopes. The occurrence of "Olympic Blue", "APEC Blue", and other "Policy-oriented Blue" demonstrated that air pollution is not untreatable. Under the central government's top-level design and with the unified management, the environmental and ecological situation is expected to be greatly improved. The 19th National Congress of the CPC proposed "reforming the environmental regulation system" and strengthening the overall planning, organization, and leadership for building an ecological civilization. It aims to raise the ecological protection to the top-level leadership of the central government on the one hand, and make significant progress in environmental protection by unified supervision on the other hand, in order to restore the lucid waters and lush mountains, the blue sky and white clouds, and to meet the people's yearning for a beautiful China.

References

Hu Jintao's report to the 17th National Congress of the CPC. October 15, 2007. Database of National Congresses of the CPC.
Hu Jintao's report to the 18th National Congress of the CPC. November 8, 2012. Database of National Congresses of the CPC.
Jiang Zemin's report to 15th National Congress of the CPC. September 12, 1997. Database of National Congresses of the CPC.
Jiang Zemin's report to the 16th National Congress of the CPC. November 8, 2002. Database of National Congresses of the CPC.
Xi Jinping's report to the 19th National Congress of the CPC. October 18, 2017. Database of National Congresses of the CPC.

CHAPTER 3

From a Moderately Prosperous Society in All Respects to a Great Modern Socialist Country

Muzi Li

It is the ultimate goal of the Communist Party of China and the Chinese people to build a moderately prosperous society in an all-round way and build China into a great modern socialist country that is prosperous, strong, democratic, culturally advanced, harmonious, and beautiful. The strategic arrangement clearly outlines the characteristics and goals of China's economic growth in different phases, charting the course for future development of China. Besides, it enriches the Overall Plan for Development in Five Areas and offers a better guide to the future, which demonstrates the inexhaustible source of the CPC's leadership in ensuring the realization of the two centenary goals.

M. Li (✉)
National Academy of Economic Strategy, Chinese Academy of Social Sciences, Beijing, China

D. He et al. (eds.), *Chinese Finance Policy for a New Era*,
https://doi.org/10.1007/978-981-33-4054-1_3

3.1 The Historical Context of the New Goal

3.1.1 China's Modernization Process

In March 1957, Mao Zedong proposed to "build China into a socialist country with modern industry, modern agriculture and modern science and culture". In 1963, he expanded this to clearly propose to "build China into a great socialist country with agricultural modernization, industrial modernization, national defense modernization and scientific and technological modernization". In August and September 1963, the first draft plan on industrial development, personally revised by Mao Zedong, outlined China's industrial development in two steps: establishing a complete and comprehensive industrial system as the first step; and moving Chinese industry closer to the internationally advanced level as the second step. Mao Zedong's thought in this regard is clearly revealed in the Report on the Work of the Government delivered by the late Premier Zhou Enlai at the third National People's Congress (NPC) of CPC held in December 1964. The "two-step approach" was formally expressed as: "First, China will take 15 years to build itself as a country with a complete and comprehensive industrial and economic system, so that China's industry will generally approach the world's level; second, China will strive to enable its industry to stand at the forefront of the world, realizing the modernization of agriculture, industry, national defense and science and technology in an all-round way by the end of the 20th century". This officially brought "the Four Modernizations" into the overall strategic goal of national development and guided the development of China over a long period since. However, limited by the combination of the international and domestic environment for economic and social development at that time, the government was not able to establish the specific level of development of modernization, and was not clear about necessary indicators to measure and criteria to make a proper judgment of progress.

Since then, the connotations and goals of socialist modernization have been adjusted to cope with the changing situation of the world, that in China and within the CPC leadership. After the introduction of the reform and opening up in late 1978, Deng Xiaoping, after much reflection, put forward new ideas such as creating the "moderately prosperous society" and the "China's modernization". Deng believed that China could not simply copy what other countries did to modernize, but should take its own path toward prosperity in accordance with its own characteristics as a populous but poor country, and work to build socialism with Chinese characteristics. Deng also adjusted the timetable to realize modernization from two to three "steps". The strategy outlined specific targets for each of the three steps. The first step of meeting the most basic needs of the people and the second step of enabling the people to enjoy a "moderately prosperous" life would be completed by the end of the twentieth century, and the third step would then take 30–50 years in the twenty-first century to reach the level of moderately developed countries. Unveiled at the 13th National Congress of CPC in October 1987, the strategy envisaged three steps for economic development: "First, the years from 1981 to 1990 would see the doubling of the 1980 GDP, thus meeting the most basic needs of the people. Second, GDP would be doubled again between 1991 and the end of the 20th century, enabling the people to enjoy a 'moderately prosperous' life. Third, with the process of modernization basically completed, per capita GDP was expected to reach the level of a moderately developed country by the mid-21st century, further improving the people's wellbeing. Then, China would continue forging ahead along this path". China's economy has developed apace under the guidance of this "three-step approach". By 2000, the first two steps had indeed been realized as scheduled, with China enabling its people to enjoy a "moderately prosperous" life.

The third step was deemed much more difficult to achieve. The "moderately prosperous society" being pursued by China at that time was not comprehensive enough, at a low, unstable, and uneven level. In 1997, the 15th National Congress of CPC further specified the third step and put forward three-phased goals: the first decade of the twenty-first century would see GDP double the 2000 level, making the people's lives more prosperous and forming a relatively comprehensive socialist market economy; in the ensuing 10 years, up to the eve of the 100th anniversary of the founding of the CPC, the national economy would be further developed and various systems much improved; by the mid-twenty-first century, when China celebrates the centenary of the founding of the People's Republic of China, it will basically realize modernization and see a prosperous, strong, democratic, and culturally advanced socialist country.[1] Here, the "two centenary goals" were put forward for the first time. As of how to walk, China has put forward specific requirements and objectives, and made it clear at the 16th National Congress of CPC: "We need to concentrate on building a well-off society of a higher standard in an all-round way to the benefit of well over one billion people in the two decades of development". Hu Jintao said in the report at the 17th National Congress of CPC: "When the goal of building a moderately prosperous society in all respects is attained by 2020, China, a large developing socialist country with an ancient civilization, will have basically accomplished industrialization, with its overall strength significantly increased and its domestic market ranking as one of the largest in the world. It will be a country whose people are better off and enjoy markedly improved quality of life and a good environment. Its citizens will have more extensive democratic rights, show higher ethical standards and look forward to greater cultural achievements. China will have better institutions in all areas and Chinese society will have greater vitality coupled with stability and unity. The country will be still more open and friendly to the outside world and make greater contributions to human civilization". The report also points out: "The following five years will be a crucial period for building a moderately prosperous society in all respects. We must enhance our confidence and work hard to lay a more solid foundation for success in building a moderately prosperous society of a higher level in all respects to the benefit of over one billion people".[2]

Since then, with the phenomenal development of science and technology and dramatic changes of situation at home and abroad, the world witnessed the big jump in China's international standing and overall development. Given this, the 18th National Congress of CPC further adjusted the goal of the original "Four Modernizations" by proposing "New Four Modernizations", namely, the Chinese-style path of carrying out industrialization in a new way and advancing IT application, urbanization, and agricultural modernization. At the same time, the Congress also added the fourth characteristic of a socialist country "harmonious" on the

[1] Jiang Zemin: *Hold High the Great Banner of Deng Xiaoping Theory and Push the Cause of Building Socialism with Chinese Characteristics to the 21st Century in an All-Round Way*—delivered at the 15th CPC National Congress, September 12, 1997.

[2] Hu Jintao: *Hold High the Great Banner of Socialism with Chinese Characteristics and Strive for New Victories in Building a Moderately Prosperous Society in all Respects*—delivered at the 17th CPC National Congress, October 15, 2007.

basis of the first three of "prosperous, democratic and culturally advanced, and "the two centenary goals" were reaffirmed. At the Third Plenary Session of the 18th CPC Central Committee, General Secretary Xi Jinping put forward the fifth modernization—modernizing the national governance system and capabilities. The 19th National Congress of CPC further enriched the content of the second centenary goal, boosted its overall strength, and advanced the time to realize it. "Beautiful", as the fifth characteristic of a great modern socialist country, proposed for the first time and was upgraded as the ultimate goal. The time to basically realize modernization was advanced to 2035. The report at the 19th National Congress of CPC points out that "the period between the 19th and the 20th National Congress is the period in which the timeframes of the two centenary goals converge. In this period, not only must we finish building a moderately prosperous society in all respects and achieve the first centenary goal; we must also build on this achievement to embark on a new journey toward the second centenary goal of fully building a modern socialist country".[3] The 19th National Congress of CPC made two-stage arrangements for the period from 2020 to the middle of the twenty-first century and put forward two-phased goals. It advances the goal of socialist modernization to a new stage of development following the trend of the world and combining with China's actual situation. As the phased tasks have been elaborated more clearly and concretely, the dream to realize socialist modernization is no longer unreachable but close enough to touch.

3.1.2 The Evolution of the Principal Tension of Socialism in China

Both the "two centenary goals" and the new "two-step approach" strategy fully reveal that the principal tension facing Chinese society is no longer that between the ever-growing material and cultural needs of the people and the backwardness of social production but one between the uneven and underdevelopment and the people's ever-growing needs for a better life. This historic judgment shows the CPC Central Committee with Xi Jinping as the core, clearly takes the interests of the people as

[3] Xi Jinping: *Secure a Decisive Victory in Building a Moderately Prosperous Society in All Respects and Strive for the Great Success of Socialism with Chinese Characteristics for a New Era*, delivered at the 19th National Congress of the Communist Party of China, October 27, 2017.

of paramount concern, putting them in the first place, and is always being concerned for and working to satisfy their changing needs. This, in turn, embodies the strong strategic planning ability and the sense of responsibility of the CPC Central Committee.

One important experience of the CPC in governance is to be good at discovering problems existing in the development stage of the country, thus summing up experiences based on the objective and practical conditions, putting forward corresponding development strategic goals, and leading the people to overcome difficulties and forge ahead. The problems in the development stage are mainly reflected in principal social tensions. Realizing that, the CPC Central Committee has made correct judgments on the principal tensions facing society, and moved to determine the development goals focused on their solutions. The history of the CPC tells us that such solutions could be traced back to the 8th National Congress of CPC in 1956. The 8th National Congress of CPC determined the principal tension facing Chinese society at that time as "one between the people's requirements for the establishment of an advanced industrial country and the reality of a backward agricultural country", as well as "one between the people's needs for the rapid development of economy and culture and the current situation that the economy and culture cannot meet the people's needs". Since the reform and opening up, the basic domestic social tensions have continued to what they were adjudged to be in 1956. In 1979, Deng Xiaoping pointed out that "the level of the development of the productive forces is very low, far from meeting the needs of the people and the country, which is the principal tension in the current period". In 1981, for the first time China declared in the *Resolution on Certain Questions in Party's History since the Founding of the PRC* that "the principal tension in our society is one between the ever-growing material and cultural needs of the people and the backwardness of social production". This is the very statement China has used for 36 years. However, it was at the 19th National Congress of CPC that it was made clear the social tensions had changed to become "one between the uneven and under development and the people's ever-growing needs for a better life". The statement focused on "uneven" and "inadequate" development, meant that as the basic food and clothing problems had been solved, it was necessary to shift focus efforts on the "uneven and under development". Of course, the change of social tensions does not mean a change in China's national conditions. The report at the 19th National Congress of CPC also made it clear, "The basic dimension of the Chinese context – that our country is still in the primary stage of socialism – has not changed. China's international status as the world's largest developing country has not changed".

In the new historical stage, it is necessary to make new judgments on the principal social tensions and, at the same time, make a series of new strategic arrangements for their solutions. The report at the 19th National Congress of CPC sets out the timetable and road map for building China into a strong and modern socialist country, and also describes the blueprint for "socialist modernization being basically realized" and "becoming a great modern socialist country" that is around the people's ever-growing needs for a better life and in pursuit of more balanced and adequate. The report points out that. By the end of that socialist modernization is basically realized, the following goals will have been met: "China's economic and technological strength has increased significantly. China has become a global leader in innovation. The rights of the people to participate and to develop as equals are adequately protected. The rule of law for the country, the government, and society is basically in place. Institutions in all fields are further improved; the modernization of China's system and capacity for governance is basically achieved. Social etiquette and civility are significantly enhanced. China's cultural soft power has grown much stronger; Chinese culture has greater appeal. People are leading more comfortable lives, and the size of the middle-income group has grown considerably. Disparities in urban-rural development, in development between regions, and in living standards are significantly reduced; equitable access to basic public services is basically ensured; and solid progress has been made toward prosperity for everyone. A modern social governance system has basically taken shape, and society is full of vitality, harmonious, and orderly. There is a fundamental improvement in the environment; the goal of building a Beautiful China is basically attained". When China is developed into a great modern socialist country that is prosperous, strong, democratic, culturally advanced, harmonious, and beautiful, the following goals will have been met: "New heights are reached in every dimension of material, political, cultural and ethical, social, and ecological advancement. Modernization of China's system and capacity for governance is achieved. China has become a global leader in terms of composite national strength and international influence. Common prosperity for everyone is basically achieved. The Chinese people enjoy happier, safer, and healthier lives. The Chinese nation will become a proud and active member of the community of nations".[4] These two paragraphs of the report outlined the strategic plan for building China into a socialist country with Chinese characteristics after the principal social tensions have been determined, and China will embark on a new journey to the great rejuvenation. As General Secretary Xi Jinping pointed out in his report at the 19th National Congress of CPC: "This is what socialism with Chinese characteristics entering a new era means: The Chinese nation, which since modern times began had endured so much for so long, has achieved a tremendous transformation: it has stood up, grown rich, and is becoming strong; it has come to embrace the brilliant prospects of rejuvenation".

3.2 Understanding "A Powerful Socialist Modern Country"

3.2.1 The New Characteristics of a Great Modern Socialist Country

Complete the building of a moderately prosperous society by 2020 is a historical responsibility to the CPC Central Committee with General Secretary Xi Jinping as its core. We now move into a new period where we review history, look ahead to the future, and shoulder heavier and greater mission on embarking on a new journey to fully build a modern socialist country. Deng Xiaoping proposed a version of "a moderately well-off society". With regard to this goal, the understanding underwent evolution from construction of the basic well-off society, primary well-off society, or a low-level well-off society to turn China into proposed at the 16th and 17th National Congresses of CPC and build into a well-off society in an all-round way proposed at the 18th National Congress of CPC. With the deepening of understanding of the connotations of a well-off society, we have stronger determination and confidence in handling this great struggle. There are both connections and differences between building a moderately prosperous society in an all-round way and embarking on a new journey of socialist modernization. Let us see how the previous national congresses of CPC talked about socialist modernization, as shown in Table 3.1.

[4] Xi Jinping, *Secure a Decisive Victory in Building a Moderately Prosperous Society in All Respects and Strive for the Great Success of Socialism with Chinese Characteristics for a New Era*, delivered at the 19th National Congress of the Communist Party of China, October 27, 2017.

Table 3.1 Statements on socialist modernization of the previous national congresses of CPC

CPC congress	*Major contents*
12th	Among all the tasks of creating a new landscape in an all-round way, the first task is to push forward the socialist modernization building and economic growth. China's total national income and major industrial and agricultural products will increase several times over, and people's material and cultural life will be able to reach a well-off level
13th	We should lead and unite the people of all ethnic groups in the country, focus on economic development, adhere to the four cardinal principles, uphold the reform and opening up, rely on ourselves and work hard to build China into a prosperous, democratic, culturally advanced, and harmonious socialist modern country
14th	We should combine the universal truth of Marxism with the specific reality of our country and take our own road to build socialism with Chinese characteristics. We decide to take two steps to achieve the goal of quadrupling the gross national product in the 20th Century, and, at the third step, basically realize socialist modernization by the middle of the twenty-first century
15th	The CPC takes Marxism–Leninism, Mao Zedong Thought, and Deng Xiaoping Theory as its guides for action. Deng Xiaoping Theory, a continuation and development of Mao Zedong Thought, is a correct theory guiding the Chinese people in successfully accomplishing their socialist modernization in the process of reform and opening to the outside world. At the beginning of the reform and opening up, our Party put forward the goal of achieving a well-off society by the end of the twentieth century. If the goal is achieved on time, it will lay a new foundation for China to achieve long-term stability and create a new starting point for the more powerful promotion of socialist modernization
16th	Hold high the great banner of Deng Xiaoping Theory, fully act on the important thought of Three Represents, carry forward our cause into the future, keep pace with the times, build a well-off society in an all-round way, speed up socialist modernization and work hard to create a new situation in building socialism with Chinese characteristics. As human society entered the twenty-first century, we will start a new phase of development for building a well-off society in an all-round way and speeding up socialist modernization

(continued)

Table 3.1 (continued)

CPC congress	*Major contents*
17th	Hold high the great banner of socialism with Chinese characteristics, follow the guidance of Deng Xiaoping Theory and the important thought of Three Represents, thoroughly apply the Scientific Outlook on Development, continue to emancipate the mind, persist in reform and opening up, pursue development in a scientific way, promote social harmony, and strive for new victories in building a moderately prosperous society in all respects. Lead the people of all our nationalities in a united, self-reliant, intensive, and pioneering effort to turn China into a prosperous, strong, democratic, culturally advanced, and modern socialist country by making economic development our central task while adhering to the Four Cardinal Principles and persevering in reform and the open policy
18th	Hold high the great banner of socialism with Chinese characteristics, take Deng Xiaoping Theory, the Theory of Three Represents, and the Scientific Outlook on Development as our guide, free up the mind, implement the policy of reform and opening up, pool our strength, overcome all difficulties, firmly march on the path of socialism with Chinese characteristics, and strive to complete the building of a moderately prosperous society in all respects; Complete the building of a moderately prosperous society in all respects, accelerate socialist modernization, and achieve the great renewal of the Chinese nation
19th	Remain true to our original aspiration and keep our mission firmly in mind, hold high the banner of socialism with Chinese characteristics, secure a decisive victory in building a moderately prosperous society in all respects, strive for the great success of socialism with Chinese characteristics for a new era, and work tirelessly to realize the Chinese Dream of national rejuvenation. The whole Party should take economic development as the central task, adhere to the Four Cardinal Principles, adhere to the reform and opening up, self-reliance, hard work, and entrepreneurship, and strive to build China into a strong, democratic, culturally advanced, harmonious, and beautiful socialist modern power

From the reports to the previous National Congress of CPC, we can see that socialist modernization building is the central and the most important task for a given period of China's national development. This means that all our development activity has been undertaken around socialist modernization. In the beginning, China put forward the idea of building a well-off society; now, we are working actively, step-by-step, to build a well-off society in an all-round way. Building such a society and embarking on a new journey of modernization are complementary.

Only by following the path set for achieving the first goal can we successfully embark on a journey to build a strong country that is the basis for realizing overall modernization. However, it needs to be stressed that embarking on a new journey of modernization is not a continuation of the effort to build a moderately prosperous society in an all-round way; it is rather a higher level of national modernization. In the future, we will inevitably encounter more difficulties, more arduous challenges, and more complex problems. General Secretary Xi Jinping has stressed many times: "Developing socialism with Chinese characteristics is a long-term arduous task of historic importance, and we must be prepared to carry out a great struggle with many new historical features". We need to review history, stay true to the Party's founding mission, and proceed with this new task with even higher morale.

3.2.2 Comparison of International Indicators of "a Great Modern Country"

The report at the 19th National Congress of CPC put forward the "Two Centennial Goals". The period between the 19th and the 20th national congresses of the CPC is the period in which the timeframes of the Two Centennial Goals converge. From 2020 to 2035, on the basis of having built a moderately prosperous society in an all-round way, China will work hard to basically realize socialist modernization. This means that the third step of China's three-step approach strategy is set to occur 15 years earlier than the original plan. In the following part of this section, I will analyze the current development process and future development momentum through comparisons in five aspects—economic, political, cultural, social livelihood, and ecological civilization building.

i. Economic building

Table 3.2 shows that, in 2015, Chinese GNI per capita reached USD7380, representing 22 percent of that achieved by high-income countries but 89.3 percent more than that of middle-income countries; it was 88.1 percent that of the world, but only 15.1 percent that of the US. Data from Yao Yang, Professor of the National School of Development of Peking University, shows our medium-term goal is to become a middle-income power by 2035, with per capita income reaching 37.5 percent of

Table 3.2 China's GNI per capita In USD

Country	*2011*	*2012*	*2013*	*2014*	*2015*
High-income country	35,103	35,022	35,150	35,705	33,537
Middle-income country	3663	3852	4015	4121	3899
World	8581	8678	8789	8926	8372
USA	42,606	44,591	45,468	47,336	48,762
China (excluding Hong Kong, Macao, and Taiwan)	4300	4940	5441	6740	7380

Source World Bank, WDI database

the American level; the long-term goal is to become a high-income power by 2049, with per capita income rising to 45 percent of the level achieved by the US. In 2016, China's economic growth rate was 6.7 percent, while the US was only about 2 percent. If China wants to reach the target of 45 percent in average income compared to the US in 2049, then it needs a growth rate of 3.7 percent.

ii. Political building

Since the 18th National Congress of CPC, General Secretary Xi Jinping has repeatedly stressed the need for law-based governance and strengthen Party self-discipline. The CPC Central Committee issued eight rules, sending a strong signal that the Party needed to be strictly governed. A comprehensive agenda for promoting the rule of law was launched by General Secretary Xi Jinping for the first time in December 2014. In the past five years, from the full-scale inspection and residence of discipline inspection and supervision groups around the country to the reforms of the country's supervisory systems, the Party and government have constantly improved self-supervision, launched activities to see members command and act on the Party's mass line, initiated a campaign for the observance of the Three Stricts and Three Earnests, regularized and institutionalized the requirement for all Party members to have a solid understanding of the Party Constitution, Party regulations, and related major policy addresses and to meet Party standards. As a result, the ideals and convictions of all Party members have been strengthened and their sense of Party consciousness has deepened, and the government's credibility and ability to govern have also enhanced a lot.

General Secretary Xi Jinping equips the whole Party with the system of theories of socialism with Chinese characteristics, fully developing the people's democratic politics. Especially in regard to guidance through theory, General Secretary Xi Jinping's new thought and strategy for the governance of China formed since the 18th National Congress of CPC represents a vivid expression of Marxism today. In terms of strategic arrangement, the four-pronged comprehensive strategy and the five-sphere integrated plan have been adopted around "Two Centennial Goals" and the Chinese Dream. Since the 18th National Congress of CPC, the systems of people's congresses go on simultaneously with reform, which democratic elections, democratic supervision, democratic management, democratic consultation, and democratic decision-making effectively implemented and continuously developed. From 2013 to 2016, the NPC Standing Committee promulgated 17 laws and amended 95 laws, thus achieving a number of new important results.

iii. Cultural building

At the grand gathering in Beijing marking the 95th anniversary of the founding of the CPC, General Secretary Xi Jinping solemnly put forward the "Four Matters of Confidence": "To remain true to our original aspirations and continue to make progress, we need to have confidence in its path to socialism with Chinese characteristics, our theory, system and culture, adhere to the Party's basic line unswervingly and keep pushing forward the great cause of socialism with Chinese characteristics". The "Four Matters of Confidence" just mentioned originate in a firm belief in the great cause of socialism with Chinese characteristics and was a new expression in practicing socialism with Chinese characteristics. Xi Jinping Thought on Socialism with Chinese Characteristics for a New Era, established at the 19th National Congress of CPC, brings the "Four Matters of Confidence" closer to the goal of building a great socialist modern country. Of them, confidence in its path brings followed shows that socialism with Chinese characteristics in the new era is the only way to ensure creation of a great modern socialist country in the new era; confidence in its theory show that socialism with Chinese characteristics in the new era is the requisite action guidance for achieving socialist modernization building; confidence in its system shows that socialist system with Chinese characteristics in the new era is the fundamental guarantee for building a great modern socialist country; confidence in its culture shows that socialist culture with Chinese characteristics in the new era is the powerful source of strength inspiring all members of the Party and the people of all ethnic groups in China to build a great modern socialist country.

As a matter of fact, same as the characteristics and objectives of socialist modernization, the establishment of these "Four Matters of Confidence" has also undergone a process of development and evolution. In his speech of July 1, 2016, Xi Jinping added "confidence in its culture" to the existing "three matters of confidence" (confidence in the socialist path, theory, and system), showing the high importance he attaches to this aspect. The reason why our Party has been able to forge ahead bravely despite various setbacks along the way is that it has maintained total faith with lofty, long-range ideals. Facing the rapid development of globalization, marketization, and informatization in the world today, China has also reached a critical period in achieving national rejuvenation and becoming a rising power. Can China accomplish the cultural tasks while comprehensively promoting the economic rise of socialism with Chinese characteristics, and no longer be a follower but a leader? Culture plays an irreplaceable role and shows soft power that cannot be ignored. The proposition of the "Four Matters of Confidence" with Chinese characteristics implies we must trace back the development of socialism with Chinese characteristics from the angle of culture. It also indicates that the CPC and the Chinese people must, in the course of striving to seek development of the cause of socialism with Chinese characteristics, work hard to continuously seek development of socialist culture with Chinese characteristics and stand firm in the cultural agitation of today's world. At the same time, we need to show Chinese culture to the whole world while continuing to explore and contribute Chinese strength to the overall cause. This requires us to consciously and firmly grasp the cultural mission, rights, and responsibilities of socialism with Chinese characteristics.

iv. Social livelihood building

The report at the 19th National Congress of CPC made a clear request to the whole Party: "Everyone in the Party must keep firmly in mind that the nature of a political party and of a government is determined by those whom they serve. To lead the people to a better life is our Party's abiding goal. We must put the people's interests above all else, see that the gains of reform and development benefit all our people in a fair way, and strive to achieve shared prosperity for everyone".

In the five years since the 18th National Congress of CPC, China has achieved astonishing development, with the number of scientific researchers ranking first in the world. The proportion of China's R&D investment in GDP has been continuously increasing, reaching 2.0 percent in 2015, a figure dwarfing the vast majority of developed countries in the world. This does not mean total investment, but only the proportion in GDP. The total number leaves most developed countries far behind. In 2016, the total amount of R&D investment in China was RMB1567.67 billion, an increase of 10.6 percent over the last year, and the growth rate increased by 1.7 percentage points. In 2016, it accounted for 2.11 percent of GDP, with the proportion having exceeded 2 percent for three consecutive years. Although China still falls a long way from the US, the proportion in China has exceeded the average level of 2.08 percent in the 15 leading countries of the European Union. It is estimated that China's R&D investment will reach about RMB2.3 trillion by 2020, accounting for about 2.4 percent of GDP. The amount of R&D investment represents a country's scientific and technological strength and innovation ability. China is steadily moving closer to high-income countries, and it will continue to increase the amount of such investment in the future. We will make concerted efforts for the great rejuvenation of the Chinese nation.

China's education level is constantly being enhanced, and its quality improved as well. Here is a very interesting discovery: young generation's income exceeds that of middle-aged group, which is not the case in many developed countries. This is fact that the quality and level of education in China have been constantly improved, and the return on human capital investment is relatively high.

v. Ecological civilization building

The 19th National Congress of CPC outlined a beautiful blueprint for the modernization of ecological civilization: "The modernization that we pursue is one characterized by harmonious coexistence between man and nature. In addition to creating more material and cultural wealth to meet people's ever-increasing needs for a better life, we need also to provide more quality ecological goods to meet people's ever-growing demands for a beautiful environment. We should, acting on the principles of prioritizing resource conservation and environmental protection and letting nature restore itself, develop spatial layouts, industrial structures, and ways of work and life that help conserve resources and protect the environment. With this, we can restore the serenity, harmony, and beauty of nature". Since the 18th CPC Congress, General Secretary Xi Jinping has attached great importance to the building of ecological civilization. He has delivered a series of important speeches, comprehensively expounding the concept, significance, principles, and measures of socialist ecological civilization building. To implement and adhere to the new development concept, we must correctly handle the relationship between economic and ecological environment, strive to achieve a win-win situation between economy and ecology, and realize the sustainable development of the Chinese nation (Xia Jiechang 2017).

3.3 Challenges in Building a Great Modern Socialist Country

In the past 40 years of reform and opening up, huge changes had taken place in the country from the economic sector to many other fields in both rural and urban areas, not only in east China but also in Central and western regions. These development achievements are incomparable to any other country in the world, with economic growth having increased more than 100-fold in nominal volume and 16–20 times in terms of actual volume. This is a rare phenomenon in human history to see such high-speed growth for so many years. This is not only a miracle in Chinese history, but also in world history. However, alongside the rapid development, there are many problems left, and, which need to be solved in the next 20–30 years and then we could move forward steadily in building a great modern socialist country.

i. Medical insurance

China is the largest developing country in the world. In 2015, its population reached 1.375 billion, including an urban population of 771.16 million, and a rural population of 603.46 million. GDP per head has reached USD7380. China introduced medical insurance reform in 2009, thus establishing a basic medical security system covering the entire population. At present, there are more than 1.3 billion insured people, so that the coverage rate has reached upwards of 95 percent. However, this is an impressive figure in terms of quantity, but poor in quality, especially in rural areas. The problem of "the difficulty and high cost of getting medical treatment" has been a prominent social problem for a long time now and the foreseeable future. One key indicator to measure a modern powerful country is to see whether it has achieved a national health system for all.

ii. Income gap

In 2015, the urban per capita disposable income was RMB31,194, and that of rural residents was RMB11,421, the former thus being almost three times that of the latter. According to the *2016 Statistical Communique of the People's Republic of China on the National Economic and Social Development* issued by the National Bureau of Statistics on February 28, 2017, he urban per capita disposable income in 2016 was RMB33,616, an increase of 7.8 percent year-on-year; while the figure for rural residents was RMB12,363, an increase of 8.2 percent year-on-year; the difference between the two was thus was 2.72 times, only a very slight improvement of 0.01.[5]

By income scale, the per capita disposable income of low-income people is only RMB5529, while that in the high-income bracket is RMB59,259, a nearly 10-fold difference. By region, the high per capita disposable income is mainly concentrated in the eastern region, while western provinces not only have a low GDP, but also low per capita disposable income. In particular, Tibet is bottom with per capita disposable income of RMB13,639, only 25 percent of the level in Shanghai. Does such a situation mean failure of the Strategy for large-scale development of western China launched by China? Of course not. In recent years, the central and western regions have all seen an increase in GDP and per capita disposable income. However, due to the large base of low-income people in the latter and infrastructure lagging far behind a growing need,

[5] http://www.chashebao.com/shebaotiaoli/17307.html.

plus a poor natural environment, there is still a long way to go before the western region can catch up with the east.

iii. Education

Education plays such a crucial role and is the lifeblood of any country. In 2015, the average length of compulsory education in the world stood at 9.1 years; It was 13 years in the US, 12 years in UK, and 11 years respectively in France and Denmark. China has pressed ahead with achieving the nine-year compulsory education level for 30 years. Its GDP ranked second in the world in 2016, second only to the US, but the duration of compulsory education is lower than the world average. In the next few decades, China will no longer face the problem of labor shortage, but the problem will shift to rising unemployment. As the introduction of more and more artificial intelligence replaces human labor, China needs to do a better job of enhancing its educational level and improving its quality, so as to cope with AI and ensure relatively full employment.

China's education development shoulders an important mission. In the new era, the nation needs to develop basic education in an all-round way, and, at the same time, cultivate a large number of world-leading high-level talents with innovative ability. The development experience of developed countries shows that, if we want to realize industrialization, we must develop basic education, secondary education, and higher education at the same time. This is because basic education is the foundation for training high-quality talents key to the development of a country leading the world. At present, China lacks a strong reserve of high-quality multifacted talents. In 2013, the number of researchers per million people was 3962.5 in high-income countries, 4018.6 in the US, 5201.3 in Japan, 6456.6 in South Korea, and 1089.2 in China.[6] Shouldering a dual mission in education, China need not only improve the overall quality of the entire nation, but also cultivate a large number of high-quality high-tech talents. This determines that education reform and development will be a road full of challenges. China hopes to become a manufacturing power by 2035 and the second largest technological power in the world by 2049.

[6] Word Bank WDI Database.

iv. Ecological environment

China is now on the verge of building into a moderately prosperous society in an all-round way. At this point of time, it finds itself at an awkward stage in terms of environmental protection, when it has to deepen reform and, at the same time, seek green development. At present, the economy has begun to follow the path of stable but slower growth. Various tensions converge and interact, so it is difficult to find a balanced commitment point between development and environmental protection.

First, the eastern region enters into the late stage of industrialization, and the environmental pressure is gradually being reduced; meanwhile, the central and western regions are in a period of going for all-out development. As 77.8 percent of the heavy chemical projects approved by the Ministry of Ecology and Environment the People's Republic of China are located in the central and western regions, this, plus relatively weak regulation, means the areas are highly likely to experience more serious pollution.

Second, China's current comprehensive competitiveness index is close to 80, which is estimated to reach about 95 in 2020. However, this is only the level achieved by the US, Japan, and other developed countries in the 1980s. China's main products in the global value chain feature low added value, and overcapacity is still prominent, and development and environmental protection are stalemated.

Third, China's coal demand far exceeds that of developed countries. Its GDP is basically equivalent to that of the US in 1979, but the demand for coal is five times that recorded by the latter in the same period. The current coal consumption of the Beijing-Tianjin-Hebei region and the Yangtze River Delta is about four times that of Europe in the same historical period (1980 in Germany and 1987 in the UK). Chemical oxygen demand and ammonia and nitrogen emissions are 1.6 times and 5.6 times of the environmental capacity respectively, and about 1/3 of the rivers are overloaded and have exceeded or approached the upper bearing limit. Many environmental problems, such as regional atmospheric oxidation, water eutrophication, and ecological balance at river sources have been in a critical state and become ever more sensitive. In 2014, eutrophication in 61 lakes (reservoirs) reached 24.6 percent. Judging by the pollutant load of per unit water resources, the chemical oxygen demand load per unit water resources in the Haihe, Huaihe, and Yellow river stood at

Table 3.3 PM2.5 in air Unit: Mg/m^3

Country	*2000*	*2005*	*2010*	*2011*	*2013*
World	26.6	29.2	30.6	30.8	31.5
USA	14.7	13.7	11.8	11.4	10.7
UK	14.6	12.7	11.4	11.2	10.8
China	44.2	51.0	54.2	54.1	54.4

Source World Bank, WDI database

39.67 mg/L, 29.30 mg/L, and 15.76 mg/L, being 6.1 times, 4.2 times, and 2.2 times that of the national average, respectively.[7] After the slowdown of economic development, the environmental problems previously covered by economic prosperity gradually come to the surface.

The photochemical smog in Los Angeles and the London smog incidents are both world-notorious environmental hazard incidents in living memory. Britain and the United States have spent nearly 100 years to recover blue sky and white clouds. Table 3.3 shows that the PM2.5 in the air of the UK and the US is far below the world average. In 1996, the US proposed to control PM2.5 when its per capita GDP was USD28,000. China proposed to control the PM2.5 level in 2011 when its per capita GDP was only USD5400. At that time, China consumed nearly 70 percent of its coal reserves, and its industrial energy consumption was 70 percent, compared to 20 percent and 7 percent of American coal and industrial energy consumption. There are huge differences in energy and economic development stages. We can see from Table 3.3 that, in 2013, China's PM2.5 in air was more than five times that of the US, and 1.7 times that of the world average. In the *International Statistical Yearbook*, China ranked first in the world in this regard. China proposed to control PM2.5 in 2011, and we can see from Table 3.3 that the figure decreased only 0.1 in that year compared to the previous one. Actually, the pollution of surface water and groundwater is more difficult to control than that of air treatment. When China is making full progress toward the goal of becoming a modern country, the task of building a beautiful China with blue sky and white clouds is a long way off.

[7] Wu Shunze: *Eight Challenges to Environmental Protection during the 13th Five-Year Plan,* China Environmental News, September 15, 2015.

3.4 Construction of a Great Modern Socialist Country at Full Steam Ahead

To maintain vigor and vitality and brave the tide, a country must conform to the law of historical development and keep up with the pace of the times. The CPC Central Committee with Xi Jinping at the core puts forward the new "two-step approach" strategy: the first step is to basically realize modernization by 2035, and the second step to develop from a modern country to a great modern socialist country by 2050. In the mid-twentieth century, China succeeded in "standing up" and then plunged into socialist transformation, and concentrated all available forces to establish a complete socialist industrial system. On this basis, it activated the economy in all aspects through modernization. During the reform and opening up that began in late 1978, China makes every effort to enable the people to live in a well-off society in an all-round way, a society featuring common prosperity. It takes 40 years for China to go from "standing up" to "becoming prosperous and strong". Building a great modern socialist country is the new task to be undertaken in the twenty-first century.

China's development has entered a new era since the 18th National Congress of CPC. During the period, it has encountered unprecedented challenges and problems. The CPC Central Committee with Xi Jinping at its core led the Chinese people to surmount difficulties, and, by summing up experiences, open up a new road to the future development. The CPC Central Committee constantly points out new directions for future development and introduces new strategic deployments. A series of new ideas, new concepts, and new augments have been put forward for the realization of the Chinese dream, including: the Four-Pronged Comprehensive Strategy, the innovative, coordinated, green, open and shared development, the Two Centennial Goals strategic deployment, the "Belt and Road Initiative", as well as promoting innovative transformation and development of traditional Chinese culture, exchange and mutual learning between civilizations, win-win cooperation, and a community with a shared future for humanity. These all form Xi Jinping Thought System on Socialism with Chinese Characteristics for a New Era. It builds on and further enriches Marxism–Leninism, Mao Zedong Thought, Deng Xiaoping Theory, the Theory of Three Represents, and the Scientific Outlook on Development. It represents the latest achievement in adapting Marxism to the Chinese context and encapsulates the practical experience and collective wisdom of our Party and the people. It is an important component of the theory of socialism with Chinese characteristics, and a guide to action for all our members and all the Chinese people as we strive to achieve national rejuvenation. This Thought must be adhered to and steadily developed on a long-term basis. It is the dream and pursuit of the generations of Chinese Communists to realize the emergence of a great modern socialist country. It is also a beautiful dream the Chinese people have been pursuing for a long time. It is more the inexhaustible power for which the CPC has been striving since its establishment.

Xi Jinping Thought on Socialism with Chinese Characteristics for a New Era innovates China's socialist theoretical system, and it is China's Marxism of the twenty-first century. Xi Jinping Thought on Socialism with Chinese Characteristics for a New Era makes the following things clear: It makes clear that the overarching goal of upholding and developing socialism with Chinese characteristics is to realize socialist modernization and national rejuvenation, and, that on the basis of finishing the building of a moderately prosperous society in all respects, a two-step approach should be taken to build China into a great modern socialist country that is prosperous, strong, democratic, culturally advanced, harmonious, and beautiful by the middle of the century. It makes clear that the principal tension facing Chinese society in the new era is that between uneven and underdevelopment and the people's ever-growing needs for a better life. We must therefore continue the commitment to our people-centered philosophy of development, and work to promote well-rounded human development and common prosperity for everyone. It makes clear that the overall plan for building socialism with Chinese characteristics is the five-sphere integrated plan, and the overall strategy is the four-pronged comprehensive strategy. It highlights the importance of fostering stronger confidence in the path, theory, system, and culture of socialism with Chinese characteristics. It makes clear that the overall goal of deepening reform in every field is to improve and develop the system of socialism with Chinese characteristics and modernize China's system and capacity for governance. It makes clear that the overall goal of comprehensively advancing law-based governance is to establish a system of socialist rule of law with Chinese characteristics and build a country of socialist rule of law. It makes clear that the Party's goal of building a strong military in the new era is to build the people's forces into world-class forces that obey the Party's command, can fight and win, and maintain excellent conduct. It makes clear that major country diplomacy with Chinese characteristics aims to foster a new type of international relations and build a community with a shared future for humanity. It makes clear that the defining feature of socialism with Chinese characteristics is the leadership of the Communist Party of China; the greatest strength of the system of socialism with Chinese characteristics is the leadership of the Communist Party of China; the Party is the highest force for political leadership. It sets forth the general requirements for Party building in the new era and underlines the importance of political work in Party building.[8]

The 19th National Congress of CPC summarized the essence and rich implications of the Xi Jinping Thought on Socialism with Chinese Characteristics for a New Era in the following 14 aspects: (1) Ensuring Party leadership overall work; (2) Committing to a people-centered approach; (3) Continuing to comprehensively deepen reform; (4) Adopting a new vision for development;(5) Seeing that the people run the country; (6) Ensuring every dimension of governance is law-based; (7) Upholding core socialist values; (8) Ensuring and improving living standards through development; (9) Ensuring harmony between human and nature; (10) Pursuing a holistic approach to national security; (11) Upholding absolute Party leadership over the people's armed forces; (12) Upholding the principle of "one country, two systems" and promoting national reunification; (13) Promoting the building of a community with a shared future for humanity; (14) Exercising full and rigorous governance over the Party.[9] The above 14 points form the basic policy that underpins our endeavors to uphold and develop socialism with Chinese characteristics in the new era.

Since the 18th National Congress of CPC, the CPC Central Committee with Xi Jinping at its core has led the Chinese people to wage

[8] Wang Junwei: Set Sail again from a New Era to a Great Modern Socialist Country, *China Youth Daily*, October 24, 2017.

[9] Xi Jinping: *Secure a Decisive Victory in Building a Moderately Prosperous Society in All Respects and Strive for the Great Success of Socialism with Chinese Characteristics for a New Era*, delivered at the 19th National Congress of the Communist Party of China, October 27, 2017.

an arduous struggle to win great achievements in various fields. The new journey is about to start. We firmly support the CPC leadership, and, with great hope in mind, we shall work hard to surmount difficulties along the path of socialism with Chinese characteristics. The Chinese dream for national rejuvenation will be bound to achieve!

Reference

Xia Jiechang. (2017). Promote Development and Transformation with the Building of Ecological Civilization. *China Economic Times*, May 10, 2018.

CHAPTER 4

The Innovation-Driven Development and Nation-Building Strategy

Chunping Zhong

Innovation has always been the crux of sustainable development in any country and society. It fills the gap between future development needs and historical reality, which is why the Chinese government is vigorously advocating an innovation-driven development strategy, highlighting the importance of innovation, and striving to make China a country and society of innovators. Out of necessity, there is not much controversy in that. However, there is still the need to further study into whether China is able to realize the desired innovation-driven development strategy so as to make China a country of innovators.

4.1 Understanding the Strategy

Innovation becomes the most important driving force for any country seeking prolonged economic growth, and technological innovation especially becomes the most critical and explicit factor in this regard. From

C. Zhong (✉)
National Academy of Economic Strategy, Chinese Academy of Social Sciences, Beijing, China

D. He et al. (eds.), *Chinese Finance Policy for a New Era*, https://doi.org/10.1007/978-981-33-4054-1_4

the theory of long-run growth of the economy, we can see how the traditional economic growth theory has been transformed from an emphasis on factor expansion to technological progress. The early growth theory attached importance to capital accumulation, which constituted the core of the initial Harrod-Dommar model [based on a Keynesian approach used in development economics to explain an economy's growth rate in terms of the level of saving and of capital]. In terms of conclusion, the crucial role of capital accumulation became the core of development economics in the 1950s–1960s. According to the theory, the capital-output ratio remains constant, thus the capital accumulation actually determines the rate of long-run growth. Therefore, lack of capital is the main obstacle to growth, so that the saving ratio of society needs to be greatly improved. As the saving ratio increases, the rate of long-run growth will increase correspondingly. This has been proved in many developing countries. Under-developed economies usually are short of capital and the capital stock per capita is low; thus, more capital input can bring higher output. In terms of policy, we can improve the capital stock in various ways so as to promote economic development. This proposition has also been widely used in China's economic practice. From 1950 to 1990, the emphasis was on promoting capital accumulation through centralized means, thus promoting the industrialization and realizing economic development. It does enable the economy to achieve greater capital accumulation and form a relatively complete industrialization system; however, due to the excessive capital accumulation through "self-reliance", the efficiency isn't paid attention to. Therefore, it was not able to achieve sustained rapid growth, with little significant improvement in per capita living standards. There was still a large demand for capital around the year 2000; however, since then, capital has not proved to be the key to the problem, despite its relative abundance.

In fact, theory of economic growth has conducted research and explained the problem in a clear-cut way: The capital is not necessarily the key. The follow-up neoclassical economic theory stresses endogenous savings or the endogenous consumption and saving decisions of households. Capital stock per capita will eventually tend toward stabilization if decide the optimal decision of households through the Harrod-Dommar model but the constant exogenous saving ration epitomized by it is relaxed. In other words, the constantly increasing capital stock is not the best way forward. What becomes truly important is for households to make the best decision between current and future consumption (realized through capital accumulation) to maximize their lifetime utility. It is not the best choice to constantly increase capital accumulation but reduce current consumption. From the perspective of the overall economic system, we see that excessive capital accumulation is relatively inefficient. In terms of policy conclusions, constantly increasing capital stock will only increase output per capita, instead of long-run sustained economic growth. In this sense, the growth theory testifies to the truth that capital is not the key to long-run growth. In other words, the continuous investment of capital will limit the final economic development.

The key to getting rid of the limit-to-growth or the constant states in the long term is long-run technological progress. As a result, the growth theory has turned to the study of the source and mode of action in regard to technological progress, and a growth theory model of endogenous technological progress has gradually emerged as the core idea. This naturally leads on to consideration of how best to promote technological progress to ensure lasting economic growth.

This theoretical problem has been verified by abundant experience in the process of economic development. If no substantial technological progress, with the continuous investment of capital and greater labor participation, an economy will eventually tend to stabilize rather than continue to advance. This is, then, the convergence hypothesis in the theory of economic growth. In under-developed economies that is far from the steady-state level, they may realize faster growth, higher return on investment of capital, enhanced accumulation of capital and the ever-faster output. However, with the increase of capital stock per capita, the marginal output of capital decreases and the accumulation impetus and final output growth rate correspondingly decreases. Once it approaches the steady-state level, an economy will become stable, thus the overall economic growth rate will tend to sink lower and lower. From the policy perspective, an economy may maintain rapid economic growth in a given period. However, it is necessary to analyze what factors form the driving force of this growth. If it starts from a low initial development level and tends to rely on increased capital investment and greater use of labor, it will lead to the continuous decline in the final economic growth rate; certainly, the previous rapid economic growth will be difficult to maintain. There are many examples of this in Southeast Asian economies. Around 1990, the "Four Asian Tigers" (referring to Hong Kong of China, Taiwan of China, Singapore, and South Korea) enjoyed rapid economic growth, and the per capita income of residents increased continuously, propelling them into the ranks of high-income economies. However, many studies expressed concern about this kind of rapid development potential. Alwyn Young (1995) decomposed the factor contribution of growth in the "Four Asian Tigers" and found that, according to the Solow residual method [describing empirical productivity growth in an economy from year to year and decade to decade devised by Nobel Economic Prize winner Robert Solow], most of the growth comes from capital accumulation and labor input, while the contribution rate from technological progress is limited. This means that growth is unsustainable. This research has aroused a lot of concern and controversy in regard to accounting method itself and data used. However, the 1997 Asian Financial Crisis generally revealed underlying problems in the economic growth of the four dragons. After the crisis, they lost economic growth momentum, which to some extent confirms the conclusion of previous economic growth accounting.

China's economic growth naturally attracts special attention of the world, and there are also continuous disputes emerging from time to time, focused on the motive power and sustainability of growth. Since 1980, China has become the second largest economy in the world after nearly 40 years of rapid growth and increasing stock accumulation. China's newly increased output every year has a significant impact on the global economy. The future of its economy has also attracted the attention of all parties concerned. The questions worthy of attention include: First, how to explain the rapid growth achieved, and what factors promoted such rapid advancement? Second, can China's economy maintain its original growth momentum for some time to come. Two of these questions are most widely considered: "China Economic Collapse" and "the Middle-income Trap". The first focuses more on short-term risks, holding that short-term debt and other issues will disrupt China's development momentum. The second mainly emphasizes that it is difficult for China to sustain long-run economic growth. This view is sustained by arguing that, after a certain stage of development, growth will be hard to sustain, and cannot exceed the middle-income level as defined by the World Bank. Both question China's economic growth. These questions are raised frequently in the process of China's economic growth, and there are even people who voice doubts about the authenticity of data provided by China. Cases in point include the academic debates around 1992, and also the large-scale discussion around 2002. The skeptical view is that China's data is not authentic as it does not reflect fluctuations of prices. If excluding price factors, China's economic growth rate will fall significantly. The positive view is that the China's economy is actually more significant than the data, finding impressive expression in loner life expectancy per capita, decreasing number of poverty-stricken population, higher living standards of residents.

The crux of the matter is whether the driving force of China's economic growth in the future can be realized by endogenous technological progress. If this enhances the driving force, rather than relying on the expansion of essential factors, including capital deepening, more migration, and employment of rural labor to urban areas, then economic growth is more driven by innovation, which means that the economy can achieve continuous growth.

From the perspective of growth theory, if the initial level of a country's economy is low, then the force derived from convergence can help under-developed economies to grow rapidly, and the return on capital and the marginal income of investment will be higher. There will be sufficient returns from increasing capital investment.

From a process viewpoint, an economy is not likely to be innovation-driven at the start-up stage. It is unrealistic to emphasize technological progress or technological dominance for under-developed economies. On the contrary, the further down the income ladder people live, the more efficient to increase capital investment and labor investment. Therefore, it is impossible, and actually unnecessary to adopt an innovation-driven development strategy growth model for a long time. In regard to China, when the economy began to develop in 1980, it was more effective and realistic to promote economic growth through capital expansion and labor force transfer, and in fact, it was in general. However, after the capital stock per capita reaches a certain level, more technological progress is needed to drive further economic growth.

In terms of results, the innovation-driven development strategy means that technological progress plays an important role in overall economic growth. From the perspective of growth accounting, the greater the contribution from TFP, the stronger the driving force technological progress will impart. If an economy has enough investment in technology research and development, and can form more new technologies, it can be called an innovation-driven economy. If a country has enough innovation, it can be called a country of innovators. However, if the technological progress contributes less, and the driving force and activities of innovation in the whole society are also moribund, it cannot be called an innovation-driven economy or country.

Some obvious characteristics may appear that, the innovation-driven development at least means the whole society attaches great importance to innovation. Investment in R&D from both public sector and private sector should account for a considerable proportion on total inputs. In terms of output, there needs to be many explicit features, such as many new patent applications and approvals every year.

Therefore, we need to compare whether China has achieved innovation-driven development, and it can be called as a country of innovators.

4.2 How Far Does China Still Have to Go?

There are certain "Black Box" problem in technology, and it is also difficult to measure technology itself. Therefore, there are great difficulties in how to measure innovation and technological progress. We try to compare and analyze the contribution of technological progress in China's economic growth from the following dimensions.

First, this can be measured by growth accounting. The general method is to measure the growth rate, the change in capital and labor inputs and other variables, and then calculate the Solow residuals on average, which is the default contribution rate of technological progress through regression. Although there are many controversies surrounding growth accounting, the general conclusion is that in the past 30 years, the China's economic growth relies heavily on increasing investment in capital and a labor force migrating from rural to urban areas, but the total factor productivity (TFP) derived from technological progress has yet to be improved. Another possible evidence is that the return on capital is still relatively high on the whole. The nongovernmental financing rate is mostly around 15–20 percent. It is a fact that the return on capital is relatively high despite many possible reasons, which may mean that there is still considerable room for more capital investment. That is, in the process of moving toward innovation-driven development, there is still much room for economic growth coming from the drive force generated by "convergence".

Second, investment index and R&D investment. China continues to invest more in scientific research. It was less than RMB35 billion in 1995, nearly RMB90 billion in 2000, nearly RMB250 billion in 2005, and more than RMB700 billion in 2010, more than RMB1 trillion in 2012, even RMB1,417 billion in 2015. But the proportion in relative economic aggregate is not high, which is less than 2.2 percent in most years.

By composition, although fundamental research funding is also growing rapidly, it still accounts for little in the total funding. In a period of more than 20 years, the proportion of fundamental research has remained at about 5 percent. Generally, it reflects the situation that there continues to be a lack of attention to basic research. However, research and experimental development funding accounts for a very high proportion, which generally shows that the government or enterprises are trying to apply advanced technology for reference to achieve economic development. This unique composition is also very strange in the global view. The point is that the proportion of fundamental research is too low, reflecting that there is a long-lasting "short-sighted" tendency about the technological innovation in general.

Third, in terms of output indicators, China has strengthened the hand of R&D workers, and the number of patents approved is increasing. However, there are hidden dangers in the indicators of import and export reflected in economic competitiveness—the import and export status of high technology, which can reflect the relative competitive strength to a certain extent. To be sure, the number of science and technology papers and monographs, akin to the indicators of fundamental research achievements, is steadily increasing. The number of inventions and patents reflecting technological achievements is rapidly increasing. Especially in recent years, both the number of applications and grants of patents have shown rapid growth, which, to a certain extent, reflects the great progress of innovation activities in technology. Various indicators have greatly improved compared with 10 years ago. The import and export of technology can best reflect the competitiveness level (of course, some areas may be subject to technology blockade by certain countries). At this level, the export capacity deserves special attention. At present, there is still a large deficiency for China in this regard. Since 2013, although the volume of high-tech exports has remained high, there has been relative stagnation. The 2015 figure shows USD665.297 billion, which is lower than 2014. That's not enough. In terms of imports, it sustains the similar trend. The overall data shows that the level in 2015 was nearly double that recorded in 2007; however, after 2013, the level has remained stable.

Therefore, on the whole, it should be understood that, investment in the fundamental research is increasing, but not much in proportion, as a result the fundamental research is increasing correspondingly. Investment in technology R&D is huge, so there will be impressive increases and promotion of technological achievements. Regarding investment in direct application of technology, it involves more input than any other aspect, and international competition is gaining momentum. The stamina is worthy of special attention given the recent situation. In this sense, we hope to gain more space for innovation growth as soon as possible, despite the fact that we have not reached the desired level of innovation-driven development.

4.3 How to Drive Economic Growth with Innovation?

i. **Uncertainty of technological progress and the source of social innovation**

Technology is a black box to a large extent, and the emergence of a single technology is random. In fact, it is hard to predict which kind of technology will become the dominant one, and even harder to predict when it will emerge. For example, energy has always occupied a very important position in social and economic life. However, which new energy technology can appear and in what form is an issue of wide concern. History proves it is very difficult to seek innovation and development in terms of energy technology. This is why the development of the so-called new energy technology is not as fast as people expected but rather extremely slow, and every step of improvement is hard-earned. We have seen more "tricks" and "traps" in the process. Although the vast majority of people can generally understand energy technology, they know little about the technology in detail, let alone be able to make an objective evaluation on the future of technological innovation. In this context, entrepreneurs obtaining some technical ability may become so-called "adventurers" and false prophets. There will be endless scams when capital works. Therefore, we must be very clear about the uncertainty of technological progress, and that it is far from easy to realize true innovation.

If we invest in technological innovation and R&D in various fields, we can generally see that new technologies will appear at a certain speed from the perspective of the whole society. The emergency of new technology is the most common form of innovation, and technology mainly comes from R&D investment, and so the latter becomes the dominant form of innovation.

Significant technological progress is full of uncertainties and unpredictable characteristics; however, for most of them, including technological improvement and more new products, if the R&D investment increases, the possibility of obtaining technological progress should increase to a certain extent generally. Therefore, the growth theory is used mainly for the study as to how monopoly firms seeking to maximize profits decide their scale of R&D investment, so as to analyze the extent to which centralized central planners can improve overall social welfare.

For society, what should be considered is that we should in no way expect innovation to come naturally; instead, we need to make all possible preparations for the realization of innovation.

ii. **Manufacturer's decision and R&D investment decision**

The incentive for micro enterprises to engage in innovation will be the key to innovation activities, and also the foundation of innovation-driven development strategy to the whole society.

The goal of manufacturers is very clear— mainly to obtain monopoly profits. They can obtain unique technology or products through technological innovation, and then acquire monopolistic advantages on the market with technological innovation thus obtained, so as to realize monopoly pricing. On the one hand, funds will be earmarked to make up for the cost of R&D, including the input of human and material resources; on the other hand, efforts will be exerted to obtain a risk premium. In the process of R&D, enterprises take the risk of innovation failure, so they seek for higher premium taking this particular risk.

Therefore, for enterprises and entrepreneurs, the decision made on investment in innovation activities is the key. First, there should be an aspiration recognizing the need to invest. It is very important for innovation to have the aspiration for change— obtaining new technology or new products via innovation, so as to obtain new markets. For entrepreneurs, investing in innovation is a kind of risk-taking activity, so investors need to possess the risk-taking spirit. Only in this way, there will be the initial power of innovation. In this sense, entrepreneurship means possession of the will to change. For the whole society, risk appetite is an important variable. Hence, there needs to be a risk-taking spirit for change; the entrepreneur should not be too conservative or too averse to risk. This is especially obvious in society with deep-rooted traditional culture or history. For example, if the authority and tradition are overemphasized, it is likely to be difficult to accept change because of the relatively low level of the acceptance of innovation in the whole society. The cultural motivation of innovation is relatively low in this kind of society too. On the other hand, it is necessary to guard against going to extremes, such as being adventurers and engaging in fraud such as pyramid selling. In particular, once it is linked to capital, it is easy to go to extremes, which then leads to become risk lovers. Society needs appropriate risk appetite—not too much risk aversion or too much recklessness. It is important to find a balance between the two situations.

In addition, there should be an appropriate return on investment. Generally speaking, entrepreneurs pursue economic interests, so they need to safeguard the interests when engaging in risky activities. Only the interests are properly safeguarded, can there be a sustained investment motivation. Therefore, innovation is not an activity without cost and a natural given, but an economic activity. At the same time, entrepreneurs will seek to monopolize profits after innovation obtained, which involves certain conflicts with the interests of society. However, it is also a necessary condition for innovation activities. Therefore, society needs to safeguard the monopoly interests after innovation properly. If there is not enough protection for business interests, it is difficult to guarantee the incentive of innovation in the long run. We thus need to overcome the idealization and protect the profit of monopoly and innovation objectively.

iii. **Innovations investment policy**

On the theoretic level, technological innovation needs to achieve a compromise or trade-off between the monopoly benefits of individual manufacturers and overall social benefits. The tension between the two provides room to action for innovation-driven development strategy. Innovation is achieved mainly through manufacturers' R&D investment, which leads to a high chance of a technological breakthrough. Usually, the higher the investment the greater the possibility of innovation being achieved. However, it is not a simple linear step increase, and at a certain point the probability will decline accordingly, meaning the difficulty of achieving the required technological breakthrough becomes enlarged. That is to say, even if there is investment, it will not necessarily achieve a real breakthrough. Technological R&D itself is a risky activity, and the investment by a single manufacturer and in a specific technological R&D achievement will not necessarily produce the desired return. Manufacturers need to weigh the possible loss, and entrepreneurs need to shoulder risks. Given the risks, there is a natural need for corresponding benefits. Therefore, in terms of a single technology, innovation is not necessarily the ideal as the goal of innovation is monopoly benefits, not the ideal contributions to Humanity. Once the technological R&D is successful, manufacturers tend to obtain exclusive right to exploit the technology and usually resort to various means to protect it in order to maintain the monopoly position and monopoly income. They will increase the pricing higher than the level in a perfectly competitive market, and decrease the output lower than the Pareto optimality. Therefore, the best choice for society is to subsidize R&D activities so as to increase investment by manufacturers in R&D activities and enhance the innovation capability of technological innovation as much as possible.

Direct governmental participation in R&D activities is generally not considered theoretically, but the best concentrate decision-making can help improve the investment of the whole society in R&D and its innovative capability. The underlying truth is that concentrate decision-making can make up for the difference between the income of a single manufacturer and that of the whole society. In essence, it is not economically feasible for the government to get involved in technological research and development directly, because innovation activities are not only full of uncertainties but also severe information asymmetry. In fact, it is difficult to control and plan the characteristics of technology. This is why many of the government's plans or technical projects fail to meet preset goals. With regard to the goal of public policy, the public interest needs to be achieved within the preset time; however, technological innovation cannot be controlled in advance, and officials engaged in public decision-making cannot know the details of the relevant technology, so the desired innovation cannot be achieved through central government involvement. More generally, governments choose to subsidize R&D activities to improve incentives for manufacturers to engage in R&D investment.

In providing a subsidy, there also exists the problem of adverse selection and moral hazard caused by information asymmetry. In short, some enterprises, in order to obtain government subsidies and reduce their own R&D expenditure, simply cheat. If the government's entrusted agent is taken into consideration, there is still the possibility for local government officials and enterprises to conspire to get financial funds. Subsidies are valuable in theory overall; however, in practice, it is very difficult for subsidies to play the role in the ideal model.

Therefore, the government should provide as much investment in technological R&D as possible as a whole society, and support more subsidies and investment for fundamental research which can play the most effective role. In fact, investment in fundamental scientific knowledge and related aspects, the foundation of innovation, should actually be the acting point of policy.

At present, increasing the investment in fundamental research and alternating the view that such work is "useless" are that require adjustment the most for public policymaking departments. The whole society is increasing investment in R&D but there is still room for further improvement. The most crucial point is that investment in fundamental research is actually very small. The neglect to fundamental research is the neglect to long-term development momentum in fact; and, if we don't pay enough attention to knowledge, this will turn innovation strategy essentially into a slogan. As compared to international level, the proportion of China's investment in fundamental research is very low. A possible explanation is that, in the catch-up stage, in order to achieve rapid technological progress, China adopts more imitation and experimental application, meaning that existing advanced technologies can be absorbed as soon as possible to achieve rapid application and immediate effect. However, this may work only in a certain stage temporarily. When the technology application and economic development have already reached a certain level, the room for future development is limited, should this same method continue to be adopted. Therefore, researches with little investment but quick result needs to be altered to improve its basic motive power. In other words, it is this seemingly "useless" fundamental research that really innovates technology and makes the biggest contribution to technological development. Only by strengthening the foundations can there be subsequent technological innovation and technological application. If this shortsightedness cannot be reduced, innovation will be more difficult to achieve, the innovation activities of entrepreneurs will be limited, and the innovation-driven innovation development strategy of the whole society will be difficult to achieve.

4.4 Building a Country of Innovators: Optimal Policy Mix and Institutional Guarantee

To build an innovation system at the national and social level, it is not only necessary to ensure that entrepreneurs and the public have the impetus to engage in innovation, but also to maintain the ability of the whole social mechanism to innovate, which can provide corresponding guarantees and guidance for social innovation, so institutional guarantees and innovation will be crucially important to any policy.

There is the need to cultivate a more patient public mood and pay more attention to long-run development momentum, rather than simply pursuing projects promising immediate and those with little investment but quick result. A single enterprise, people who make the research rules, and even the whole society need to be more patient as patience is of substantive significance. In innovation activities, investment also involves patience. Economics uses time preference to show patience. The more one pays attention to the future the more patience it has. It will reduce current consumption and increase investment in the future. So it is with innovation. Innovation means that there will be more development in the future, so we need to have a long-term vision and reduce current consumption. If one is short-sighted in understanding the overall social environment, it may lead to more current aspects such as higher inflation, more emphasis on quick results. Such haste actions may lead to waste, which is incompatible with the pursuit of long-run development. Therefore, it is necessary to establish a long-run development mechanism featuring social patience to guide society look more forward and reduce depreciation factors. In this sense, culture also plays an important role in long-term economic development, while innovation culture also plays the same important role in regard to innovation-driven development strategy. It needs to be placed under cultural guidance, and more groups should be encouraged to discard old-fashioned behavior by going from tolerating changes to constantly realizing changes, and from traditional authority-oriented culture to features that respect personality.

The whole social mechanism needs to encourage and guarantee innovation activities, with an emphasis on flexibility. To ensure sound innovation, there is a need to find a balance between the private benefits of entrepreneurs and public benefit. First of all, efforts must be made to protect the former, and give necessary support to the intellectual property and monopoly benefits. We cannot damage the interests of enterprises because they have the right to obtain high monopoly profits from innovation. The monopoly benefits enterprises obtain, to certain extent reflect risk compensation for early innovation activities, so monopoly profit based on innovation of technology should be tolerated by society. In regard to the protection of intellectual property rights and other interests, it is important to have a broader vision to guide more entrepreneurs to engage in innovative activities and obtain more patents, so as to create more innovation incentives for the whole society. Short-term benefits such as paying more patent fees due to the current lack of advantages should not be the limit. More importantly, we should avoid reaping other's profits, and make it possible for innovators to enjoy the returns they deserve. Meanwhile, we need to make appropriate institutional arrangements for bankruptcy to protect the basic interests of entrepreneurs engaged in but failing to achieve innovation. In fact, most innovative activities end in failure in general. Therefore, there should be more social tolerance of failed innovators to act as another incentive. We need to provide positive incentives for innovation, and safeguard innovation activities attracting a broader spectrum of society. Finally, we should weigh the compromise and trade-off among social risks. Innovation-driven development strategy and society of innovators need the existence of certain amount of players who have growing risk appetite; however, the whole society could not encourage overindulgence in such risk appetite. Innovation could be linked to fraud, so we need to tolerate risk activities, but guide and warn against the overall risk at the society level. It is often difficult to distinguish between entrepreneurs engaging in risk activities and speculators involved in fraudulent activities. Therefore, society needs to emphasize the integrity mechanism and honesty culture, and expose and severely punish anyone convicted of fraud. On the whole, in regard to institutional development, innovation-driven society needs to have a flexible but regular social system, which can tolerate change and failure, and, at the same time, keep society from being too fanatical and disordered.

Total investment in R&D should be guaranteed, but the subsidy should be provided indirectly. Innovation activities yield public benefits, and entrepreneurs' innovation activities bear externality, so they need to be given corresponding subsidies. To build a country of innovators and implement the innovation-driven development strategy naturally requires sufficient R&D investment. Due to the characteristics of innovation activities, the overall investment and new ways of investment should be guaranteed in a certain proportion. More funds should be directly invested in fundamental research, and enterprises should be guided to engage in more technology development and application. Among fundamental research, applied research and experiment, more enterprises are encouraged to directly link up these three R&D activities. To guide more entities who are mainly entrepreneurs to engage in innovation, society only needs to give proper guidance, pay more attention to fundamental R&D and cultivate more scientists and engineers, thus making the innovation activities of entrepreneurs easier to achieve.

Opening up will continue to promote more international competition. Innovation is a competitive behavior, so there is the need to include competition in any innovation-driven development strategy and building of a country of innovators. Viewed from a country's perspective, international competition should be encouraged and guided to maximize the promotion of innovation activities. If China wants to realize the innovation-driven development strategy and become a country of innovators, it will be an important arrangement for it with broader participation in the international division of labor. External pressure could provide more pressure and incentives to participate in innovation. China has to be patient enough and maintain focus to external competition. In fact, the longer we participate in international market competition, the stronger innovative capability can be formed. Chinese enterprises and entrepreneurs can gradually transform from imitation and learning to self-development in the context of opening up. This process calls for time and capital accumulation, as well as the need for institutional guarantee. In fact, we can maintain enough confidence in the ability of Chinese entrepreneurs and enterprises to participate in international competition.

Reference

Young, A. (1995). The Tyranny of Numbers:Confronting the Statistical Realities of the East Asian Growth Experience. *Quarterly Journal of Economics*, 110, 641–680.

CHAPTER 5

Expediting the Creation of a Modern Public Finance System: Goals and Strategies

Zhiyong Yang

General Secretary Xi Jinping made the proposal in his report at the 19th National Congress of CPC, "We will expedite the creation of a modern public finance system, and establish a fiscal relationship between the central and local governments built upon clearly defined powers and responsibilities, appropriate financial resource allocation, and greater balance between regions. We will put in place a comprehensive, procedure-based, transparent budget system that uses well-conceived standards and imposes effective constraints; and we will implement performance-based management nationwide. We will deepen reform of the tax system, and improve the local tax system". This important statement clearly indicates the direction for the reform of China's fiscal and tax system, and tells us what to do the next step is to expedite the creation of a modern public finance system to meet the needs of building a great modern socialist country.

Z. Yang (✉)
Chinese Academy of Social Sciences, National Academy of Economic Strategy, Beijing, China

D. He et al. (eds.), *Chinese Finance Policy for a New Era*,
https://doi.org/10.1007/978-981-33-4054-1_5

5.1 Significance

According to the report at the 19th National Congress of CPC, China will "expedite the creation of a modern public finance system", highlighting the importance of finance in the building of great modern socialist country. The third plenary session of the 18th CPC Central Committee made clear that the goal of public finance system reform was to create a modern public finance system and endow the new position that finance would form the foundation and become an important pillar of national governance. The fiscal and tax system are thus being reformed according to this decision in an all-round way, with important progress in budget and tax system reform, along with reform of the fiscal relationship between the central and local governments. However, as the principal tension facing Chinese society in the new era has changed to a tension between uneven and under development on the one side and the people's ever-growing desire for a better life on the other, there is still a considerable gap between the achievements of fiscal and taxation reform and the requirements of developing socialism with Chinese characteristics for a New Era. To help achieve the goals for a better life, China has to expedite the creation of modern public finance system based on clear goals and strategies.

To unleash and develop productive forces is the essential requirement of socialism, without which the people's ever-growing desire for a better life will only look unlikely. There will certainly be no real solution to the problem of uneven and under development. In the past 40 years, China's reform and opening up has made brilliant achievements—making it possible to build itself into a great modern socialist country. However, we must never forget that the basic dimension of the Chinese context—that our country is still and will long remain in the primary stage of socialism—has not changed and China's international status as the world's largest developing country has not changed. The basic dimension in the primary stage is determined by the reality that the productive forces are not yet developed. Sweeping reforms, including fiscal and taxation reform, are important means to boost the development vitality and greater creativity throughout society. According to Marx, the forces of production of a society determine the society's relations of production. The relations can further the development of the forces. We can learn from this that only by deepening reform can China achieve higher quality, more efficient, fairer, and more sustainable development!

Fiscal and taxation reform is the most important part of deepening reform. To build China into a great modern socialist country that is prosperous, strong, democratic, culturally advanced, harmonious, and beautiful will not be possible without fiscal support. In order to play its due role, what should first be done is to ensure that a modern public finance system is put in place as quickly as possible. This is truly an important part of promoting the modernization process of the national governance system and the overall governance capacity.

5.2 Goals[1]

5.2.1 Expediting the Creation of a System That Meets the Needs of a Great Modern Socialist Country

Finance is the foundation and important pillar of national governance. The building of great modern socialist country calls for a modern public finance system that meets its needs. The modernization process of big countries involves clear promotion of industrialization and urbanization at global level. Industrialization alters the economic structure, migrates more rural population to urban areas, and brings urbanization. The creation of a modern public finance system should adapt to the progress of both industrialization and urbanization, and be devoted to providing public services matching the progress in both aspects. The revenue of government should be consistent with such progress. The modernization process of the country is related to the transformation of government functions. In the early stage of modernization, the government function of a market economy country is relatively simple. With the development of economy and society, the role of the country shows comprehensive characteristics, with the scope of national economic regulation changing from a micro approach to placing equal importance on both micro and macro regulation. This naturally involves the government playing an increasingly important role in promoting of an all-embracing social security system. At present, the problem of the urban–rural division in China has yet been resolved, while the new-type urbanization is still in progress. The rural vitalization program has begun to be implemented, while the building of a modern economic system is also underway. The creation

[1] This part is mainly based on the explanation of Yang Zhiyong (2014, 2015) on the basic characteristics of modern finance system.

of a modern public finance system should adapt to the different requirements appearing at different stages of modernization. The finance system should cover both urban and rural areas, and work on principal social tensions. The reverse growth of China's market economy determines that the modern public finance system should focus equally on the public sector and the non-public sector and support development of mixed-ownership economic entities, fundamentally changing the situation where the government is not fully playing its proper role.

5.2.2 *Accelerating the Establishment of Special Finance Management Organization*

The fiscal authorities undertake overall responsibility of national wealth management, including government revenue and expenditure, assets and liabilities, and government capital stock and flow management. A special finance management organization is an indispensable part of a modern public finance system. Professional management of specific affairs goes hand in hand with specialized finance management. Specialization of work cannot replace special financial management. The unreasonable division of responsibilities among fiscal authorities, especially overlapping of functions, not only makes it difficult to give full play to the advantages of specialized departments, but also leads to the waste of resources and is not conducive to the improvement of government efficiency. Each of the central departments, more or less functions as a special finance management organization. In addition to the Ministry of Finance, there are also a large number of government funds, which form a lot of ministries of finance. Moreover, there are many departments specialized in financial management. In addition to the Ministry of Finance, the State Taxation Administration and the General Administration of Customs have special responsibilities for collecting financial revenue; the Ministry of Natural Resources manages over state-owned resources and land as a national wealth manager, the responsibility of the Ministry of Finance; the State-owned Assets Supervision and Administration Commission (SASAC) shoulders responsibilities as the state investor sharing the same responsibility of the Ministry of Finance. Meanwhile, the foreign exchange reserves are state-owned assets, but are not managed by the Ministry of Finance.

The fact that several government departments are involved in such specific financial responsibilities has affected the exertion of joint efforts for national financial management; it also increases the coordination cost between departments, which is not conducive to the transformation of government functions and the effective deliver of public services. To form the special finance management organization is bound to reduce government power, to allow various government departments to perform their own duties rather than by one to provide the nation with more effective public services. The creation of a modern public finance system cannot help but destroy such power in one hand and form a large finance department. Now that a company cannot have multiple finance departments with overlapping functions, how can a country decentralize its revenue and expenditure and wealth management authority among different departments? In a word, efforts must be made to concentrate the power to handle government revenue and expenditure affairs and national wealth management affairs in one financial sector in order to build it into a specialized modern finance management institution.

5.2.3 Accelerating the Development of Socialist Democracy in Finance

Modern finance is the democratic finance, or the system of institutions through which the people run. A modern country differs from a traditional monarchy. Both the ruling party and the government accept the mandate of the people to provide public services. The state has many identities such as wealth manager, production organizer, redistributor, and public service provider, a fact illustrating the complexity of modern state affairs, which have assumed "black box" properties to some extent. Without opening this "black box", there can be no supervision. The government is entrusted by the people to manage national wealth, and the special financial management organization, integrating state wealth management and government revenue and expenditure, must be supervised effectively. In the creation of modern public finance system, we need to give full play to the role of the system of people's congresses, so as to enable public opinion to be fully expressed. Efforts should be undertaken giving full play to the supervisory role of the people in the collecting and use of financial funds, actively enhancing financial transparency. In addition to a few items involving state secrets, government budgetary and final accounting information should be made public as effectively as possible to provide necessary conditions for people to supervise financial affairs.

Democratic financial operations should also be reflected in effective public opinion supervision over financial affairs.

The democratic financial development of a great power features multi-levels. Specific responsibilities shall distribute across different levels of central government and local government, which is favorable for bringing into full play the incentive and constraint roles involved in a modern public finance system. From a global perspective, the legislature restrains the government revenues and expenditures in two aspects: system and daily operation. Institutionally, a system should be introduced for government revenue, expenditure and national wealth to be managed within the bounds of the legislature in accordance with public opinion. The presentation and implementation of the government's annual budget and multi-year revenue and expenditure plan are routine matters subject to supervision of the legislature.

5.2.4 *Speeding Up the Development of the Rule of Law in Finance*

Modern countries practice the market economy, and the rule of law guarantees its efficient operation. The building of a country ruled by law is an important part of modernizing the national governance system and its capacity. Public property is just as inviolable as private property. The process of a state obtaining revenue is one involving property transfer, which should be carried out with the rule of law. Taxation must be based on established laws, both substantive law and special legislation for tax collection and administration. Legislation should be both for taxation and all government charges and government funds that burden the market and society. Slapping taxation should be avoided, which may lead to the uncertainty of government burden and interfere with the decisive role of the market in resource allocation.

In reality, as long as it belongs to the functions an effective government should perform, it comes within the scope of finance guarantees. The development of the rule of law in finance cannot be put in a double squeeze. In a certain period of time, the statutory expenditure proportion of certain duties is helpful in the implementation of government duties. However, the changing reality, and the attempt to solve the problem of financial fund guarantees once and for all, are based on the premise of a flexible response to the loss of space. At present, about half of China's financial funds are restricted by this proportion, which is extremely unfavorable to the development of the rule of law in finance.[2]

5.2.5 *Speeding Up the Formation of Specialized Modern Financial Management Techniques*

Different from the traditional financial system, modern public finance system is based on a set of special financial governance techniques. A government budget is not only the basic plan of governmental revenue and expenditure to brief government activities, but also the link between policy and expenditure. Accurate prediction of fiscal revenue is fundamental to the arrangement of budget expenditure. It is one of the contents of the building of modern public finance system that helps form an accurate forecasting method of fiscal revenue. The arrangement of financial expenditure should be consistent with the policy objectives and reflect policy priorities. Any government budget is based on a sound accounting system. In order to meet the needs of economic and social development and government reform, the accrual system needs to be gradually reflected in government accounting procedures. The revised PAYG (pay-as-you-go) schemes in developed countries affect the choice of other governmental accounting system. The compliance and performance budgets should receive equal attention, and special attention should be paid to the development of performance budget technique to evaluate public sector performance in an appropriate way. Government purchasing expenditure is changing from simple and direct market purchase of goods and services to a unified and standardized government procurement system. The government purchases goods at first and then more services, which profoundly reflects the trend of public–private partnership. The main purpose of government procurement is to reduce costs. Due to the complexity of the centralized procurement process and insufficient follow-up to market changes, decentralized procurement, which was previously excluded, must be taken seriously.

[2] In 2012, the fiscal arrangements for seven key expenditures in education, science and technology, agriculture, culture, health care, social security and family planning that are linked to the growth of fiscal revenue and expenditure or GDP accounted for 48 percent of the national fiscal expenditure. In recent years, there has been little change in this area (Lou Jiwei 2013).

From the perspective of financial management, we should form a modern treasury management system to maximize efficiency of the centralized payment system of treasury. With the popularization of computer technology and the development of the Internet, access to decision-making information for financial management is changing, the cost of access is decreasing, and the radius of financial management expanding. Responding to the needs of the Internet era, it is becoming an important part of the creation of a modern public finance system.

The special governance in a modern public finance system is based on multiple consultation and checks and balances. Modern state governance is different from traditional national rule. In traditional countries, the ruler and the ruled are unequal. This has now changed to refined state governance.

5.2.6 *Accelerating the Establishment of a System Meeting the Needs of Dynamic Financial Governance*

In the face of the complexity and uncertainty of both current reality and the future, a modern public finance system is committed to mobilize the activities of all parties and realize dynamic governance of finance on the basis of equal consultation among the main entities.

Technological progress and institutional change are deeply changing the world. Financial governance is facing severe challenges in regard to population structure, informatization, and globalization. A modern public finance system should not only offer stable expectations to the market and society, but also be dynamic and change. It must coordinate the needs of both stability and change. The deterministic demand calls for systemic stability, and the changing economic, political, social, cultural, and ecological civilization tasks require adjustments according to the demands of the times. The acceleration of population aging is bound to increase the future financial burden. Dynamic financial governance needs to take precautions, pay attention to the changing trend of the financial expenditure structure as early as possible, and grasp the evolutionary trend in key areas. It must also reexamine some old assumptions and values to deal with emerging new problems. Dynamic governance of finance aims to transform a series of fragmented intuitions into the overall concept of "governance", and enhance the systematization and feasibility of actual operation.

5.3 Strategies

5.3.1 Comprehensively Expediting the Creation of a Modern Public Finance System

5.3.1.1 Significant Progress Made in Fiscal and Taxation Reform

The 18th National Congress of CPC has determined the task of comprehensively deepening reform. The *Decision of the CPC Central Committee on Several Important Issues of Comprehensively Deepening Reform* adopted at the third plenary session of the 18th CPC Central Committee makes clear that the goal of the fiscal and taxation reform is to create a modern public finance system. On June 30, 2014, the Political Bureau of the CPC Central Committee reviewed and approved the *Overall Plan for the Reform of the Fiscal and Tax System*. The aim was to make the position of "finance the foundation and an important pillar of state governance" in reality and not just name. Fiscal and taxation reform not only ensure the modern public finance system of China become more modernized by the day, but also ensures that finance plays a proper supporting and promoting role in overall economic and social development. There are three breakthroughs in fiscal and taxation reform. In 2014, the *Budget Law* was amended, moving reform forward toward the goal of "being comprehensive and procedure-based, open and transparent". We should strengthen unified budget management, put idle assets to better use, and enhance overall planning of funds among various sub-budgets. Provincial government could issue local government bonds. Budget and final account information become more open. All these efforts not only promote modernization of financial governance, but also advances modernization of the national governance system and its overall capacity.

The fiscal and taxation reform is well-underway. The process of rule of law in taxation is also accelerating, and the goal of China's rule of law in taxation will be basically completed by 2020. The new environmental protection tax was due to be levied as of January 1, 2018, based on the Environmental Protection Tax Law, rather than regulations or provisional regulations. The principle of replacing tax rules and regulations with tax legislation is well-received by the general public. The legislation concerning the tobacco tax, land occupation tax, and vehicle purchase tax has been overhauled. The pilot project of "replacing business tax with value-added tax (VAT)" was launched in 2012, and achieved marked progress on May 1, 2016. The nationwide pilot project means the creation of a modern value-added tax system has taken an important step forward as the business tax is gradually withdrawn. Value-added tax legislation will also make new progress based on experiences with the nationwide pilot. In order to establish a comprehensive and classified personal income tax system, much progress has been made in the basic work of tax collection and management. The personal income and property information system building program has been adopted. Special attention should also be paid to the coordination of tax system reform and fiscal policy. Active fiscal policy needs to be supported by tax cuts. Paying attention to the implementation of tax reduction policy in the pilot program of "replacing business tax with VAT" is a good match for the implementation of active fiscal policy. Accelerated depreciation and tax preferential tax policies for small and micro enterprises not only make up an important part of corporate income tax system reform, but also the implementation of active fiscal policy.

The most difficult financial relationship between the central and local governments has also witnessed important breakthroughs. In 2016, the *Guiding Opinion of the State Council on Promoting the Reform to Define the Respective Fiscal Powers and Expenditure Responsibilities of Central and Local Governments* was adopted, pointing the way for the fiscal powers and expenditure responsibilities. According to the opinion, new progress was made in the common fiscal powers and expenditure responsibilities in 2017 and 2018. In order to cooperate with the nationwide pilot program of "replacing business tax with VAT" the central and local sharing proportion of value-added tax revenue has been adjusted accordingly, and the insufficient part of local financial resources has been covered by the corresponding tax return system, which has accumulated experience for exploring a new central and local fiscal revenue division scheme. Local debt management has also been further regulated. "Increasing investment and avoiding risks" play an important role in mobilizing activities at levels of both central and local governments.

5.3.1.2 Only by Further Accelerating the Reform of Fiscal and Taxation Reform Can Meet the Requirements of Comprehensively Deepening Reform

The fiscal and taxation reform covers a wide range and has far-reaching effect. Since the 18th National Congress of CPC, the fiscal and taxation has overcome various difficulties and made due progress against the background of the economic slowdown, and entered the new normal.

The fiscal and taxation reform is highly professional. The choice of steps to be undertaken needs to change with time and place. Rashly pushing forward reform that is not well-prepared, although it can be viewed as being brave enough, is not good for deepening change in an all-round way. Some specific plans of fiscal and taxation reform are already under study, which is actually the performance of the reform progress. Reform is not about "superficial practice", but continuing with a task until it is completed. The fiscal and taxation reform has made important progress, but the road ahead is still long and the task is arduous. The modernization of state governance needs to give full play to and highlight the basic and important pillar role of finance. At present, the function of the financial department is not in line with this requirement, so it needs to be adjusted as soon as possible, so that the fiscal and taxation reform can be more strongly supported, and the creation of a modern public finance system can be accelerated.

The fiscal and taxation reform should not only seek to make a breakthrough, but also to facilitate the development of the economy and society. To evaluate the process of fiscal and taxation reform, we can base on the number of reform tasks that have been completed, and also pay attention to and respect the laws of fiscal and taxation reform and cope with it. Steady progress and reform need to be well-coordinated. The report at the 19th National Congress of CPC clearly put forward the need to "expedite the creation of a modern public finance system". The process and speed of introducing the system raises new requirements. In the process of the fiscal and tax system reform, it is necessary to adjust the idea of forcing the reform of the administrative management system through the fragmented fiscal and taxation reform measures witnessed in the past. For example, the reform to place county public finances directly under the management of provincial governments, which started in 2009, cannot achieve the goal of promoting proper administrative system reform. The fiscal and taxation reform should be carried out in a highly accurate way. We can start with the reform of the administrative system, so that the overall process can advance faster.

5.3.2 *Accelerating the Establishment of a Regulated Fiscal Relationship Between the Central and Local Governments*

5.3.2.1 *Reform of the Fiscal Relationship Between Central and Local Governments Must Come First*

The report at the 19th National Congress of CPC on the creation of a modern public finance system includes three aspects: budget reform, tax system reform, and the fiscal relationship between the central and local governments, in which the third comes first in deepening reform of the fiscal and tax system.

However, it is the most difficult aspect of the three fiscal and taxation reform areas determined by the third plenary session of the 18th CPC Central Committee, and it is a universal issue involving the mobilization of both central and local activities. In the past, it was necessary to put reforms in the field of budget and tax system in first place. And now, great progress has been made in both areas. The *Budget Law* has been amended and the pilot reform of "replacing business tax with VAT" has been unfolded. However, efforts made to adjust the fiscal relationship between the central and local governments remain in the initial stage where guiding opinions introduced to the defining of the respective fiscal powers, and many interests and technical problems in common powers and responsibilities still need to be solved, which are very difficult. In this way, the priority of specific fiscal and taxation reform areas has been adjusted in terms of statement, and can receive more attention. Of course, the adjustment of the statement order does not mean that other reforms are unimportant, let alone that the completion of other reform tasks can be easily achieved. There are also many institutional and technical problems to be faced in the reform of budget and tax systems.

5.3.2.2 *New Statement on the Fiscal Relationship Between the Central and Local Governments*

In the report at the 19th National Congress of CPC, the fiscal relationship between the central and local governments is not summarized by the common fiscal rights and financial resources, fiscal powers and expenditure responsibilities as was done in the past, but to build a fiscal relationship between the central and local governments built upon clearly defined powers and responsibilities, appropriate financial resource allocation, and greater balance between regions. Clearly defined powers and responsibilities can mobilize the initiative at all governmental levels. The modern public finance system is stable, which is the premise and foundation for the better performance of financial functions. However, the realization of rights and responsibilities must have sufficient financial support, so appropriate financial resource allocation is also an indispensable part of building a modern fiscal relationship between the central and local governments. Facing the problem of uneven and under development, including the problem of regional development imbalance, equalizing access to basic public services is undoubtedly an important way to solve this problem. No matter how the statement changes, the fiscal relationship between the central and local governments is still focused on three aspects: division of expenditure, division of revenue, and the determination of the transfer payment system. The fiscal relationship between the central and local governments becomes clearer when viewed from the perspective of government function. How to define the relationship among government, market and society, namely the government functions, is an unavoidable problem for financial research to tackle. The fiscal relationship between the central and local governments should first resolve the problem of division of powers, which is not a summary of the current situation, but needs to be based on national conditions, with corresponding changes to the existing unreasonable situation. Financial management and professional management perform their duties respectively. The promotion of efficient coordination of financial departments and functional departments are reliant on comprehensive fiscal and taxation reform.

5.3.2.3 What Is the Fiscal Relationship Between the Central and Local Governments

Only by standardizing and modernizing the fiscal relationship between the central and local governments can we fully mobilize activities at all levels and come to an end to uneven and under development. There are many reasons for imbalance and insufficiency. Some developed regions make full use of their comparative advantages, and the special preferential policies implemented by the state have made great contributions. Now, China has entered a new era in which the developed regions feed back to the relatively backward regions. The central government's tax return and transfer payment system to local governments have greatly equalized more regions in public services. Paring assistance from developed regions to relatively backward ones has also promoted the latter's development. It should be stressed that, in recent years, finance has done a lot in achieving regional public service equality, and the results are remarkable. However, compared with the requirements of the new era, there is still considerable room for improvement. We need to realize that some causes of regional imbalance and insufficiency can be eliminated by handling the fiscal relationship between the central and local governments, while other causes need more efforts. Under the premise of reasonable positioning, only by clarifying central and local fiscal powers and responsibilities can we make the expenditure responsibilities of governments at all levels in the equalizing of public services, and enable the fiscal work at all levels play its due role in promoting a solution to uneven and under development. The expenditure responsibility at all levels of government, especially local governments, cannot be fulfilled without the corresponding financial resources. However, in reality, the difference of economic development in different regions determines the level of imbalance in disposable financial resources. The imbalance of economic development will cause these in balance problems. In addition to accelerating the development of backward regions, improving the financial transfer payment system, and improving the financial revenue division system can solve some of them.

The modernization of the fiscal relationship between the central and local governments concerns the mobilization of activities at the two levels. China is a big nation where the central government cannot take everything on itself, thus many functions of the government need to be implemented by local governments. The experience of developed countries needs to be absorbed and used as reference, but even the practices of developed countries differ from each other. Not only do federal states and unitary states have different practices, but they are also have witnessed differences internally. In different historical periods, the fiscal relationship between the central and local governments of different countries shows different characteristics. In recent years, the fact that the centralization of powers in federal states and the decentralization of powers in unitary states undoubtedly deserve our special attention. However, there are many challenges in learning from the experience of developed countries.

The division of central and local powers is the first step in regulating the fiscal relationship between the two governmental levels. Based on China's national conditions, it is full of challenges but indispensable to creatively put forward a plan of division of powers suitable for the needs of China's new era. The division plan of fiscal powers should not only evaluate the rationality and effectiveness, but also be forward-looking and meet the requirements of the medium to long-term goal of national building of a division of government functions at all levels. The division of fiscal power is not only about interests, but also techniques. For example, is running a university the responsibility of the central or local government? Does the division of power involve the existing system of running a university? The answers to these questions certainly depend on the practice, but the forward-looking reform plan is more meaningful.

The division of central and local fiscal revenue is also very difficult. The goal of fiscal management system reform in regard to the tax sharing system established in 1994 stressed that there must be a local tax system; however, the reality that the sharing tax revenue accounts for a significant proportion of tax revenue means such a local tax system must have a far sight. A large amount of sharing tax revenue does not mean that the local tax system cannot be sound. It is important to understand the local tax situation. The idea that disposable local tax revenue is the local tax needs to be accepted by more. The improvement of local tax system needs to be combined with the deepening of overall tax system reform.

Fiscal transfer payments are an important measure to push forward the balanced development of all regions. The structure of fiscal transfer payment needs to be further improved to allow general transfer payments and special transfer payments to perform their respective duties and be more effective. We should abandon the idea that the efficiency of special transfer payments can be lower than that of general transfer payments. The former is far superior to the general transfer payment in realizing central policy goals. Transfer payments could facilitate regional balance mainly in equality of public services. Here, we should not only pay attention to the positive role of transfer payments, but also prevent reverse regulation.

5.3.3 Speeding Up the Establishment of a Modern Budget System

5.3.3.1 New Requirements for Budget Reform in the Report at the 19th National Congress of CPC

The third plenary session of the 18th CPC Central Committee set the goal of budget reform as "a comprehensive and procedure-based, open and transparent budget system". On this basis, the report at the 19th National Congress of CPC further refined and put forward the principle to put in place a comprehensive, procedure-based, transparent budget system that uses well-conceived standards and imposes effective constraints. This puts forward higher requirements for budget reform, especially that effective constraints must be imposed to budget system the budget management must focus on performance. Obviously, this is also the most important content of a modern budget system.

5.3.3.2 *Focus of Budget Reform*

There are many activities of financial expenditure in the non-market field, lacking market prices as an evaluation standard, so that an evaluation index system needs to be developed, and technical problems such as the independence and operability of developing such a system needs to be further explored. Budget management is the requirement of improving the efficiency of financial funds. To this end, constraints on budget need to be further strengthened. Budget expenditure should be more aligned with public policies to reflect the requirements of national governance goals. To achieve the goal of a better life for all, the problems related to people's lives must be solved. Areas of weakness in this regard will need financial assistance to a large extent, especially in recognition that poverty alleviation is an area in urgent need of finance. Income distribution also needs the adjustment of financial policy tools. The compliance of financial revenue and expenditure is the basis for the budget to fully play its due role.

In a modern public finance system, the professionalism of financial investment is of high concern. Not all the financial funds invested in the areas where the government should are supposed to be, and it is about the evaluation of budget performance here. The scarcity of financial resources determines that the investment efficiency needs to be evaluated and financial resources need to be allocated to the most needed areas. The establishment of performance-based budget system is indeed a professional work. There is always a lack of market price as a reference frame in financial capital operation, and the performance-based evaluation within the public sector may be interfered by other factors.

5.3.4 *Accelerating the Establishment of a Modern Tax System*

5.3.4.1 *New Statement on the Tax System Reform in the Report at the 19th National Congress of CPC*

In the report at the 19th National Congress of CPC, the statement on tax system reform—"to deepen reform of the tax system, and improve the local tax system" is simple but full of meaning. To improve the local tax system could also be put in the fiscal relationship between the central and local governments. It appears here to express the meaning that the reform of the tax system needs to be connected with the improvement of the local tax system.

At present, the local categories of taxes provide less tax revenue, and the central and local tax revenue mainly depends on the sharing of tax revenue. We should therefore gain new understanding of the local tax: as long as it is relatively stable for local use, it can be regarded as local tax. The tax sharing system does not have to be based on the tax categories but should be based on tiered financial management, which is to realize the relative independence of all levels of finance under the leadership of the unified central government. In this way, the scale effect and incentive effect of tax collection and management can be reflected, and at the same time, the constraints on finance will be stronger.

5.3.4.2 *Focus of Tax System Reform*

Deepening reform of tax system requires a reasonable tax burden and a tax system structure adapted to national conditions. It requires that the tax system can play its due role in promoting effective allocation of resources, that it can promote the realization of social equity and justice, and that tax plays its due role in macroeconomic control.

A reasonable tax burden is not only a matter for consideration at the national level, but is also directly related to the people's need for a better life. Tariff and consumption tax cuts may create more domestic opportunities for consumption, and the reduction of the latter needs to be further accelerated. It is true that there are difficulties in the level of adjustment, but this does not mean they cannot be implemented. The enthusiasm for overseas shopping and the long line of duty-free shops are inconsistent with China's image as a big state and the requirements of great modern socialist country. The nationwide pilot involving replacement of the business tax with VAT will help establish a more neutral value-added tax system as soon as possible. Therefore, it is necessary to summarize the experiences learned from pilot projects, simplify the tax rate, and speed up legislation on VAT. The reform of the integration and classification of personal income tax, especially the special expense deductions accompanying the reform, are closely related to a better life. These special expense deductions directly relate to such livelihood issues as pension, medical care, childcare, and education. The environmental protection tax will also make our sky bluer and air quality better.

The local tax system mentioned in the report at the 19th National Congress of CPC does not necessarily depend on the collection of real estate tax. This, in the context of international standards, should be generally levied and based on the assessment on the real estate value. Under the current conditions, this will face a problem that if the tax is assessed according to the value of the real estate, even if a certain range of tax exemption rules are set, it is difficult to avoid the problem that the owner of the real estate is unable to bear the tax burden. For example, welfare housing, is at an income level not meeting the conditions of buying commercial housing. For example, a decade ago, the price of commercial housing was very low, but has now greatly increased. However, their income level has not increased with it. If the tax is reduced because of their insufficient ability to pay, it means latecomers who have paid a great deal to buy a property will pay a high real estate tax, which will create an issue of fairness, leading to other problems. In addition, from the perspective of fairness and tax capacity, it is not feasible for inheritance tax to become a major local tax in the short term. Therefore, we need to look at the whole issue of local tax afresh.

The core problem of deepening reform of tax system relates to the law. The principle of replacing tax rules and regulations with tax legislation requires taxation regulations and provisional regulations to be made into law, with significant changes in content. Although the nationwide pilot of replacing business tax with VAT in China is well-underway, so that the former no longer exists, the current action is still accumulating experiences for the creation of relevant VAT legislation. Only when the VAT system is improved, can related legislation be introduced smoothly. Consumption tax reform is of equal importance. Since the State Council executive meeting revealed on April 28, 2015 called for the adjustment of tariff rates and consumption tax, although the former has indeed been lowered the latter remain unchanged. The technical difficulty may be that consumption tax is not only levied on imported goods, but also on domestically produced ones. However, to realize reform goals, the reduction of consumption tax will provide more convenient and reasonable consumption conditions for its own people, and, at the same time, be conducive to the establishment of an image of China as a great power.

To expedite the creation of a modern public finance system requires courage to break through the system of vested interests, and wisdom. The creation of modern public finance system will create high professionalism, which needs to concentrate on the wisdom of all parties and make accurate decisions. In the process of system exploration, we should pay special attention to drawing lessons from the existing experience. As long as it is beneficial to the modernization of modern public finance system and the national governance system and capacity, we can try it. In the building of a modern public finance system, it is necessary to clearly analyze the gap between the existing system and the target system, and then move forward step-by-step in the right direction and be closer to the target. To expedite the creation of this modern public finance system can only be smoothly promoted based on coordinating the interests and conflicts, and it is an important step to meet the people's ever-growing needs for a better life. This modern public finance system could set up a basic framework to solve the principal social tension. In reality, in accordance with the new requirements of new ideas in the New Era and the new journey, we should constantly develop new fiscal policies, and pay attention to the changes of the actual situation in financial operations, so as to better serve the overall situation and make due contributions to the national rejuvenation.

References

Lou Jiwei, Establishing a Modern Public Finance System, *People's Daily*, December 16, 2013.

Yang Zhiyong (2014), Modern Public Finance System: Basic Principles and Main Features, *Sub National Fiscal Research*, issue 6.

Yang Zhiyong (2015), *Exploration of Modern Public Finance System: China's Fiscal and Taxation Reform from the Perspective of National Governance*, Guangzhou: Guangdong Economic Publishing House.

CHAPTER 6

Deepening Reform of the Tax System and Improving Local Tax Systems

Zhang Bin

The report at the 19th National Congress of CPC emphasizes the need to expedite the creation of a modern public finance system from an overall and strategic perspective, and clarifies the goals and main tasks for deepening reform of the tax system and improving the local tax system. Taxation work should, under the guidance of Xi Jinping Thought on Socialism with Chinese Characteristics for a New Era, start from solving problems related to imbalanced and under development, and focus on in-depth study of how to better meet people's ever-growing needs for a better life, so as to make due contributions to fulfillment of the goals of basically realizing socialist modernization by 2035 and developing China into a great modern socialist country that is prosperous, strong, democratic, culturally advanced, harmonious, and beautiful by the middle of the twenty-first century.

Z. Bin (✉)
Chinese Academy of Social Sciences, National Academy of Economic Strategy, Beijing, China

D. He et al. (eds.), *Chinese Finance Policy for a New Era*,
https://doi.org/10.1007/978-981-33-4054-1_6

6.1 Socialism with Chinese Characteristics in a New Era Calls for Furthering Taxation Reform

In recent years, China has made significant progress in the reform of the tax system. The pilot reform of replacing business tax with VAT has been carried out nationwide. Ad valorem resource tax reform has been fully advanced. The Environmental Protection Tax Law has been issued and steady progress has been made in real estate tax legislation and the reform of personal income tax and local tax system. The *Plan on Deepening Reform of Central and Local Tax Collection Systems* was issued, a remarkable progress in modernization of tax collection and management.

However, as the socialism with Chinese characteristics enters into a new era, changes in principal social tensions require to expedite creation of a modern tax system. The system must ensure sufficient financial revenue to lay a solid financial foundation for offering better public services. Moreover, the formulation and implementation of the tax system must better meet people's needs in regard to democracy, rule of law, fairness, justice, security and environment, and so on. Specifically, the new requirements on the tax system in the new era can be summarized as follows:

Firstly, to meet the needs of the people for democracy and the rule of law and the requirement of advancing law-based governance, the building of law-based tax system should be further promoted in accordance with the principle of replacing tax rules and regulations with tax legislation that should be applied to all types of compulsory revenue, including special revenue and government-managed funds. To this end, efforts should also be made to improve the legislative procedures of taxation, expand orderly political participation of the people, and support and ensure the people's exercise of state power through people's congresses. At the same time, taxation by law and law-based tax system are also an important part of the work to ensure the security of people's property and meet their need for safety.

Secondly, as for people's demands for fairness and justice and requirements of safeguarding and improving their lives in the course of development, work is needed to further improve the structure of tax system, tighten tax collection and management, gradually increase the proportion of direct taxes and give full play to the role of taxation in regulating income distribution, so as to promote social equity and justice through creation of a fair tax.

Thirdly, with respect to people's need for a more beautiful environment and requirement of harmonious coexistence between humans and nature, it is necessary to further strengthen the role of taxation as a policy tool in promoting resource conservation and environmental protection, so as to put forward the development of an ecological civilization.

Fourthly, in regard to the more diversified and higher quality of material and cultural needs and the requirements of implementing new concept for development and building a modern economic system, the tax system must play its due role in developing an economy with more effective market mechanisms, dynamic micro entities, and sound macro regulation, and continuously enhancing China's economic innovation abilities and competitiveness by promoting market unification, encouraging innovation and strengthening coordination of the international tax system.

6.2 Changing Status of Tax Codes: Replacing Rules and Regulations with Legislation

"Running of the country by the people" and "Advancing law-based governance" are important components of 14 basic strategies for developing socialism with Chinese characteristics for a new era. Following the principle of replacing tax rules and regulations with tax legislation is the fundamental requirement for adherence to the two aforesaid basic strategies and also the only way to meet the people's ever-growing needs for democracy, the rule of law, fairness and justice.

6.2.1 Replacing Tax Rules and Regulations with Tax Legislation

Since the reform and opening up, in order to meet the needs of the economic system reform, China has formed a taxation legislation system mainly authorized by administrative bodies, playing an irreplaceable role in establishing a tax system that is compatible with the socialist market economy. However, as China's economic and social development has entered into a new chapter, the tax system must not only adapt to the needs of the socialist market economy, but also give play to its roles as the foundation and important pillar for state governance. The tax law, as a basic rule regulating the state's power to tax and citizens' property rights, determines the distribution of resources between the government and society and the tax burden among members in society. It not only directly affects the relationship between the government and the market, but also plays an important role in income distribution and social equity.

To codify the country's tax rules in the form of legislation, the first step is to regulate all newly levied taxes by law according to the requirements of the *Opinions on Codifying Tax Rules in the Form of Legislation* approved by the CPC Central Committee. For example, the *Environmental Protection Tax Law*, adopted by the National People's Congress at the end of 2016, came into effect on January 1, 2018. Moreover, the current taxes ruled by the administrative regulations of the State Council should be subject to laws, and relevant tax regulations should be abolished. All legislative procedures for the work are expected to be completed in 2019, and the reform task of "implementing the taxation by law" to be completed in 2020.

To codify the country's tax rules in the form of legislation, we must not only change government revenues gathered under the name of "tax" as legal norms, but also coordinate work promoting the reform of non-tax government revenues and accelerate the legislative process to cover these. In particular, we must continue to advance the transforming administrative fees into taxes and strictly control all kinds of special revenues and government funds of a tax nature and compulsorily levied on society. They should be suspended in time when they are due. If it is really necessary to collect for a longer period, they should be changed into taxes when feasible, and then be regulated by law as newly levied tax.

To implement the tax legislation principle, we should not only change the existing interim regulations into laws, but also, in accordance with the report of the fourth plenary session of the 18th CPC Central Committee and the report at the 19th National Congress of CPC, bring into play the leading role of people's congresses and their standing committees in the legislative work, so as to prevent legalization of departmental interests. Judged by content, the legislative tendency of "being general rather than detailed" lasting for a long time should be changed, and the basic elements of the tax law should be detailed and comprehensive as far as possible, and the discretion of administrative bodies should be minimized.

To codify the country's tax rules in the form of legislation, it is also necessary to properly expand the tax management authority of local governments, mainly provincial governments, based on the characteristics of different taxes and legislative authorization and on the premise of unified legislation and right to tax by the central government. Meanwhile, ensuring standardized management and strict supervision, part of the non-tax revenue management authority should be properly delegated. As a legislative body, local people's congresses should play their due roles in replacing tax rules and regulations with tax legislation, laying a more solid institutional foundation for improving the local tax system.

6.2.2 Improving Administrative Regulations and Ministerial Rules on Taxation

While replacing tax rules and regulations with tax legislation, the building of the law-based tax system also includes taxation approved by the legislature. With social and economic development, the increasingly complicated system of specialized division of labor leads to a high degree of asymmetry in the distribution of public information. This further results in complicated social coordination and management activities, and expanded and increasingly professional government functions, forming advantages for the administrative bodies in many aspects such as information and efficiency.

The performance of taxation legislation is particularly obvious in this respect. Taxation is based on the confirmation of transactions and other actions between civil subjects. With economic development, the transactions become increasingly diversified, new forms have emerged, and each taxable transaction attains certain particularities. This makes it difficult for statute tax laws to pre-determine each transaction, so the tax authorities inevitably have a lot of discretion.

In addition, the modern tax system is not only a means for the government to raise funds, but also an important tool to exercise macro control and achieve various economic and social policy goals. As a policy tool, its effectiveness is crucial. Therefore, greater power is required by administrative bodies for formulation of taxation policies, and by tax authorities for taxation management. In such case, as a supplement to the tax law, administrative regulations formulated by administrative bodies and ministerial rules promulgated by the financial and tax authorities become an indispensable and important part of the taxation legislation system.

To formulate accurate administrative regulations and ministerial rules on taxation, it is first necessary to establish and improve the legislative body's review mechanism on administrative legislation. Administrative regulations and ministerial rules on taxation are only supplements to tax laws, and must not conflict with the provisions and principles of the tax laws. Secondly, the administrative bodies and financial and tax authorities should improve the capacity and level of administrative legislation, strengthen and improve the government's legislative system, improve the procedures for formulating administrative regulations and rules as well as the mechanism for public participation in governmental legislation. The system of administrative regulations and ministerial rules will be continuously improved within the scope and authority provided by the laws. Finally, tax authorities should formulate and promulgate comprehensive, meticulous and operable rules for dealing with the emerging transactional forms and tax-related matters in a timely manner in accordance with the provisions and principles of relevant laws and regulations so as to achieve nationwide unification of tax law enforcement, and provide taxpayers with fair and confirmed tax law interpretation and services.

6.2.3 *Improving the System of Taxation Judiciary and Judicial Interpretation*

To restrict the expansion of administrative discretion, not only the legislative review process involving legislative bodies needs to be strengthened, the role of judicial authorities should also be given full play to. To effectively protect the citizens' property rights, when participating in the formulation of tax law through exercise of political rights, taxpayers as the administrative counterparts can also obtain remedies through administrative litigation when they believe that the tax authorities have violated their legitimate rights.

The judicial authorities can not only correct the violation of tax authorities in specific tax cases handled in administrative litigation, but also correct or negate relevant provisions of ministerial rules substantially through judicial interpretation of common cases the tax authorities deal with in accordance with ministerial rules. In other words, tax-related judicial interpretations may also form effective supervision over the administrative legislative power, and the judicial interpretations generally followed by judicial authorities at all levels also constitute an important part of the taxation legislation system. In the future, general administrative acts should be incorporated into the scope of administrative litigation, and the power of judicial review to ministerial rules should be granted to judicial authorities, thus forming an administrative legislative supervisory mechanism attaching equal importance to legislative and judicial review.

6.3 Improving Tax Structure and Building a Fairer Tax System

A modern tax system is an important part of the modern financial system, playing a fundamental role in the modernization of national governance system and governance capabilities. Tax fairness is the basic feature of the modern tax system, and is also an inevitable requirement to achieve social fairness and justice and meet people's desires and needs for a better life.

This requires regulating income distribution through taxation. Currently, improving the structure of tax system and focusing on improving the direct tax system are the main measures to achieve such fairness. The personal income tax system that combines comprehensive and classified tax systems is established to give full play to the adjustment function of the personal income tax; and making progress in legislation on real estate tax and its implementation in accordance with the principle of "legislation first, full authorization and step-by-step promotion" is a major part to improve the direct tax system.

6.3.1 Main Problems in the Current Taxation Structure

China's current tax structure, with circulation tax as the main tax, was established via the taxation reform in 1994. Such a structure had a significant advantage in raising revenues during the period of rapid economic growth. However, as economic and social development entering into a new period, the disadvantage of this structure has become obvious. Specifically, it is mainly reflected in the following four aspects.

First, the tax burden on residents' incomes is lighter while that on consumption is heavier. However, according to the law of diminishing marginal propensity to consume, such a structure is regressive, that is, the tax burden decreases with the increase of incomes, which makes it difficult for tax to play a role in regulating income distribution.

Second, the circulation tax, as the cost of business operations, is mostly passed to consumers by increasing prices. The higher circulation tax burden is an important factor in the large price gap of the same commodity at home and abroad, which is not conducive to promoting household consumption.

Third, the tax structure with circulation tax as the main tax means that income mainly comes from the scale of production and transactions, rather than corporate profits and residents' incomes. As a result, local governments may focus on scale and output value rather than efficiency, and be high on attracting investment but neglect the work of providing public services for residents.

Fourth, with the development of the economy and the increase of residents' incomes, compared with progressive personal income tax in excess of specific amount and the circulation tax levied at the tax rate in transactions, especially the value-added tax with inelastic revenue, the shift of tax structure to direct tax with higher income elasticity is conducive to the stabilization of macro tax burdens and the function of "automatic stabilizer" in macroeconomic regulation.

6.3.2 *Promoting the Reform of Personal Income Tax System that Combines Comprehensive and Classified Tax Systems*

The reform of personal income tax system that combines comprehensive and classified tax systems is to strengthen the tax regulation on people with high income, and gradually increase the revenue of personal income tax and its proportion in tax revenue. While gradually increasing the proportion of personal income tax, the proportion of value-added tax should be reduced, to improve the tax structure without increasing the macro tax burden, which is conducive to better regulation of income distribution through taxation and improving the progressiveness of the overall tax system. At the same time, the decline in the proportion of circulation tax will also play a role in expanding consumption by reducing the prices of goods and services.

China's current personal income tax system distinguishes between different categories of income, calculating the tax amount depending on the income type and collecting it monthly or based on how often such income occurs. This taxation model has income tax withheld at source at a relatively low cost. However, its biggest disadvantage is that it focuses on taxable income but fails to distinguish taxpayers. It's not possible to identify all various incomes of each individual or household, and also hard to make differential tax deduction as per the annual total income. However, as residents' income sources become diversified, this taxation model cannot fully reflect a taxpayer's capacity of tax payment, nor does it take into account their actual financial burdens. This is not conducive to the role of personal income tax in income distribution.

In promoting the personal income tax reform that intends to combine the comprehensive and classified taxation models, the following five questions need to be considered.

First, which income items should be included as comprehensive taxable income? One proposal is to separate labor income from capital income. The labor income is collected together, and the capital income is levied by rate and classification. An alternative is to include sustainable and regular income into the category of comprehensive income, including labor income and dividends, bonuses and incomes from interest and lease of property, but tax the income from transfer of property by classification. In addition, the cost of collection and compliance need to be considered. The more income items included in the comprehensive income, the fairer the tax burden distribution will be; however, the cost of collection and that of taxpayer declaration will also be relatively high. Especially when it's hard to provide the supporting facilities at one go, the cost of collection and compliance are important factors to consider when designing the tax system.

Second, should taxpayers be allowed to pay on a household basis? This requires consideration of various factors such as information and collection and management costs and the impact of this policy on labor supply.

Third, what should be included as itemized deductions, and in which order they should be included? For example, can deductions be allowed for children or elderly family members the taxpayer supports, or for interest on mortgage loans and rents within a certain limit? Meanwhile, we need to make a careful choice between the forms of tax incentive: tax deductions or tax credits. The tax system with a longer list of itemized deductions is generally thought to be more equitable. However, doing so would lead to a significant increase in the cost of tax collection and compliance. In addition, when designing the itemized deduction scheme, we must fully consider the fact that personal income tax payers account for only a small proportion of the total population in China, and thus fiscal expenditure policies and taxation policies need to be well-coordinated. For example, providing a prescribed level of government subsidies for qualified individuals and families with children would be a more equitable practice than dependent tax deductions.

Fourth, how should the progressive tax rates be designed for comprehensive tax levying? Should the maximum marginal tax rate be reduced accordingly and the tax rate bracket further simplified? The reduction of the maximum marginal tax rate is conducive to improving the work enthusiasm of high-income groups and also attracting high-end talents to work in China for a long time, but the function in income regulation will be relatively weakened. In addition, the progressive tax rate in excess of specific amount needs to be coordinated with the tax rates for categorized incomes. This involves the final settlement of the number of taxpayers who apply for tax refunds or supplements, and the actual amount of the refunds or supplements.

Fifth, how should tax collection, management, and other supporting measures be taken? Implementation of a personal income tax system that combines comprehensive and classified tax systems first requires the amendment and improvement of relevant laws and regulations such as the *Law on Tax Collection and Management* to establish a legal system of tax collection and management for natural persons. Secondly, it is necessary to establish an interdepartmental information sharing mechanism that meets the requirements of comprehensive tax levying, and establish and improve the personal income and property information systems. Finally, since the personal income tax is a sharing tax between the central and local governments, it should also determine the distribution mechanism of tax refunds and supplements between the central and local governments in the stage of comprehensive tax levying.

6.3.3 Promoting the Reform of Real Estate Tax

The core of reform of real estate tax is to levy real estate possession tax of residential houses for personal use, involving the benefits of millions of households. Unlike value-added tax, consumption and business tax, for which circulation taxes are levied on enterprises, the reform of real estate tax must directly involve a large number of taxpayers who are natural persons. The key to advancing the reform is to first draft law first so as to build wide consensus.

As a direct tax, real estate tax has a clear distribution of tax burdens among members of society. Real estate tax is a property tax, and is levied on the property value as the tax base. The tax authorities do not have corresponding cash flow as a basis for taxation of real estate tax, so taxpayers should pay taxes on their own. Under such circumstances, the reform of real estate tax must inevitably face diverse and conflicting interest claims of different interested parties. To successfully advance real estate tax reform and improve taxation efficiency, it is necessary to seek the opinions of all parties throughout the legislative process of the national people's congress. On the basis of full coordination and communication, we seek solutions that can achieve the greatest consensus of all sectors of society. In this sense, scientific and democratically-based real estate tax legislation is not only an inevitable requirement of "improving the socialist democratic and political system", but also an institutional guarantee for smooth and effective real estate tax reform.

The reform of real estate tax is an important move to improve the local tax system. If real estate tax becomes the main tax category for city- and county-level primary governments in the future, it will have an important and far-reaching impact on the relationship between local governments and taxpayers and the governance model of local governments. If natural person taxpayers in the jurisdiction regularly pay real estate taxes directly to local government, this means taxpayers and the government have established a more direct link, and the former will link more closely the taxes they pay with the public services they enjoy, and thus have greater motivation to participate in socialist democratic decision-making. Therefore, the reform of real estate tax is not only about taxation, it is directly or indirectly connected with the building of socialist democratic and political systems and even the modernization of the national governance system and governance capabilities. In this sense, in the next step, the reform of real estate tax will break through current limitations as it stands, and to understand the significance of "expediting the legislation on real estate tax" from the perspective of the reconstruction of the relationship between the government and residents in the jurisdiction as well as national governance. Moreover, local governments should be given greater tax management authority on the principle of "full authorization".

The reform of real estate tax should also cover various categories of taxes covering real estate development, transaction, and possession such as city and town land use tax, farmland conversion tax, deed tax and land value increment tax and so on, and involve urban infrastructure supporting fees and other charge items. At present, there are large amount of local government revenue from land and real estate, including real estate-related taxes, urban infrastructure supporting fees in government funds, and income from state-owned land transfer. Therefore, to carry out real estate tax reform, we should appropriately reduce the tax and fee burden on construction and transactions, and gradually establish a comprehensive modern real estate tax system, to bring into full play the role of real estate tax in "establishing a long-term mechanism for the stable and healthy development of real estate in line with national conditions and market rules".

In terms of path of reform of real estate tax, it is reliable and reasonable to carry out the reform step-by-step, given the current higher house prices, inconsistent urban and rural real estate systems, diverse properties, and the existing multiple taxes and fees covering real estate development, construction, and transaction.

6.4 Establishing a Modern Multiple Tax System Serving Different Objectives

6.4.1 *Further Improving the Value-Added Tax System*

While to keep tax fairness, the reform of the tax system must also promote market unification through the consolidation of various tax laws, and create a tax system environment featuring fair competition for all market players. In a modern multiple tax system, the value-added tax generally imposed on goods and services has a "neutral" feature, and plays an important role in promoting market unification and fair competition.

After the nationwide pilot reform of "replacing business tax with value-added tax" on May 1, 2016, value-added tax has covered all goods and services, and transformational reforms have also been completed, which has basically eliminated double imposing and opened up a deduction chain between the secondary and tertiary industries. This is helpful to deepen the division of professional labor and social collaboration, and will play a significant role in promoting the development of the service industry and the transformation and upgrading of the manufacturing sector. Next, following the principle of tax neutrality and based on the nationwide pilot reform, it is necessary to further perfect the deduction chain, improve the tax rate structure and export tax rebates and other policy measures to build a fairer and concise value-added tax system. Specifically, further reforms are needed in the following areas.

The first is to simplify and consolidate the value-added tax rate, standardize preferential policies for value-added tax, and further improve the value-added tax system. Based on the abolition of the 13 percent of tax rate, further studies are needed to consolidate the current three-bracket tax rates of 17, 11, and 6 percent, and at the same time, standardize preferential policies for value-added tax to better utilize the fair and neutral advantages of value-added tax, and create a favorable tax environment for the market to play a decisive role in resource allocation.

Secondly, there are two brackets of tax rate related to entertainment tax within the business tax—10 and 20 percent. After the reform of "replacing business tax with value-added tax", in accordance with the requirement of "including some high-end consumer goods and high-spending behaviors into the category of consumption tax" as proposed in the 13th Five-Year Plan, the high-end consumption which are originally subject to the high tax rate of business tax should be effectively adjusted by levying consumption tax.

Thirdly, in accordance with the principle of giving play to the enthusiasm of central and local governments, and the overall plan for improving the system and mechanism under which the authority and fiscal powers of central and local governments are compatible, the implementation effect of the plan of sharing value-added tax during the transition period should be summarized in a timely manner, and the proportion of value-added tax sharing should also be adjusted reasonably and properly.

Fourthly, on the basis of improving the tax system and in accordance with the principle of replace tax rules and regulations with tax legislation, the *Interim Regulations on Value Added Tax* should be abolished and the *Value Added Tax Law* should be formulated.

6.4.2 Bringing into Better Play the Role of Taxation in Regulating Income Distribution

In recent years, China has enacted the *Environmental Protection Tax Law*, promoted the reform of ad valorem resource tax and the pilot reform of water resource taxation, and adjusted the collection scope of consumption tax in due course. Next, we need to continue to deepen the reform of the resource and environment tax and fee system in the following aspects:

Firstly, proactive and steady expansion of the taxation scope. Resources include not only minerals, but also water resources and various types of natural ecological space. Next, we should sum up the experience of the pilot project of water resource taxation in due course and gradually implement it nationwide. At the same time, it is necessary to actively encourage provincial governments to formulate plans for levying resource taxes on forests, grasslands, tidal flats and so on according to local conditions, and guide and give full play to the initiative of local government in institutional innovation. In terms of environmental tax, further research should be carried out to tax carbon dioxide emissions.

Secondly, in a policy system that seeks to promote resource conservation, policy tools such as resource renting, charging and pricing are also important. To promote resource conservation through reform of tax, the key is to guide the allocation of resources via price mechanism. Therefore, the resource tax system should be further upgraded in combination with reforms in resource renting, charging and pricing in the future.

Thirdly, a fiscal and taxation policy system conducive to green development should be promoted by strengthening the connection and coordination among resource tax, environmental protection tax, consumption tax and other taxes as well as fiscal subsidy and other expenditure policies. Green development runs through the entire process of resource exploitation, processing, and consumption. Resource tax, environmental protection tax, consumption tax, and corresponding tax incentives and fiscal subsidies play different roles in different links and fields. How to make full use of the advantages of different policy tools and connect various policies is essential and requires further research in the follow-up tax reform. In the long run, however, the increase in resource tax and environmental protection tax may cause a rise in the price of daily necessities. Therefore, it is necessary to adopt a tiered pricing mechanism and provide necessary and appropriate fiscal subsidies to reduce or offset the impact of resource tax reform and environmental protection tax collection on low-income groups.

6.4.3 Further Improving Preferential Tax Policies to Encourage Innovation and Entrepreneurship

According to the report at the 19th National Congress of CPC, "China's economy has been transitioning from a phase of rapid growth to a stage of high-quality development. This is a pivotal stage for transforming our growth model, improving our economic structure, and fostering new drivers of growth. It is imperative that we develop a modernized economy. This is both an urgent requirement for getting us smoothly through this critical transition and a strategic goal for China's development." Taxation, as an important policy tool, should conform to the requirement of "implementing new development concept" and play a due role in "developing a modernized economy" by establishing and improving preferential tax policies that encourages research and development, and promotes innovation and entrepreneurship.

In order to implement the strategy of innovation-driven development, in recent years, China has successively introduced a series of preferential tax policies based on the existing ones for high-tech enterprises, including accelerated depreciation of fixed assets, additional tax-deductible R&D costs, pre-tax deductions for employee training fees, personal income tax preference for equity incentive, and enterprise income tax preference for legal partners of limited partnership venture capital investment enterprises, enterprise income tax preference for technology transfer and personal income tax preference for converting to stock capital. These policies have been promoted nationwide following pilot projects in national innovation demonstration zones such as Zhongguancun, playing an important role in promoting implementation of the strategy of innovation-driven development.

In the future, while further improving the system of preferential tax policies, it is also necessary to improve the overall tax system in accordance with the requirements of functional industrial policies, starting from reducing the innovation cost of market players and cultivating long-run economic growth drivers. Specifically, it involves the following key aspects:

First, according to the functional industrial policies, we should comprehensively evaluate the existing preferential tax policies, make efforts to narrow down policies for selection, gradually increase the inclusiveness of preferential tax policies, and reduce interference with the innovation activities of market players.

Second, we should improve the efficiency of tax collection and management and reduce enterprises' compliance cost. While reducing selective preferential policies and expanding the coverage of inclusive policies, tax authorities should further improve the tax collection and management process, strengthen publicity and improve tax services. They should also reduce various examination and approval items and procedures, in an effort to reduce compliance cost for enterprises, so as to effectively benefit eligible venture business with tax preference.

Third, since the rise of the Internet in the 1990s brought about innovation in technology and business models, the digital economy has moved "from edge to center", representing the most dynamic innovation force and exerting sustained and profound impact on all sectors of the economy. However, the development of the digital economy also brings challenges to the current tax system and collection and management. How to transform and improve the current tax system under the premise of "taxation neutrality" and "taxation fairness" to guide and encourage innovation and development in the digital economy era is an important task of taxation reform guided by the strategy of innovation-driven development.

6.5 Improving Local Tax Systems and Central-Local Fiscal Coordination

6.5.1 *Local Tax System Improved in Combination with Taxation Reform*

Local tax system must be improved in combination with taxation reform. The international experience shows that, real estate tax is more suitable to be the exclusive tax for municipal, county and other governments at primary level. On the principle of "full authorization", local governments should be given greater autonomy in real estate tax collection, and real estate tax reform should be actively and steadily promoted to improve the revenue system at the primary level. Considering the reform of revenue distribution between central and local governments, studies should be focused on adjustment of the collection of some consumption tax items and their attribution. In addition, while accelerating the legislative process of local non-tax revenue, it is necessary to expand the scope of local taxes by transforming administrative fees into taxes.

In market economy, in order to ensure the free flow of resources across the country, the central government has a natural advantage in tax collection. Therefore, on the premise of maintaining overall stability of the central and local financial resources, methods and proportions of sharing tax between the two governmental levels should be determined to form a reasonable revenue distribution system based on sharing tax supplemented by the exclusive tax. At present, value-added tax, enterprise income tax, and personal income tax are the main components of sharing tax. Given the overall plan of maintaining market unity, promoting regional balance, and giving full play to enthusiasm of local government, full consideration should be given to the optimization and upgrading of the economic structure and the impact of emerging business development so as to determine the sharing methods and proportions of major taxes appropriately.

6.5.2 *A Sound Local Tax System Should Be Based on a Fiscal Relationship Between the Central and Local Governments Built Upon Clearly Defined Powers and Responsibilities*

A sound local tax system is based on the clearly defined fiscal powers and expenditure responsibilities of central and local governments, and the fiscal relationship between the central and local governments built upon clearly defined powers and responsibilities.

For public services that fall within the scope of local government fiscal powers, such as compulsory education and medical services, if the local government has insufficient financial resources to meet the minimum standards set by the government at a higher level, the difference will be covered by general transfer payments. For those that belong to a higher level government but do need to be implemented by one or more lower-level governments, the higher level government should provide sufficient funds through special transfer payments and may not require local governments to provide support. For public services that have revenue spillovers and fall within the scope of local government fiscal powers, the higher level government can encourage the local government below to increase supply accordingly via special transfer payments. Therefore, the optimal combination of local government revenue based on fiscal powers and expenditure responsibilities should be: the self-owned financial resources resulting from local government's fiscal powers plus the general transfer payments match with local government's fiscal powers, and fiscal powers of the lower-level government undertaking for the higher level government and expenditure responsibilities as required by the higher level government are made up by special transfer payments.

As an important part of a local government's own financial resources, the main function of local tax is to raise funds for recurrent expenditures within its fiscal powers. Therefore, the optimal scale of local tax is also affected by the structure of local government expenditures in a certain period. At the peak of the urbanization drive, a large amount of funds required by local governments for infrastructure construction cannot be obtained through local tax revenue. At this time, funds should be mainly raised through local government bonds or PPP models, and also the proceeds from the transfer of land use rights in China. The function of local tax in infrastructure construction is mainly to repay capital with interest in the future and offer subsidies and funds to social capitals.

6.5.3 Basic Idea for Improving the Local Tax System

In the long run, a relatively stable local tax system should be established on the base of an overall optimized fiscal relationship between central and local governments.

First of all, the central government's fiscal powers and expenditure responsibilities should be appropriately increased, and the expenditure pressure and funding requirements of local governments should be reduced, such as bringing social security funds under national unified management.

Secondly, from the perspective of the overall financial resource structure of local governments, tax rebates and general transfer payments also constitute disposable financial resources corresponding to fiscal powers of local government. If no major adjustment is made within central and local fiscal powers and expenditure responsibilities, to avoid an excessive proportion of the value-added tax revenue gained by local governments that makes them more impulsive in interfering with the resource allocation within the market, while all the value-added tax is collected as a central tax, 50 percent of the revenue can be allocated in proportion to the population or consumption of each province.

Finally, as far as the local tax system is concerned, with the comprehensive reform of taxes and fees, the scale of special-purpose non-tax revenue such as special revenue and government funds should be gradually reduced, and local tax that can be coordinated by local governments should be enlarged accordingly. At the same time, with the gradual improvement of local government's governance system, local government's legislation on tax can be expanded accordingly and empower the local people's congresses to add tax items under certain conditions, determine tax rates, and levy local tax or complementary tax.

6.6 Establishing a Modern Tax Collection and Management System

The modern tax collection and management system is an important part of the modern tax system. The General Offices of the Communist Party of China (CPC) Central Committee and the State Council published the *Plan on Deepening Reform of Central and Local Tax Collection Systems*, proposing that "to continuously push forward the modernization of the tax collection and management system and capabilities, and further strengthen the basic, pillar and guarantee roles of taxation in national governance", and making clear the reform goal of building a modern tax collection and management system that will match the modernization of national governance systems and capabilities by 2020.

The basic, pillar, and guarantee roles of taxation in national governance is mainly reflected in two aspects in the field of tax collection and management: First, the modern tax collection and management system will reduce collection costs, improve collection and management efficiency, and enhance tax law compliance and taxpayer satisfaction. Second, it is to serve economic and social development and give full play to the functional role of taxation in promoting healthy economic development and social fairness and justice. In addition to meeting the common requirements in terms of collection and management efficiency and tax law compliance, China's tax collection and management reform should also focus on the following aspects in the future:

First, the reform of the tax collection and management system have to promote the market to play a decisive role in the resource allocation. As the economy enters the "new normal", the cross-region operation of enterprises, the implementation of regional development strategies beyond the administrative division represented by the "Beijing-Tianjin-Hebei region" and "Yangtze River Economic Belt" and other changes challenge the tax collection and management system based on administrative divisions. This requires the tax authorities to promote cross-region central tax, sharing of local tax information, mutual recognition of qualifications, mutual assistance in collection and management, continuously expand the regional taxation cooperation, and play an active role in facilitating the cross-region flow of resources and improving the efficiency in resource allocation.

Second, tax collection and management should deeply engage with international cooperation and actively serve the strategy of opening up. To keep pace the trend of economic globalization and meet China's requirement of establishing the economic system to achieve a higher level of opening up, tax authorities should set up a tax concept as a leading nation, actively participate in the formulation of international tax rules, and effectively strengthen international tax cooperation. While cracking down on international tax evasion, tax authorities should also take the initiative in serving the strategy of opening up and providing high-quality foreign-related services for enterprises going global.

Third, it is necessary to establish a tax collection and management mechanism that promotes paying tax by credibility. The market economy based on specialized division of labor and exchange is a contract economy or credit economy, and its effective operation depends on the credibility of parties involved in the division of labor and transactions. Tax-paying credit is an important part of the social credit system. Tax authorities should not only apply different rules to taxpayers of different credit levels in the process of tax collection and management, but also strengthen bank-tax cooperation, and jointly take disciplinary actions with relevant departments implementing prohibition of high consumption, restriction on credit extension prohibiting participation in government procurement, restricting access to government-supplied land and government funding support, and going abroad and so on. Therefore, tax authorities could realize the linkage management of tax-paying credit and other social credits through the cross-department credit information sharing mechanism, which is of great significance for improving the social credit system and establishing a comprehensive social credit system that covers every citizen.

Fourth, it is of great importance to give play to the role of taxation big data to serve national governance. Comprehensive, timely, and accurate data is the technical basis for the modernization of national governance capabilities. In the "big data era", big data is viewed as a country's basic strategic resource. The "big data" development by tax authorities is an important part of the national big data strategy, playing a key role in implementing law-based taxation management, improving the efficiency of tax collection and management, and improving tax services. As the tax authorities' data cover most of the transactions of economic entities, with the development of the taxation management system for natural persons in the future, it will also further cover most of the natural persons' income, spending and property information. The nearly full-sampled dynamic micro data will reflect the economic indicators in a timely, comprehensive and profound way. The collection, processing and utilization of these data will enable taxation big data to play a pivotal role in enhancing national governance capabilities.

CHAPTER 7

Building a Transparent, Standardized, Scientifically Sound and Binding Budget System

Dehua Wang and Zaozao Zhao

The report at the 19th National Congress of CPC solemnly announced: "As socialism with Chinese characteristics has entered a new era, the principal tension facing Chinese society has evolved. What we now face is the tension between uneven and under development and the people's ever-growing needs for a better life". This clarifies the strategic objectives for the building of a modern budget system, and provides a development direction for deepening reform. That is to strive to put in place a comprehensive, procedure-based, transparent budget system that uses well-conceived standards and imposes effective constraints, and implement performance-based management nationwide.

D. Wang (✉) · Z. Zhao
National Academy of Economic Strategy, Chinese Academy of Social Sciences, Beijing, China

D. He et al. (eds.), *Chinese Finance Policy for a New Era*,
https://doi.org/10.1007/978-981-33-4054-1_7

7.1 A Modern Budget System: Cornerstone of a Modern Public Finance System

To drive forward the reform of a modern budget system and fully build the system of socialism with Chinese characteristics, China needs to absorb the achievements of human civilization. The 19th National Congress of CPC proposed to "put in place a comprehensive, procedure-based, transparent budget system that uses well-conceived standards and imposes effective constraints". This statement contains the basic principles of a modern budget system and is consistent with the international experience in such a development. There are seven basic principles involved. The rule of law. Government should set the budget under the current legal framework and be subject to the budget system. All government budget revenues and expenditures have to be approved by the legislature, and budget enforcement upon approval has to also be carried out in accordance with laws. All budget participants have to act within the bounds of related laws. The first is comprehensiveness. All the revenues and expenditures related to public resources shall be fully included in the budget, handled by the budget process, and be subject to the budget system. The second is consistency. All budget resources have to be allocated and managed under the same rule, and all decision-making processes regarding financial revenue and expenditure must be unified. The third is annuality. The government budget-related decisions must be made annually. In other words, the government must make timely adjustments to the budget for the new situations emerging each year. Mid- to long-term fiscal planning should also be combined with the annual budget process. The fourth is openness and transparency. The process of setting government budgets should be transparent and subject to public supervision. Budget documents and information disclosed by the government must be truthful, detailed, and accurate to make them easy to understand and review by the public. The enforcement, audit, and final accounts shall also be subject to full public disclosure. The fifth is performance-based. In the use of public resources and funds, the government shall lay emphasis on results and performance, evaluate the relationship between input and output rationally, and guide the government to make budget decisions and enforcement to solve social problems more effectively. The sixth is audit. All organizations that use budget resources, including the government, have to accept the audit supervision of an independent auditor every year, and the problems found therefrom need to be corrected in time (Lou Jiwei 2016; Ma Jun and Zhao Zaozao 2012).

To establish a modern budget system in China, in addition to the above-mentioned seven principles, six basic requirements, namely integrity, well-informed preparation, standardized implementation, effective supervision, performance orientation, and openness and transparency are also important (Xiao Jie 2017). Specifically, these are mainly reflected in the following aspects: First, any such system should clarify the budget goals, strengthen control over the total amount, enhance forecasting capacity building of budgetary revenue and expenditure, and prevent risks. Second, it should standardize the budget decision-making process, define budget allocation rules, and reduce repeatability of budget resource allocation results to improve allocation efficiency. Third, it should speed up the budget enforcement and improve its performance, establish and form an open and transparent budget reporting system, with both internal and external administrative supervision. Fourth, it should keep a close watch on the actual effects of the budget fund use, make full use of big data and other information technologies that allow an objective evaluation of actual effects imparted by the government and its public sectors in regard to economic, social, cultural, and other sectors using public funds and resources.

7.2 Making Budgets and Final Accounts More Standardized and Transparent

7.2.1 *Making Budget and Final Accounts More Comprehensive and Procedure-Based*

i. **According to the requirements of the third plenary session of the 18th CPC Central Committee, all proceeds from the state-owned assets that be turned over are included in the budget for general public finance, and the budget for state capital operations will be phased out.**

In particular, during the reform of the Industrial and Commercial Bank of China (ICBC) and the Agricultural Bank of China (ABC), the government did not actually provide funds, instead, it owned up to the asset losses through the establishment of the joint management account with the two banks, and the banks will repay with taxes and equity dividends afterward. In regard to the source, the equities held by the finance system are regular financial revenue. The practice is de-normalized, especially in case of financial difficulties, it is unreasonable to continue to purchase equities with general financial revenue. The unified budget management shall be further combined with standardized budget management and revenue from state capital operation. De-normalized practices such as fund co-management shall be improved by reducing part of holding-shares, so as to increase financial revenue.

ii. **Accelerating the reform of various government-managed funds, treating them differently by nature, and finally phasing out budget for government-managed funds.**

The revenue from some government-managed funds are of the nature of consumption tax, which can be booked to subitems over time; some government-managed funds have a collection deadline, and when they are collected, they can be canceled; some government-managed funds are suitable to be changed into special revenue and included in the general budget. Some are mainly fund budget management tasks. If local government special bonds should be included in the government-managed fund budget according to existing requirements, they can be included in off-balance-sheet information as supplementary information in the budget report in the future.

iii. **Preparing a separate budget for social security funds based on international experience.**

The budget for social insurance funds mainly covers revenues and expenditures of funds including enterprise employees' basic aged-care insurance, unemployment insurance, urban workers' basic medical insurance, employment injury insurance, maternity insurance, aged-care pension benefits for rural and nonworking urban residents, and medical insurance for rural and nonworking urban residents. Various types of social insurance are closely related to the interests of residents. Based on international experience, independent funds for budget management are most often set up. China should also keep the budget for social insurance fund and manage all types of social insurance funds in a unified manner to provide safe and sustainable social security for the people.

iv. **Deducting duplicate items and preparing a comprehensive separate budget based on "reducing four budgets into two".**

Via the reform of the system of turning over proceeds from the state-owned assets and the classification of government-managed funds, the reform goals of incorporating the budget for state capital operations and budget for government-managed funds into budget for general public finance. Thus, the reform process of "reducing four budgets into two" in the unified budget system will be achieved, with the independent budget for social insurance funds. Based on this, a separate comprehensive budget should also be prepared, deducting duplicate items in the budget for general public finance and social insurance funds, and reflecting the government revenue and expenditure in an overall and comprehensive manner. Eventually, a budget management system will come into being, including the budget for general public finance and the budget for social insurance funds as well as a separate comprehensive budget, with legal effect upon approval by the National People's Congress.

7.2.2 Making the Information on Budget and Final Accounts More Transparent

i. **Further improving the open system of budget and final accounts and strengthening social supervision.**

We should adhere to the principle that information is withheld only in exceptional circumstances, constantly seeking to expand the budget content and scope to be disclosed, and improve the methods of budget disclosure (Xiao Jie 2017). The openness and transparency refers to the information provided by the government and departments, including its content, way, and method (Stephen 2014). Transparent government budget and final accounts information means government providing the public more reliable information to evaluate the effectiveness of the use of public funds. Due to the government budget and final account information is highly professional, if the government as an information provider, does not actively and consciously cooperate to enhance transparency, it is difficult for the public to obtain accurate information on the budget management and evaluation process. It will directly affect the public's understanding on the government and its budget performance (Ma Yuan 2014). Transparency of government budget and final accounts performance information is like the "disinfectant", could act as a tool for curbing national and official corruption, while encouraging the government to be more responsible, and resulting in good economic performance (Zhuo Yue and Zhang Hongchun 2016). Therefore, the main goal of making government budget and final accounts performance information as transparent as possible is to ensure that the public has access to effective information of interest, helps them judge the government's spending effect, and understand government behaviors. This will further improve the quality of public service.

ii. **Continuing to expand the content and scope of disclosure.**

With the existing scope of disclosure, two areas of work can be accelerated: First, more detailed disclosure of the special transfer payments. Except for confidential content, the project name and budget arrangement of the special transfer payment should be disclosed, together with management measures, distribution results, budget enforcement, and final accounts. Second, the reform of comprehensive financial reporting system on an accrual basis. We should actively promote the disclosure of local government assets and government debts, intensify the evaluation and identification of government assets, and gradually disclose the balance of government debt and its changes, government guarantee commitments, risk control, and other debt information and management information (Lou Jiwei 2016).

iii. **Exploring and innovating disclosure methods.**

Disclosure is a means and its purpose is to allow the public and all sectors of society to fully know, correctly understand and effectively interpret the disclosed information and the content and effectiveness of the government work behind it. At the same time, it can also foster public awareness of modern budget supervision to make it more effective. To this end, innovations should be undertaken in regard to the methods of disclosure, and the report should be easy to understand, mainly adopting tables rather than abstract data. Moreover, it should be easy for the public to receive and read.

7.3 Approaches to Preparing Scientifically Sound Budgets

The key and path of budgeting must follow the basic law of a modern budget system, and pay attention to the effective connection to macro policy and micro management. The total budget revenues and expenditures should be determined, and the basic norms of budget arrangements for key expenditures and the standards of those for basic expenditures should be clarified according to economic and social development goals, national macro-control requirements and industry development needs as well as the mid-term financial plan. The aim is to achieve effective connection to national strategic planning and budget. As human rationality is limited, a completely rational, well-conceived budgeting method is not possible for the real budget process. Therefore, another meaning of "well-conceived standards" put forward at the 19th National Congress of CPC is to recognize the adjustability of standards, and give the budgeting system a reasonable and dynamic adjustment space according to the changes in the macro environment, the needs of micro management and the characteristics of the project itself.

7.3.1 Paying Full Attention to Correlation of National Strategy and Budget

Through top-level design and in combination with means such as institutional adjustment and process reengineering, an effective connection to the national strategic plan/policy and budget decision-making and budgeting can be truly achieved. This makes it necessary to effectively distribute policy priorities and special projects among various departments, reduce policy duplication and overlapping projects, and fundamentally solve problems of overlapping projects and poor fund utilization, so as to achieve the same goal.

7.3.2 Improving the Basic Expenditure Standard System

The development of the basic expenditure standard system has deepened along with the advancement of departmental budget reform. The scope of the standard system has been continuously expanded and is becoming more and more refined. What cannot be ignored is that the standards for setting basic expenditure have always been affected by external factors such as political, economic, social development, and regional differences. It is not fixed, but needs to be constantly adjusted and improved. In the future, we need to improve the basic expenditure standard system from three aspects: First, we should expand the scope of basic expenditure quota management, especially in combination with the administration reform and the reform of public institutions to promote the development of a basic expenditure quota system for different types of units, and check the accurate number of personnel in cooperation with the staffing work to ensure that the basic expenditures are real and effective. Second, we should establish and improve the dynamic adjustment mechanism for quota standards. Besides, we should also calculate the scope of dynamic adjustment based on factors such as the performance of the budgeting units, relevant policy adjustments, changes in price and economic development, to ensure the objective basic expenditure budgeting under the standards. Third, we should strengthen the building of the basic expenditure database, including collecting, analyzing and collating data in a timely manner, and try to analyze the correlation between basic expenditure and the actual effect of budget expenditure (Xiao Jie 2017; Budget Department of the Ministry of Finance 2014).

7.3.3 Further Improving the Project Expenditure Standard System

It is relatively difficult to establish a project expenditure indicator system, mainly because of the many different types and salient characteristics of projects. Nonetheless, it is still necessary to gradually standardize the project expenditure standard system, and bring into play the basic role of standards in budgeting. First of all, we should carry out in-depth research on project classification, with classification standard as the first tier of the system. At present, project expenditures can be roughly divided into goods and services expenditure by government departments, their capital expenditure, and expenditures for guaranteeing people's livelihood that can be subdivided by functional classification, into education, health care, science and technology, infrastructure construction, culture and so on, according to the economic classification standards in budget subjects. Second, on the basis of the first-tier classification, we could summarize the expenditure rules of each major category, explore establishment of a standardized expenditure system for similar projects following common standards, and then explore the individual standards that can be used, and gradually improve them. At the same time, we must realize that the project expenditure standard system should be improved gradually, and that requires space for dynamic adjustment according to the actual situation.

7.4 Strengthening Budgetary Constraint on Government Investment and Other Expenditure

In order to realize the sustainable development of public finance and build a modern budget system, it is vital to impose strict control over the total amount and scale of budget expenditure, improve the structure, and pay close attention to the substantial relationship between the effect of budget expenditure and the realization of policy goals. The aim is to build an effective institutional environment in which hard constraints are imposed through the budget to truly ensure the cost-effective policy effect.

7.4.1 Strictly Implementing the Budget Law *to Enhance the Constraints on Budget*

According to the principle of the rule of law and the requirements of the new *Budget Law*, the government budget must be reviewed and approved by the National People's Congress. During the annual budget enforcement, we should strictly implement what was approved by the People's Congress and reduce budget adjustments and transfers in the year. If they are necessary, an application should be submitted to the People's Congress in strict accordance with the *Budget Law*, and the adjustment can only be made upon full approval. Hard budget constraints impose higher requirements on budget decision-making and budgeting. Under the framework of interim financial planning reform, considerations should be given to the matching relation between strategic planning and actual financial resources, total budget control, moderate balance of revenue and expenditure, and reasonable coordination of various debts, with a view to preventing and controlling risks and ensuring the sustainable development of the public finance.

7.4.2 *Collecting Financial Revenue in Strict Accordance with Laws and Regulations and in Combination with Law-Based Taxation*

The modern budget system requires the collection of financial revenue in accordance with laws and regulations, thus promoting law-based taxation. To this end, we should first coordinate the relationship between reform and legislation. Legislation helps increase the authority of the reform and consolidate reform results. However, reform breaks the status quo. If the reform matters have been legislated, the amendment process is long with many uncontrollable factors hindering reform. At present, the main legal basis for China's reform in the fields of public finance and taxation are the documents mostly issued by the State Council with authorization of the National People's Congress in the 1980s. This type of reform, especially in the field of taxation, raised much discussion in society. First of all, it is necessary to publish a general plan for tax reform, in which the basic objectives and framework of various tax reforms, the planning on various tax types should be clarified and made public. This is the thing in terms of the rule of law. Secondly, it is important to determine the basic principles. All newly introduced taxes, such as resident's real estate tax and environmental protection tax, should be reformed in step with legislation. The moment the law is implemented, the moment the reform can be initiated. Finally, active lawmaking for reform on taxes already levied. Depending on the situation, we can reform first and then legislate to consolidate the achievements of reform with the law, or reform in step with legislation to improve the authority of reform with law.

7.4.3 *Prevention and Control of Local Government Debt Risks*

We should build a government debt financing mechanism with standardized management and controllable risks, and make it clear that governments at all levels are responsible for their debts, in order to enhance fiscal sustainability (Xiao Jie 2017). There are two problems needed to be solved for local government debt management. One is to clarify the vision and stabilize social expectations, and the other is to improve the management system and increase the investment efficiency of debt funds. First of all, it should be made clear that the vision of China's local government debt is a long-term progressive development. Local governments should assume corresponding responsibilities of risk control and management. There is no problem that it must be fully returned all the funds at certain time, and the central government has no responsibility to repay local debts. This vision should be clearly announced to society to stabilize social expectations. Secondly, on the basis of the pilot reform, prefecture-level cities can be appropriately granted the right to issue bonds independently, and the debt funds required by the county-level governments are still raised by the provincial government. The purpose of this reform is to shorten the management chain, improve allocation and investment efficiency of debt funds, and actually help prevent risks. The National People's Congress and the State Council should actively explore rules for the reasonable determination of local government debt limits. Provincial governments should also actively explore rules for allocating local government debt funds among counties and cities to improve funding efficiency. Finally, we should make solid progress in liquidation, standardization, and market-oriented transformation of local financing platforms, continue to properly dispose of existing local government debt, evaluate the impact of the special construction funds of the China Development Bank and Agricultural Development Bank of China on local government debts, and gradually include them into the scope of government information disclosure.

7.5 Implementing Performance-Based Budget Management Nationwide

To implement performance-based management nationwide, work should be undertaken to improve the budget performance management process through the evaluation on budget performance. The reform of budget performance management in the new era is not only the job of the financial departments of governments at all levels, but also makes higher requirements for all administrative units, public institutions, and other organizations that use public finance funds. Government departments at all levels are required to improve their efficiency in the use of financial funds, deeply integrate performance concepts and methods into the entire process of budgeting, enforcement, and supervision, pay attention to cost–benefit analysis, and focus more on the results of expenditures and how far the policy goes (Xiao Jie 2017).

7.5.1 Strengthening Performance Objective Management to Meet Demand

Budget performance objective can bridge the "needs for better life" and "effective service supply". The starting point of budget performance management is to set legal, reasonable, compliant, and well-convinced performance objectives based on the national strategies and their core policies. Generally speaking, the goal of national strategies and major policies is to resolve the tension between uneven and under development and the people's ever-growing needs for a better life. Therefore, the performance objective and its determination process can serve as a bridge connecting public service supply and demand. On the one hand, we should clearly define the service goal. The process of determining performance objective is the one to implement national strategies and major policies, the one to clarify specific work objectives for governments at all levels and their departments to implement major national strategies, and the one to determine what public services are provided. To attach importance to performance objectives is to attach importance to the implementation of national strategies and plans, that is, to attach importance to how national strategies and plans can better meet the needs of the public. On the other hand, we should clarify the current status of the demand and its changes. The process of determining performance objective is also the one for governments at all levels and their departments to fully understand the needs of the public. The demand information collected from the bottom up could make ensure that the work is more accurate and practicable, push forward the implementation of the national strategies in a more solid manner through understanding the needs, and promote the matchmaking of strategy objectives, financial input, public needs, and fiscal expenditure results as far as possible.

7.5.2 Improving the Performance Indicator System

Audience demand survey is the starting point and key of establishing the performance objectives and evaluation indicators for people's livelihood projects. Through the demand survey in the field of people's livelihood, the principal social tension in the new era will be more clearly understood. The audience satisfaction indicator is more like a "window", through which the government can timely understand the status quo between the public demand for a better life and uneven and under development, providing a strong basis for future policy formulation and improving financial investment and management and so on. The establishment of the performance evaluation indicator system is the technical core of budget performance management, including inspection of multi-dimensional indicators such as compliance, economy, efficiency, and effectiveness. According to the characteristics of the projects indicated by indicators, they can be divided into common and personality indicators. They can then be further divided into quantitative indicators and qualitative ones. By data source, they can be divided into objective indicators and subjective ones, in which the latter mainly contain the audience satisfaction indicator on fiscal expenditure.

7.5.3 Better Budget Execution Reporting

Improving the quality of budget performance information and enriching the content of reports is the premise and foundation for transparency of budget performance. In the future, we need to clearly define performance evaluation objects (mainly projects) and their performance objectives and scope, including complete project information; complete the organization/institution goals of the project, clarifying the goals the organization/institution should achieve with public resources; clarify the performance evaluation indicator system, which should be related to the tasks the organization has agreed to and committed to complete; make clear the cost of the resources and services used, and the information about the relation between costs and results; contain comparison information, including comparison with the information of other periods, with established objectives, and with actual needs of the public. Such comparison information will help the public or relevant government departments to analyze project performance more efficiently. The systematical organization and timely analysis on the performance evaluation information could help us understand the effects of financial investment and its projects, identify gaps between performance goals and enforcement effects, and the reasons behind them, thus ensuing the service performance.

7.5.4 Reform of Performance-Based Budget Management System

The reform of performance-based budget management will promote the building of a responsible government through the disclosure and use of performance results. On the one hand, the transparency of performance information is one of the institutional characteristics of budget performance management, which is needed to encourage the government and its departments to publish performance evaluation information to the public in an easily accessible and understandable manner (Alfred Tat-Kei Ho 2007; Joyce 2007). Transparency of government budget performance management and evaluation information is like the "disinfectant", acting as a tool for curbing national and official corruption, and, at the same time, making the government more responsible and even bringing good economic performance (China Development Research Foundation 2010), and could also help improve the people's understanding on the government and its budget performance (Ma Yuan 2014). On the other hand, as an information provider, the government will be required to cooperate more actively, consciously, and positively to enhance information transparency throughout the reform process. By promoting the use of budget performance results in a step-by-step manner, and enhancing transparency in evaluation results, we can gradually improve the budget behavior of various government departments, form a performance culture of "cost-effectiveness", and cultivate the theory understanding and work ability of performance management practitioners, so as to promote the building of a responsible government.

Based on international experience of budget reform, the tension between control orientation and performance orientation of budget has always been the main tension. At present, China's budget reform has a strong control orientation. A budget dominated by fine control helps reduce loopholes, curb waste, and avoid corruption; however, as the budget set annually, the specific content of expenditures is generally determined one year in advance, which is somewhat incompatible with the rapid development of China. To a certain extent, it will affect the performance of financial expenditure. To de-conflict, the basic idea is to streamline administration and delegate power, strengthen supervision, and then replace externally imposed procedural control with self-control. We should strengthen social supervision and external supervision, reduce internal process control, and moderately shift the focus from control to performance.

In short, the reform of budget performance management needs to be coordinated with the administrative management reform. We should promote the comprehensive performance-based budget reform from the perspective of government reengineering. By embedding performance-based budget concepts, frameworks, and methods into China's existing budget framework and management process, we can remodel the internal control system of the public sector, gradually complete the reform of the budget performance management system and ensure establishment of a modern budget system, so as to ultimately improve the service and its quality of the public sector, enhance public satisfaction, and solve the tension between the people's demand for public services and uneven and inadequate supply.

A modernized budget system is the cornerstone of a modern public finance system. In order to build socialism with Chinese characteristics, realize the modernization of national governance capabilities, and resolve the principal social tensions in the new era, it is of great importance to achieve this goal as soon as possible. From 1999, China initiated the first round of budget system reform, including in areas of departmental budget, revenue and expenditure, systems for treasury's centralized revenue collection and expenditure payments and government procurement. After more than a decade of efforts, the main frame of the modern budget system has been basically established. Since the third plenary session of the 18th CPC Central Committee, especially the successful convening of the 19th National Congress of CPC, new and higher requirements have been put forward to further improve the system. We should make steady progress in the deepening of reforms, focusing on the coordination between the plan and the budget; emphasize "top-down" total amount control to curb the expanding "economic man" behavior of various expenditure departments; effectively promote the unified budget reform, advance effective integration of budget for public finance, budget for government-managed funds, budget for state capital operations, and budget for social insurance funds from the perspective of total amount control, and attempt to formulate a unified budget framework for the budgeting and accounting. Meanwhile, we have to pay attention to the development of related systems, and provide a good external environment for reforms to realize the coordinated development with other system development. We should promote the development of the budget supervision system by enhancing the capabilities of supervision by the people's congress, audit and citizens, and explore more effective supervisory methods. Efforts should be made to advance the reform of the government's accounting system, especially the comprehensive financial reporting system on an accrual basis. More citizens should participate in the budget development, including the budget process and budget performance evaluation with a more open attitude and in a more flexible way, in order to make budget decisions more well-convinced and the enforcement results more effective.

References

Alfred Tat-Kei Ho. (2007). Performance Budgeting—Promises, Myths, and Possibilities—Lessons from the U.S. Experience and Challenges for China. *Performance-Based Budget: Foreign Experience and Reference* (ed. Liu Kun). Beijing: China Financial and Economic Publishing House.

Budget Department of the Ministry of Finance. (2014). *Guidelines for the Budgeting of Central Departments in 2015*. Beijing: China Financial and Economic Publishing House.

China Development Research Foundation. (2010). Research on Transparency in the Budget Process of Local Governments.

Joyce, P. (USA, 2007). Linking Performance and Budgeting. *Performance-Based Budget: Foreign Experience and Reference* (ed. Liu Kun). Beijing: China Financial and Economic Publishing House.

Lou Jiwei. (ed. 2016). *Deepening the Reform of Fiscal and Tax System*. Beijing: People's Publishing House.

Ma Jun & Zhao Zaozao. (2012). *Public Budget: A Comparative Study*. Beijing: Central Compilation and Translation Press.

Ma Yuan. (2014). *Performance Information in the Government Performance-Based Budget*. Beijing: National School of Administration Press.

Stephen, K. (USA, 2014). Does Transparency Improve Governance? *China Governance Review: Vol 2* (ed. Yu Keping). Beijing: Central Compilation and Translation Press.

Xiao Jie. (2017). Accelerating the Establishment of a Modern Public Finance System. *Tutorial of the Report at the 19th National Congress of CPC*. Beijing: People's Publishing House.

Zhuo Yue & Zhang Hongchun. (2016). Standard Construction and Experiential Evaluation of Government Performance Information Transparency. *Chinese Public Administration*, issue 7.

CHAPTER 8

Priorities of Financial Reform in the New Era

Dexu He and Chaoyang Wang

The report at the 19th National Congress of the Communist Party of China clearly pointed out: "With decades of hard work, socialism with Chinese characteristics has crossed the threshold into a new era. This is a new historic juncture in China's development". This significant strategic judgment provides solid foundations for correctly understanding and accurately grasping the characteristics of China's current development, and for putting forward new ideas, new strategies, new layouts, and new initiatives at this fresh starting point. Financial system is the core element in national economic operation, financial security is an important part of national security, and the financial system is a primary fundamental system in economic and social development. It is an extremely important strategic task to deepen institutional reform in the financial sector and make China strong in finance in the new era of socialism with Chinese characteristics.

D. He (✉) · C. Wang
National Academy of Economic Strategy, Chinese Academy of Social Sciences, Beijing, China

D. He et al. (eds.), *Chinese Finance Policy for a New Era*,
https://doi.org/10.1007/978-981-33-4054-1_8

8.1 The Financial Sector Must Serve the Interest of the Real Economy

Finance is the lifeblood of the real economy. It is closely connected with the real economy and they are interlinked with each other. History suggests that, if the finance deviates from the real economy for a long time, its development will become unsustainable, likely leading to large-scale accumulated risks and even an all-out crisis. In the past two years, China has seen many salient problems in its economic operation, such as "funds circulating within the financial sector without entering the real economy or being diverted out of the real economy", which are reflected in the coexistence of high growth in the financial sector and decline in the manufacturing industry. A large amount of capital flows circulating within the financial system, but are unwilling to enter the real economy, which prolongs the credit chain of the finance serving the real economy. This results in raising the latter's financing costs, reducing availability of financial services, and deviating from the bounden duty of the financial industry serving the real economy. In terms of the added value of the financial sector of GDP, although the indicator has reached 8 percent at the end of the 12th Five-Year Plan period, it's not veritable. The rapid growths of the financial sector in 2015 and 2016 were somewhat "exaggerated" because of "funds circulating within the financial sector without entering the real economy or being diverted out of the real economy". It's a "nominal value" rather than the "actual value" created by the financial sector in effectively serving the real economy. The most direct evidence is that the rapid growth of the financial sector is accompanied by a rapid decline in the proportion of manufacturing industry. From 2011 to 2015, the added value of the manufacturing sector accounted for 39.88 percent, 38.66 percent, 37.35 percent, 36.31 percent, and 34.5 percent of GDP, respectively. It fell further to 33.31 percent in 2016. The decline of the real economy means that finance has become "stagnant water", which indicates that the growth mode of the financial sector will never be sustainable. If the proportion of the financial sector is further increased, the consequence will inevitably be the bubble and the bubble burst.

The real economy is an overall concept. To implement the purpose of the financial sector serving the real economy, we need to answer two questions. First, which parts of the real economy should the financial sector focus on? Second, how should the financial sector effectively serve the real economy? As China's economy has entered the "new normal" and shifted gear from the previous high to medium-high growth, it is necessary to further optimize the economic structure in the future, and cultivate and form new engines for economic growth. In this context, a financial sector serving the real economy should pursue the vision of "innovative, coordinated, green and open development that is for everyone", implement the task of supply-side structural reform, and focus on economic activities conducive to promoting innovation, entrepreneurship, and upgrading of the industrial structure as well as the formation of new growth drivers. For economic activities with overcapacity and pollution that are low-level and redundant, although they belong to the real economy, they should not be served by finance.

How can finance effectively serve the real economy? This depends on the nature of the corresponding economic activity. To this end, the means of macro control, the way of financial services, and financial functions need to be adjusted accordingly. First, in the context of an international economic environment still facing more uncertainties and a world economy still in the slow recovery after crisis, macro-economic regulation and control have to upheld the underlying principle of pursuing progress while ensuring stability and constantly improve the accuracy of policy operations in the implementation of prudent monetary policy so as to ensure the appropriate growth of monetary credit, keep the liquidity basically stable and create a favorable monetary environment for economic development. Second, we should handle the relationship between direct and indirect financing, give more priority to the development of direct financing, and focus development of indirect financing on structural adjustment. The reason is that, the development of direct financing, especially equity financing, such as improving the National Equities Exchange and Quotations (NEEQ), developing regional equity markets, and conducting pilot equity crowdfunding financing, is more conducive to completing the supply-side structural reform tasks, such as deleveraging and cost reduction. The domestic listing of start-up enterprises, issuing start-up bonds, and establishing the strategic emerging board market are better for the innovation-driven development strategy and revitalizing the real economy. The key to the adjustment of indirect financing structure is to vigorously develop small and medium-sized banks and private financial institutions to enrich financial service providers. At the same time, the inclusive and green development concepts should be formed in leading banks, thus making financial services available to more small and micro businesses and more impoverished people to more remote areas. Third, work should be undertaken to bring back to origins of financial services serving the real economy. For example, insurance as a financial arrangement to disperse loss is a means of risk management. Therefore, the key to the development of the insurance industry is to bring into full play its role in risk management and protection.

Vigorously developing direct financing is an important manifestation of the financial sector serving the real economy. From 2011 to 2015, the direct financing of China's non-financial enterprises accounted for 14 percent, 15.9 percent, 11.74 percent, 17.38 percent, and 24 percent of the total financing respectively, falling slightly to 23.8 percent in 2016. Although the proportion of direct financing in the total social financing has increased significantly in recent years, compared with the growing, more diversified and more personalized financial needs of the real economy, it is far from enough. Hence, the proportion of direct financing should be increased significantly. Based on a comprehensive analysis, we suggest that the proportion of direct financing of nonfinancial companies in the total financing should be raised to about 30 percent by 2020.

First, the increase in the proportion of direct financing is an inevitable result from the competition and development of the banking industry. On the one hand, due to the acceleration of interest rate liberalization and the boost of Internet finance and other factors, the profit margin of commercial banks has shown a clear downward trend. Take listed commercial banks as an example. From 2012 to 2015, the return on average equity (ROAE, weighted arithmetical average) of listed banks were 20.77 percent, 19.96 percent, 17.93 percent, and 15.68 percent, respectively, further falling to 13.83 percent in 2016. On the other hand, due to the downturn in economic growth and the decrease in profits of the real economy, the scale and ratio of non-performing loans (NPLs) of commercial banks are both rising in recent years. According to the statistics of the China Banking and Insurance Regulatory Commission (CBIRC), from 2012 to 2016, the balance of NPLs of commercial banks were RMB492.9 billion, RMB592.1 billion, RMB842.6 billion, RMB1,274.4 billion, and RMB1,493.9 billion, respectively, and the NPL ratios were 0.95 percent, 1 percent, 1.25 percent, 1.67 percent, and 1.76 percent, respectively. It can be expected that under the policy requirements of reducing overcapacity and addressing zombie enterprises, the risk of bad debts of commercial banks will be further exposed. This part of loss provisioning will inevitably further erode profits of the banking industry, thereby weakening the banking industry in the financial sector.

Second, the tasks of supply-side structural reform, such as deleveraging and cost reduction, request further development of direct financing. Deleveraging is one of the important contents of the supply-side structural reform, since a high leverage ratio has become a lingering concern in regard to China's economic development. Data shows that, as of the end of 2015, China's total debt was RMB168.48 trillion, and the overall leverage ratio was 249 percent. Among them, the debt problems of the nonfinancial enterprises were particularly prominent, with a debt ratio up to 156 percent. Meanwhile, an important connotation of cost reduction is to reduce the financial costs of enterprises, the largest burden being bank interest and various expenses incurred during the loan process. It can be said that, under the financing structure dominated by commercial banks, the high leverage ratio and costs in the real sector, and the rapid growth of the financial sector are actually two sides of the coin. To address these problems, the most important way is to vigorously develop direct financing, especially different forms of equity financing, such as establishing strategic emerging board, promoting domestic listing of startups, improving the NEEQ, developing regional equity markets, and carrying out pilot equity crowdfunding financing.

Third, development of direct financing is an inevitable choice for implementing the innovation-driven development strategy and revitalizing the real economy. The key to revitalization is innovation, but whether this involves implementing an innovation-driven development strategy or to practice "mass entrepreneurship and innovation", it is necessary to further enrich direct financing tools. As entrepreneurship and innovation are highly uncertain, indirect finance represented by commercial banks cannot accomplish this task. To build an investment and financing system conducive to entrepreneurship and innovation, it is necessary to further expand direct financing channels and constantly improve the building of multi-tiered capital markets, including the development of stock markets to provide equity funds, bond markets to provide long- and short-term debt funds, and commercial paper market to provide short-term liquidity for enterprises, and so on. Besides, work should also be undertaken to promote the development of venture investment and expand the scale of venture capital investment, especially for startups in the initial growth.

Fourth, determining the proportion of direct financing in nonfinancial enterprises' total financing as 30 percent is a "significant" increase. At the end of 2015, the State Council reviewed and approved the *Opinions on Further Significantly Increasing the Proportion of Direct Financing and Optimizing the Financial Structure*. If the proportion of direct financing in 2020 is to be 30 percent, it means the proportion will increase by six percentage points on the basis of 24 percent in 2015, which can be regarded as "significant". More importantly, trying to increase the proportion of direct financing to more than 30 percent while stabilizing the proportion of the financial sector at 8 percent is in fact transforming the past extensive, external expansion of the financial sector into the intensive development and development of substance, which is a comprehensive manifestation of an improved financial structure, enhanced financial efficiency, and better financial services for the real economy.

8.2 Improving Financial Regulation to Reduce Systemic Risks

Finance is risky, and risks are inherent in any financial activity. Millions of economic activities and financial activities constitute the macroeconomic operation. The risks generated by a single activity are individual and nonsystemic risks. Although they are managed by finance, they are not the subject of financial work, otherwise it means the stagnation and even demise of financial activities. However, if a large number of individual risks are interrelated and quickly spread, they may combine to the systemic risk affecting the operation of the entire economy. Because it is extremely destructive and even lethal, it must be strictly under control, and thus becomes an eternal theme of financial work. It starts small. The systemic risk emerges as individual risks at first. Therefore, to prevent this happening, we should not only focus on the source of the risks, but also emphasize coordinated regulation. For a period of time, the limitations in the current regulation have made problems such as gaps, conflicts, interest arbitrage, and race to the bottom more prominent. Regional and local financial risks occur frequently, if not addressed properly, it may evolve into a systemic financial risk.

Since the establishment of the China Banking Regulatory Commission (CBRC) in 2003, China has adopted a separate regulatory framework.[1] From the perspective of division of labor, the People's Bank of China focuses on monetary policies, interbank financial markets, financial stability, payment and settlement and so on, and plays a role in promoting economic growth and ensuring financial security at the macroeconomic level. The CBRC mainly regulated banking and some nonbanking financial institutions (such as trust companies, financial asset management companies, enterprise groups, finance companies, and so on), involving institution establishment, business activities, appointment of senior managers, risk disposal and so on, and its internal departments are basically set according to the types of institutions. The China Securities Regulatory Commission (CSRC) is mainly responsible for the regulation of securities industry and listed companies, and its setting of internal departments considers various business functions and market players but focus on the latter, involving securities issuance, institutions, listed companies and funds as well as audit. The China Insurance Regulatory Commission focuses on the insurance sector, and its internal departments are formed based on the properties of relevant institutions, involving property insurance, life insurance, insurance intermediaries, and insurance fund investment. In short, under the existing framework, the regulatory authorities just care their own businesses according to the attributes of the regulatory subjects. However, in recent years, with the rapid advancement of interest rate liberalization and the enrichment of financial activities, more and more financial innovations emerge, such as bank financing, interbank deposit certificates, entrusted investment (outsourcing), various asset management plans, Internet finance, and so on. These activities tend to blur boundaries between the original banks, securities, and insurance, resulting in corresponding regulatory arbitrage, that is, financial institutions choose regulatory standards that are more favorable to them. As a result, the criticism of China's financial regulation is mainly due to the fact that there are obvious regulatory conflicts and gaps in the existing framework, and the coordination between regulatory authorities is inadequate.

[1] On April 8, 2018, the China Banking and Insurance Regulatory Commission (CBIRC) unveiled in Beijing, marking the formal merger of the former the China Banking Regulatory Commission and the China Insurance Regulatory Commission.

At the fifth National Financial Work Conference, it was decided to establish the Financial Stability and Development Committee under the State Council, the purpose of which is to strengthen the overall planning and coordination of regulation and provide institutional guarantees for preventing systemic financial risks. In terms of concept, the conference proposed "strengthening comprehensive regulation, highlighting functional regulation and behavioral regulation". With respect to action, it proposed to cultivate a regulation spirit of "performing due diligence, daring to regulate, being adept at regulation and implementing strict accountability system". We believe that comprehensive regulation, functional regulation, and behavioral regulation reflect the improvement of the concept of institutional regulation, and the new regulation spirit requires the regulation departments to form four kinds of consciousness—responsibility, act, technology, and accountability.

Institutional regulation has been implemented in China for more than 10 years, that is, to define the regulatory subjects and categorize them according to the properties of the institutions. Financial institutions of the same property are all regulated by the same regulators, regardless of the type of business they operate and what kind of financial functions they perform. This regulatory concept focuses on institutions means they can be regulated as a whole, and its specific operations are clearer. The disadvantage is that, if the financial business becomes complicated, especially in cross-border business, which can lead to inconsistent regulatory standards. In recent years, the scope of comprehensive operation in China's financial sector has been continuously expanded, and horizontal business cooperation among the banking, insurance, and securities sectors has become increasingly frequent. At the same time, more and more cross-investments in equity and cross-business operations have emerged, which is particularly prominent in financial holding groups. These changes have broken through the original business areas and traditional regulatory scope, and have become increasingly challenging to the concept of institutional regulation.

Unlike institutional regulation, functional regulation focuses on financial functions rather than institutions. That is, for different forms of financial activities, as long as they perform the same financial function, they will be subject to the same standard, regardless of the property of the institution. The concept of functional regulation comes from the concept of financial function proposed by American economists Zvi Bodie and Robert C. Merton. According to their theory, the financial system may have many forms in terms of organizational structure with changes in time and space, and the names of financial institutions are even more varied; however, the functions of the financial system are relatively stable, including payment and clearing, fund collection, resource allocation across time and space, risk management, price discovery and alleviation of information asymmetry. Compared with the concept of institutional regulation, the concept of functional regulation has obvious advantages in terms of uniformity, fairness, and professionalism. However, functional regulation is not perfect, and its disadvantages are precisely the advantages of it. On the one hand, due to the focus on the performance of various specific financial functions, under the guidance of this concept, the problem of "only trees but no forests" may arise, which is especially critical for systemically important financial institutions; on the other hand, some financial business may have more than one financial function. For example, the reason why many financial activities can optimize resource allocation is that it reduces the degree of information asymmetry. At this time, as for what kind of regulatory standards should be adopted, there will be controversy and even conflicts. Therefore, we cannot simply think that functional regulation is superior to institutional regulation, nor can we negate the importance of the latter.

Behavioral regulation supplements financial regulation from another perspective, focusing on the compliance of specific behaviors of institutions or individuals engaged in financial activities. Its purpose is to maintain the fairness and justice of the financial market and provide protection for the rights and interests of financial consumers. Internationally, the concept of behavioral regulation began with the *Market Behavior Inspection Manual* issued by the National Association of Insurance Commissioners of the United States in the 1970s. A wave of theoretical research and practical operations emerged thus around 2000. After the U.S. financial crisis in 2008, this concept attracted more attention, and received the attention of government departments together with prudential regulation (both micro-prudential and macro-prudential aspects). In practice, the combined effects of fraud and greed of financial institutions, highly complex derivative contracts, the ignorance of financial consumers, and the absence of effective regulation may accelerate the formation of risks and lead to the outbreak of crises. In China's securities markets, collusion between major investors and listed companies for joint market manipulation and exploitation of retail investors is widespread despite repeated prohibitions. Information disclosure in some

Internet financial activities is not timely or even concealed, and fraudulent contracts are fabricated. All these problems create more urgent requirements on the concept of behavioral regulation.

Relying on the leadership of the Financial Stability and Development Committee under the State Council, comprehensive regulation is feasible. On the one hand, the traditional financial activities with clear boundaries are still regulated according to the concept of institutional regulation; on the other hand, for cross-business, cross-market, and cross-industry financial activities, unified standards should be formulated based on the concept of functional regulation. In this way, not only can all financial activities be regulated according to the same standards, but also the major issues involved in deepening financial reforms, such as capital account opening and RMB internationalization, can be solved with more comprehensive and well-conceived reform plans through effective planning and coordination among financial regulators. In this process, two basic tasks need to be done. One is to strengthen the overall regulation and interconnection of the financial infrastructure. The other is to promote the sharing of comprehensive statistics and regulatory information within the sector. For example, third-party payment business emerging in recent years should be included in the statistics and regulation regime.

Efforts should be made to foster a regulation spirit of "performing due diligence, daring to regulate, being adept at regulation and implementing a strict accountability system". The first thing is to make clear the responsibilities and how they are performed. Under the new regulatory framework, the responsibilities of the People's Bank of China are no longer limited to monetary policy operations, but focus more on macro-prudential management. Compared with micro-prudential regulation, which pays more attention to the security and stability of individual financial institutions, the key point of macro-prudential management is to maintain the stability of the entire financial system. Since 2016, the People's Bank of China launched the macro-prudential assessment system (MPA). It evaluates commercial banks, financial companies, auto finance companies, and financial leasing companies based on indicators include capital and leverage, balance sheets, liquidity, pricing, asset quality, cross-border financing risk, credit policy implementation. And a counter-cyclical adjustment evaluation system based on the difference in system importance and properties of the institutions was established by shifting the focus from loans in a narrow sense to macro-prudential management over credits in a broad sense (including loans, securities, investment, repurchase, and so on). In the coming period, the evaluation system should be further improved according to the development of relevant work, especially in the threshold setting of key indicators and the differences between institutions with different properties. At the same time, the responsibilities of financial regulators are no longer limited to traditional ones, such as access and exit of institutions, business approval, and market regulation, but pay more attention to behavior regulation. This requires regulators to encourage financial institutions to further improve their internal control system, make more precise instructions on product design, contract terms, disclaimers, risk levels, price standards, and personal information protection and so on, so as to give proper guidance, education, and protection to financial consumers.

In order to do a good job, regulators should continuously improve their technical level, and be good at using new technologies, new methods, and new thinking in the work. In recent years, with the advancement of modern information and communication technologies, the concept of FinTech has rapidly emerged and brought great challenges to regulatory work. In March 2016, the Financial Stability Board (FSB) issued the *Fintech: Describing the Landscape and a Framework for Analysis*, initially defining the concept of FinTech, It summarized "Fintech" as a technology that promotes financial innovation, forming business models, technology applications, and processes and products that have a significant impact on financial markets, institutions, and financial services. In practice, the Basel Committee on Banking Supervision divides this into four categories: payment and settlement, deposit and loan and capital raising, investment management, and market facilities. There are many forms of financial technologies in each category, such as online third-party payment, P2P online lending, equity crowdfunding, intelligent investment consulting, distributed bookkeeping, blockchain technology, and so on. In view of the rapid development of FinTech, international regulatory organizations and governments have paid great attention to it, among which the regulatory sandbox approach is exemplary. In 2015, the Financial Conduct Authority of the UK launched a regulatory sandbox mechanism that allows FinTech companies to carry out relevant innovative business in specific scenarios under limited conditions and on the premise of limited licenses. Through this exploratory approach, regulators can determine whether to grant a full license based on the test results. FinTech companies can also think deeply about whether they can meet relevant regulatory standards, and then decide whether to apply for or give up making further applications for licenses. This approach not only improves the regulators' inclusiveness for financial innovation, but also effectively controls the scope and scale of risks.

To implement strict accountability system, regulators should set up a sense of accountability. On the one hand, we should realize that "it is negligence of duty of duty if any risk is not found in time". Therefore, we need to establish and improve a risk warning system. The formation of systemic risks always starts with individual, discrete risks, and gradually accumulates and enlarges through spreading among different institutions, different industries, and different markets. Therefore, we should not only focus on micro-individual risk indicators from the perspective of economic and financial fundamentals, such as economic growth rate, inflation rate, asset price volatility, capital adequacy ratio of financial institutions, and debt ratio of economic entities, but also pay attention to the ways and channels of risk transmission so as to cut the chain of spreading in time. On the other hand, it is necessary to realize that "it is dereliction of duty to fail to point out and address detected risks". To this end, it is necessary to establish and improve risk emergency response mechanisms, including a series of work arrangements and rules and regulations for different types of risks, covering decision-making departments, decision-making procedures, trend assessment, scheme formulation, disposal tools, and so on.

Looking from the relationship between financial regulation and financial innovation, the former lags far behind. The questions that need further consideration in the future include: First, how should the internal departments of financial regulators be set up? How to address the relationship between these departments and financial industry and financial business? This requires a profound understanding of the characteristics of financial activities, the basic law of financial development, and the financial development trend in the future. The second question is the timing of further reform. The goal of financial regulation is to improve the efficiency and coverage, protect the legitimate rights and interests of investors and consumers, and enable the financial system to better serve the real economy. In terms of risk forestalling, the goal of financial regulation is not to eliminate risks, but to effectively prevent systemic risks. Third, there are some specific problems such as the financial business models, financial functions and regulatory rules, the decision-making procedures and organizational efficiency under the new framework, regulation over financial holding companies and emerging large Internet financial companies (regulatory gaps), overall planning of financial infrastructure, matchmaking and unification (payment and clearing, trading platform, registration, and settlement), comprehensive financial statistics, whether it is possible to establish balance sheets of the financial system, coordination of monetary policies, regulatory policies, and macro-prudential policies.

8.3 Deeping Comprehensive Financial Reform and Pursuing Greater Openness

The financial development and economic growth may be led by demand or supply, but any kind of development model is inseparable from the continuous deepening of financial reform. The real economic activities are ever-changing, and the financial sector can only meet the needs of economic development through continuous changes. If the financial sector wants to take the initiative to guide economic activities through supply, only by continuously making changes and innovations can it achieve this goal. Tracing back to various problems and risks in financial operations in recent years, we could find that the crux lies precisely in the irregularities of financial institutions and the imperfections of financial systems themselves, and this can only be solved through reform.

The subjects of financial reform at the micro level are various financial institutions, and the focus of reform is to improve the modern financial enterprise system and corporate governance structure. The modern enterprise system has clearly established ownership, well-defined power and responsibility, separation of enterprise from administration, and scientific management. Among them, clearly established ownership is the core of the modern enterprise system. Therefore, to optimize the equity structure of financial institutions has become the core of financial reform. The typical corporate governance structure includes shareholders, board of directors, board of supervisors, senior management members, and stakeholders to form an effective incentive and restraint mechanism, internal control mechanism, risk management mechanism, and external supervision mechanism. For state-owned financial institutions, another important subject is the Party organization. To address the relationship between it and other subjects, we should combine the Party's leadership with corporate governance. We should bring into full play the discipline inspection and supervision, inspection tour, and auditing functions. We should also apply the principle of the Party supervising the performance of officials to the practice of the board of directors in selecting and appointing the senior management, so as to form a good modern corporate governance framework with Chinese characteristics. Obviously, these reforms are not temporary, but to get to the root of the problem.

The key to financial reform at the macro level is to straighten out systems and mechanisms, including interest rate liberalization mechanism, RMB exchange rate formation mechanism, and clear objectives and order of financial openness. Although the lift of the ceiling on RMB deposit interest rates marks the nominal completion of the interest rate liberalization, to realize the interest rate liberalization in a very real sense, we should also establish a benchmark interest rate formation mechanism, an effective interest rate transmission and regulation mechanism, so as to let the market determine the price of capital and give full play to the decisive role of the market in the allocation of resources. The RMB exchange rate formation mechanism, capital account convertibility, and RMB internationalization are the three main goals of the opening up of finance. What relationship among them, and in what order should they be advanced? For a developing country like China, there is no ready-made experience that can be copied directly. What we can do is to make steady progress going with the flow, and adhere to the basic principles of protecting the rights and interests of financial consumers, enhancing the orderly competition of finance, and preventing financial risks.

In the near term, the five key tasks of financial reform are perfecting the financial regulatory system, improving the financial organization system, building the financial market system, strengthening the financial regulation system, and optimizing the financial environment system. (1) The objective of perfecting the financial regulatory system is to strengthen and improve the financial macro control, address well the relationship among maintaining stable and rapid economic development, managing inflation expectations, and adjusting the economic structure, enhance policy predictability, flexibility and effectiveness, and ensure stability in the overall price level to promote stable and healthy economic development. (2) The goal of improving the financial organization system is to optimize the industrial and regional layout of financial institutions, build and improve a modern financial organization system, improve financial innovation capabilities and service level, and enhance the overall strength, international competitiveness, and risk resistance capacity of the financial sector. To this end, it is necessary to improve the banking organizational system, promote standardized development of securities institutions, and encourage the innovative development of insurance institutions. It should also continue to promote the comprehensive operation of the financial industry, and encourage and guide private capital to enter financial services. (3) To build a financial market system, it is necessary to focus on promoting innovation in financial products, constantly enriching product types, and improving product structure. It should improve market systems and infrastructure as well as market operation mechanism, promote the orderly flow of funds across markets and improve market linkage and efficiency, and gradually form a financial market system with reasonable structure and complementary functions to better serve the development of the real economy. (4) The goal of strengthening the financial regulation system is to improve the risk management level of financial institutions, enhance regulation capacity to avoid the absence and misalignment of regulation and effectively prevent the interaction of economic and financial risks, the transmission of financial and public finance risks, and the spread of external risks to the internal markets. It also aims to actively and steadily resolve hidden risks, and firmly hold the bulwark against systemic or regional financial risks. (5) It is important to optimize the financial environment system, including improving financial laws and regulations, strengthening financial infrastructure construction; standardizing the financial accounting statistical system, improving the informatization level of the financial industry, and building a financial talent team to ensure the safe and efficient operation of the financial system.

The overall goal of the above-mentioned reforms is to establish a modern financial system, featuring vibrant financial institutions, a financial market of efficient resource allocation, strict and orderly financial regulation, mature and improved financial infrastructure, and flexible and coordinated financial macro control. (1) There should be large, medium, small, and micro-scale financial institutions as well as both state-owned and private ones, represented by banks, securities institutions, insurance companies, and other financial businesses, and widely covering urban and rural areas. (2) The guiding function and basic role of the financial market in resource allocation should be prominent, the interest rate liberalization reform should be basically realized, and the price mechanism should play a leading role in transactions. A multitiered financial market system with reasonable structure, clear functional positioning and complementary functions should be established, and the building of market mechanisms should achieve progress. (3) Financial products are rich and diverse, the proportion of direct financing and indirect financing of nonfinancial enterprises is more coordinated, and the industrial structure and organizational system of major financial sectors such as banks, securities, and insurance are more reasonable. (4) The financial rule of law is enabled to function better, the modern payment system and social credit system are more developed, and the financial informatization is continuously improved. The ability to protect the rights and interests of financial consumers is continuously enhanced, the self-discipline organizations of the financial industry and the building of talent teams are more effective, so that the overall environment for financial development is more favorable. (5) A sound state-owned financial asset management system and local government's financial management system are established and improved. The coordination of financial regulation and the ability to forestall and warn against systemic risks have been continuously enhanced, able to guarantee financial stability and security in all aspects.

In conclusion, the three tasks of building a modern financial system, namely serving the real economy, forestalling and controlling financial risks, and deepening reform and opening up, are organically unified. The explanation is as follows. (1) Serving the real economy is a fundamental measure to forestall financial risks. The financial sector has to serve the needs of production and life, and its profits should only come from the real economy it serves. Although the over-financialization of the economy or the over-expansion of the financial sector is prosperous for a while, it is going too far, because once the risk is formed, it can only be transferred but not be eliminated. Relying on the financial self-circulation, it is always like "a water or tree without source". Only by serving the real economy, and creating value and obtaining reasonable profits in services, can it achieve a virtuous circle of economic and financial development for common prosperity. (2) Serving the real economy is the criterion for deepening financial reform. All efforts in financial reform and financial opening up are for better service to the real economy. They must be based on China's current development stage and national conditions. They should not be done for reform and opening up purpose, or simply imitate the experience of the so-called "developed", "advanced" countries, or blindly follow so-called "international standards" leading to loss of necessary discernment. Only in this way can there be a basis for judgment on the speed of the opening up of the financial industry and the pace of financial reform. (3) Since the reform and opening up is to serve the real economy, and the latter is able to fundamentally forestall the formation of systemic financial risks, the deepening of reform and the forestalling of risks are inherently uniform and compatible. In other words, reasonable and correct reforms will not lead to the accumulation of risks, but contribute to the resolution of risks and the sustainable development of the financial industry. As a result, financial reform can achieve endogenous impetus rather than an externally imposed result. With the above three tasks supporting each other, China could be more capable in serving the real economy by its financial sector, in financial innovation and in forestalling and control financial risk. With its greater international influence in finance, it is just a matter of time for China to be an important financial power in the world.

CHAPTER 9

Deeping Pricing System Reform and Managing Price Expectations

Qunqun Zhang, Zhenxia Wang, Di Sheng, and Yongsheng Feng

The report delivered at the 19th National Congress of the Communist Party of China states that efforts to improve the socialist market economy need to be accelerated. In our economic reforms, we must concentrate on improving the property rights system and ensuring the market-based allocation of factors of production, so that property rights act as effective incentives. We should ensure free flows of factors, flexible prices, fair and orderly competition, and that business survival is determined by competition. To do that, it is important for us to introduce a negative list for market access nationwide, sort through and do away with regulations and practices that impede the development of a unified market and fair competition, support the growth of private businesses, and stimulate the vitality of various market entities. It is also critical for us to deepen reforms in the business sector, break administrative monopolies, preclude the forming

Q. Zhang (✉) · Z. Wang · D. Sheng · Y. Feng
National Academy of Economic Strategy, Chinese Academy of Social Sciences, Beijing, China

D. He et al. (eds.), *Chinese Finance Policy for a New Era*,
https://doi.org/10.1007/978-981-33-4054-1_9

of market monopolies, speed up the reform of market-based pricing of factors of production, relax control over market access in the service sector, and improve market oversight mechanisms. The report shows us the priorities and goals of the price reform in the future. This chapter will analyze the difficulties and key points in deepening the reform and make policy recommendations to tackle the issues.

9.1 Challenges of Pricing System Reform

9.1.1 New Challenges in Adjusting the Overall Price Level in the Context of New Normal

i. **Acute Structural Problems Affecting Price Movements and Varying Trends in CPI and PPI**

Since the second half of 2016, PPI has been picking up quickly. The concern is whether the rising PPI will lead to widespread inflation due to its interaction with CPI. We believe that it is hard for producers to pass the increase in costs onto end consumers in a market where supply outweighs demand. There are several main reasons. First, the prices of many producer goods affecting the PPI trend like oil, electricity, and coal are determined or regulated by the government instead of being market based. Apart from the changes of supply and demand, the government may adjust the prices of those goods according to the economic situation, thus preventing the PPI trend from fully reflecting the changes of supply and demand. Second, in recent years, the PPI has been mainly decided by the prices of producer goods. The prices of consumer goods which the CPI measures constitute merely a small proportion of PPI and fluctuate gently, which also causes the two indexes to change differently. Third, the labor costs, which are critical to both indexes, fluctuate differently in producer goods sector and in the sector of consumer goods and services. This is yet another reason for the different trends in the indexes. If such divergence continues in the near future, it will present increasing challenges for policymakers in the area of price regulation. Great importance needs to be attached to the issue since the influence of the international market is getting stronger and the domestic fiscal and monetary policies are increasingly unpredictable.

ii. **Weakened Government Role in Direct Pricing Makes It More Difficult to Influence Market Expectations**

Since the prices of goods are now mostly market based, and only a small fraction have their prices set or regulated by the government, the authorities lack the instruments to manage the prices directly, which results in their declining capacity of guiding market expectations. It is necessary to create new measures and tools to manage prices in an efficient and feasible way. Of special note in this process is the changing pattern of consumption. With the thriving of e-commerce, online shopping has become an important pattern of consumption in China. As a result of the emergence of new forms of business such as e-commerce and diversified patterns of consumption including online shopping, price frauds are getting elusive. The yet-to-be-improved legal system makes it even more difficult to regulate prices and maintain the market order.

iii. **Growing Uncertainties over the Trend of Key Commodity Prices in the Chinese and Overseas Market**

An Important challenge in the future is to manage the impact from the overseas market. It is more and more difficult to predict the prices as the world economy is recovering, the shale gas revolution and flammable ice technologies are making breakthroughs, the US dollar exchange rate is fluctuating, the geo-political situation is experiencing new changes, and the factors that determine the trend of the international commodity prices are getting more complicated. In order to cushion the domestic prices from any excessive international commodity price fluctuations, it is important to make the prices more sensitive and effectively leverage financial market instruments to avoid price risks. Apart from that, we also have to improve our commodities reserve system so as to improve the management of supply and demand.

9.1.2 The Price Reform Is in the Deep-Water Zone and Its Impacts Are Uncertain

In recent years, the price reform focused on service products such as resources, energies and medical services and industries such as transportation. The philosophy of the reform is to lift the price control in competitive sectors and links. The purpose is to balance the price relationships, lower down the business costs of real economy, and promote the transformation of the economic system. From the perspective of price reform of resources and energies, the key measures taken by the government include continuing the promotion of multistep electricity and water prices, improving the reform of the price forming mechanism for residential use of natural gas, implementing the reform of electricity and coal prices, carrying on the reform of electricity transmission and distribution prices and promoting the implementation of the green and environment protection strategy by reforming the taxation and fee charges of resources.

But the reform is pushing forward slowly and has shown signs of regression. In particular, the price reform of the monopoly industries is moving forward slowly and achieves less than market expectation. For example, the electricity pricing mechanism at the moment gets back to on-grid price bidding again which was written in the No. 5 document (2002) of the State Council. The reform to make the energy prices to be based on market, especially the reform of power system, has lagged behind, which will fail the new plans such as direct power-purchase for large end-users and the goal of reducing energy-use costs for enterprises. Furthermore, the implementation rules of the price reform measures in sectors such as electricity, water, medical service, and education need to be improved. At present, there are still problems such as cross subsidy, improper setting-up of the multistep prices, and infeasibility of reform measures.

9.1.3 Market Environment Needs to Be Improved for Fair Competition

After several years of reform, a market-based price forming mechanism has been basically established. The proportion of government pricing and government control with guiding prices has been limited. But there are still many acute problems in building a fair and competitive market environment that need to be solved.

First, the market-oriented reform of monopoly industries has lagged behind. For industries like power, oil and gas, we are still exploring new ways to reform their price forming mechanisms. There are still issues not well resolved, such as how to let the monopoly industries to be more open to the market in terms of pricing, when to allow private businesses to be gradually involved in, and how to extend the pilot experiences of natural gas price reform to other parts of China.

Second, the delayed price reform of factors restricts the transformation of economic growth pattern and impedes the development of private business. Some researches describe the grave consequences of such delay as "new double-track system"—seeking from bottom up the huge rents between the price system of goods and services which are priced by the market, on the one hand, and the price system of factors such as funds, land and labor force which are far from being priced by the market, on the other hand. The current price forming mechanism of factors after the reform has not achieved any breakthrough compared with that in the planned economy, which in turn suggests that the price reform in China is far from being successful.

Finally, problems such as local protectionism, regional block, industrial barriers, business monopoly, and arbitrary fee charges are the major factors affecting fair competition among various economic entities. Only by resolving those issues as soon as possible can we ensure a good environment for free competition among different economic entities. Less competitive businesses stepping out of the market and excellent ones getting more resources from competition to grow up will help bring vitality into relevant industries and even the whole economy.

9.1.4 The Long-Term Mechanism to Stabilize the Prices of Essential Goods Is not Sound

A mechanism to stabilize the prices of essential goods is key to protecting the basic life of low-income earners. In recent years, the prices of essential goods for people's livelihood such as pork and agricultural products often fluctuate drastically. Apart from that, rapid increase of service prices such as those of rental, education, and medical service is critical to the increase of the core CPI. Since 2014, the service prices of preschool education and medical service have been increasing. The price increase of rental and services leads to substantial increase of core CPI in 2016, compared with that in 2014 and 2015. People's life expense also increases fast because of that. Moreover, price violations such as raising the prices of goods reserved beforehand when the demand cannot be met and arbitrary fee charges that undermine people's interest occur from time to time, which suggests that the long-term mechanism to stabilize the prices of essential goods is still not sound.

9.2 Explorations and Innovations in Pricing Regulation

9.2.1 Clarifying the Role of Price Supervision in Price Management

The central government requires to lift the price control overall goods and services in competitive sectors and links and speed up the improvement of the modern market system and the market-based price mechanism. According to such requirement, in the process of deepening the reform and establishing a new market oversight system, how will the price management authorities leverage their management advantages and play a positive role in a better way while promoting the price reform? We believe that the key is to make clear the pivotal position of price supervision in the overall price management.

According to the organizational structure of National Development and Reform Commission, the Department of Price is mainly responsible for promoting the price reform, improving the market-based price mechanism, organizing the investigations and supervisions of the costs in the prices of agricultural products, monopoly industries, public utilities, and public welfare services. Bureau of Price Supervision and Anti-Monopoly is responsible for supervising the implementation of the price reform plan and price regulation measures, penalize the price violations such as price monopoly and unjust pricing exercises. Apart from the price reform itself, the responsibilities of the department and the bureau can be generalized as price supervision.

In terms of the tasks of the price reform, the near and mid-term goal set by the central leading team for "comprehensively deepening the reform" is to lift the price control oveall goods and services in the competitive sectors and links, improve the market-based price mechanism, establish a price supervision system and a law enforcement system, and set up a price regulation mechanism. The essential step and measure of the price reform is to lift the price control in the competitive sectors and links. The goal of the reform is to improve the market-based price mechanism, which is the micro basis of price management. The establishment of a price regulation mechanism serves the economic operation targets of the macro control, and will become part of the whole macro control system. The price supervision system turns the vision and plan of price reform into reality and details the market-based price mechanism into viable transaction system, pricing rules, laws and regulations.

The price supervision has become a regular task of price management in market economy. It is essential for the price management authorities to promote the price reform, improve the market-based price mechanism, establish the price regulation system, intensify the understanding of the concept of price supervision and its importance, and stick firm to price supervision as the key, so that they can enter into a new phase of price management, make use of their management advantages and play a positive role in deepening the comprehensive reform and establishing a new and unified market oversight system.

9.2.2 Balancing Price Supervision and Price Regulation

The *Several Opinions on Advancing the Reform of Price Mechanism* sets forth different requirements to the reform of market-based price mechanism, of the price supervision system and law enforcement system, and of the price regulation mechanism, separating clearly the micro and macro features of price. The academic circle thinks highly of such arrangement and believes that it can help us avoid misunderstandings and policy mistakes in macro-economic management, which we had in the past. On the basis, we can draw a clear line between the micro features of prices of all goods and services and the macro ones of the overall price level. The former is formed in an effective market operation and reflects the supply and demand of goods and services and the latter is linked with the goal of stabilizing the general price level in the macro economy.

The issue of overall price level in macro economy needs to be resolved by enhancing and improving the macro regulation. Apart from the regulation measures such as fiscal, monetary, and investment policies, price policies and price regulation measures are also part of the macro regulation system. The price issue in the micro area will be resolved mainly by the market mechanism, letting the market play its role on the one hand and maintaining price supervision to ensure fair competition and a healthy market on the other hand. Fair and effective price supervision is the precondition of ensuring the market-based price mechanism to fully play its role. However, in the planned economy, the special period of economic transition and the period under unusual circumstances in the past, micro intervention measures aimed at lowering down the prices such as direct price control and limits of transactions could not fix the macro economic problems such as inflation and sharp increase of assets prices.

In contrast, it led to misallocation of resources and loss of efficiency due to the distorted prices.

According to the requirements of deepening the comprehensive reform, a price supervision system established as required by the socialist market economy system can ensure the proper operation of the market mechanism, maintain the market order and keep the prices of goods and services sensitive in sending out signals. Thanks to price supervision, macro policies such as price regulation can be made and play their roles in transmission on the basis of accurate market information and smooth channels. The effective implementation of macro policies like price regulation can help realize the goal of basically stabilizing the overall price level, avoid the violent fluctuation in the market and create a tolerant environment for maintaining the normal operation of the market mechanism. Separating the micro and macro implications of price and balancing price supervision and price regulation will help us avoid mistakes in price management exercises.

9.2.3 *Clarifying the Goal of Price Supervision*

There are many new challenges in price supervision in the process of deepening the comprehensive reform.

First, the trend of integration of price supervision and market oversight is getting clearer. To let the market mechanism decide the prices, it means that prices reflect the pricing behaviors, take part in the process of transaction and market operation, are restricted by the transaction systems, pricing rules and market standards under certain market structure, and represent themselves as a result of effective market operation. It is impossible to set aside those preconditions and restrictions or ignore the price forming process in price regulation. It is also impossible to disregard the transaction process, pricing behaviors, and prices as a result of the market mechanism in market oversight. It is certain that the price regulation will be integrated with market oversight.

Second, it is urgent to reform the market oversight system. Within the current management system, the similar or correlated functions, such as establishing market standards, maintaining market order, building market systems, supervising online transactions, implementing anti-monopoly, and curbing unfair competition, which are classified as the same category, are scattered in relevant departments of different ministries and commissions. Moreover, the market oversight and price supervision of different types of products, services, and industries are under management of many other industry-managing departments and functional departments. The reform of market oversight system is estimated to be related to the price managing departments. Unified market oversight will be the vision and common choice of all the regulatory bodies.

Finally, it is the most important and challenging to do a good job in anti-monopoly and anti-unfair competition exercises in terms of price supervision. Ensuring fair price competition and opposing price monopoly are important ways to supervise the prices and enforce the relevant laws and regulations of price management. It is the best way for the functional departments of relevant ministries and commissions to compete and cooperate in encouraging competition and anti-monopoly practices.

In order to deal with the challenges, we have to consolidate the price supervision system, improve the policies and the law enforcement system of price supervision, and create more instruments to supervise prices. The key objective is to make price supervision comprehensive, accountable, and effective.

9.2.4 Ideas and Suggestions on Price Supervision

1. Make efforts in the following areas recently: enhancing the review and the publication of costs of goods and services whose prices are decided by the government; developing the market in the process of promoting the price reform in the competitive links of monopoly sectors; maintaining the market order after the price control in the competitive sectors is lifted; ensuring fair competition, enhancing anti-monopoly law enforcement; making competition-encouraging policies be the foundation and implementing the censorship of fair competition.
2. Establish a system of coordinated supervision and cooperative governance. The initiative should be taken to overcome the obstacles of the organizational structure, promote cross-department and cross-ministry coordination and cooperation and establish and improve the supervision system that allows interaction of the upper and lower level of the organization in order to promote price supervision in a comprehensive way. Experiences of the operation of the online price whistle blowing system on the price supervision platform should be reviewed so as to balance the development of the platform in different regions. It is necessary to improve the management system

of the platform, optimize its operational rules, better its functions, enhance its analysis of big data and strengthen its capabilities in dealing with emergencies.

3. Conduct detailed and systematic researches in areas of the market system of all goods and services, the price forming mechanism, the transaction system and the pricing rules, so as to evaluate the current achievements of the supervision and make clear the next steps and the efforts that will be made in the future.
4. Follow up the price forming process and the price operation in new industries, business forms and models, so as to clarify the supervision rules and highlight the key items of work in supervision right now and find out the future direction.
5. Leverage the talents in and out of the government to play a role as a think tank. The intermediary organizations and social force such as the universities, research institutions, and price associations should be invited to join the building of research bases and the education of high-end talents. New ways of improving the researches of price theory and policies should be explored so as to turn a new page in price regulation.

9.3 Deepening Pricing System Reform in Resource and Energy Sectors to Promote Green Development

9.3.1 *Suggestions on Deepening the Reform of Oil and Natural Gas Industry Systems*

In May 2017, the central committee of the CPC and the State Council issued *Several Opinions on Deepening the Reform of the System of Petroleum and Natural Gas* and made clear the guidelines, basic rules, general principle, and major tasks in deepening the reform of the system of petroleum and natural gas. The main idea is to stick to the problem-solving principle and market mechanism on the basis of ensuring China's energy security and safe production and promoting energy reservation and environment protection, so as to reflect the commodity attribute of energies.

In terms of key areas of the oil price reform, first, from the perspective of short term, the domestic retail market of refined oil should be opened up as soon as possible by introducing competition and encouraging producing enterprises to reduce costs. At present, in China, the whole industry of oil exploitation, processing, and selling is monopolized by three major oil groups. The three groups have clear geographic boundaries in business operation, which leads to high level of monopoly. To relax control of market access to the refined oil retailing industry and encourage capable enterprises to join the production, processing, and selling of oil can help create effective competition, improve business operation, reduce costs, and generate proper prices.

Second, monopoly of oil refining should be broken gradually. Domestic enterprises are encouraged to adopt the international cost-accounting standards for refined oil and set up proper upper and lower limits for price adjustment. Competition in the retail sector is helpful in improving the business efficiency and reducing the cost. Introducing refined oil product enterprises of various ownerships will not only improve our competitiveness in the world, but also introduce advanced experiences of management. The rate of return of domestic oil enterprises should be determined by incentive regulation, transformed from the fair rate of return regulation gradually. The incentive regulation practices include price cap, yardstick competition between regions, and franchise bidding. Enterprises stimulated by profit or competition will then rationalize the profit standards.

Third, great importance should be attached to the positive role of energy finance in price discovery. The development of the oil financial system reflects that the financial instruments currently have the function of price discovery, which is helpful to bring our refined oil pricing mechanism in line with international practices. In recent years, the pricing of oil, as a financial product rather than a commodity, has been increasingly financialized. Oil transaction has become a financial instrument. Its futures market is expanding in scale and imposes greater influence on oil compared to the spot market. Pricing has become the key to the financialization of the oil market. The development of financial derivatives such as futures has become the major way in determining the price of oil in modern world. As a core mechanism and important tool of oil pricing in the international market, oil financial derivatives not only provide convenience for oil enterprises to get funds, but also function in price discovering, hedging, and risk hedging.

Fourth, the government cannot compromise on the transparency and predictability of the price mechanism while regulating the prices. The relevant departments of macro-economic management mainly use economic means such as taxation to influence the prices instead of determining the prices directly at the moment. But if the policymaking is not transparent enough, for example, obviously arbitrary tax collection, it will mislead the expectation of consumers and impede the promotion of price regulation in the future.

Similar to the reform of refined oil price, the key to the reform of natural gas price is to let the supply and demand of the market decide the gate station price. On the basis of that, the gate station price of residential use will be gradually in line with that of nonresidential use. The supervision of pipeline transmission price and gas distribution price needs to be further improved afterward. Various sources of funding can be introduced into pipeline transmission, which will provide support for the building of the pipeline network and allow the pipeline companies to be independent in business operation with the hope that all users will be granted the Third-Party Access by the pipeline companies without discrimination.

Monopoly of the exploration and import of natural gas should be gradually dismantled when the natural gas industry develops to certain level. It is encouraged to introduce various sources of capital to the business of natural gas exploration and import and increase the reserves of gas sources to ensure competition in production of natural gas. Agencies such as natural gas brokerage companies should be established to negotiate with natural gas producing enterprises on behalf of users. It is important to make use of Shanghai Petroleum and Natural Gas Exchange to develop domestic spot and futures transactions of natural gas and improve the market-based price mechanism. Moreover, it is necessary to research on and launch the policy of peak-valley gas price and encourage the building of gas reserve facilities. It is also helpful to allow the seasonal price differences for nonresidential use of gas so as to encourage users to reserve gas for peak time.

9.3.2 Principles of Deepening the Price Reform of Electric Power and Suggestions of Relevant Policies

i. **Major Issues of Electric Power Price Management**

1. The reform of electric power price mechanism is not well-coordinated with the reduction of costs of energy. The reform requires the establishment of resources allocation mechanism that can effectively guide electric power production, consumption, and investment, drive the energy revolution and promote the energy

transformation for the purpose of sustainable economic development. But the reduction of costs of energy is dragged by the periodical demand of current situation of economic downturn. Although the *Work Plan on Reducing the Cost of Real Economy Enterprises* refers to the principle of reforming the electric power system to properly reduce the cost of energy of enterprises, there is huge pressure for the electric power industry to adjust its short-term interests. The government departments usually decide the prices of electric power in the name of the reform, which deviates from the best practices of the reform.

2. The development of the electric power market is still slow. There is a long way to go to let the market decide the price of electric power. Although the control over power generation and usage has been lifted and electric power transaction in the market is expanding, the government intervention is still serious. Large users transact directly with power generation enterprises with the help of local governments, so that the enterprises can get business and the users can get low price. Although the electric power transaction market begins to take shape in places such as Guangdong and Yunnan Provinces, the market rule of electric power distribution is presented as a disguised plan and the direct government control over the market is embedded in the rule (such as supply-demand ratio in the rule of Guangdong). With the expansion of the market transaction, the main players face great pressure, which leads to noncompetitive behaviors in some regions. For example, there is a case of price monopoly agreement among electric power generation enterprises in Shanxi Province and conspiracy in other regions.
3. Policies on independent transmission and distribution prices of electric power need to be further improved. The way to form the transmission and distribution prices needs to be bettered. The local governments and power users over-emphasize the reduction of cost of electric power use, which leads to conflicts of interests of all stakeholders and improper forming of the transmission and distribution prices. Besides, the process of cost supervision and review and accounting of the electric power price is not transparent and sound. The method of properly determining the electric power price needs to be improved. The transmission and distribution price system is not sound yet. Such prices are mainly set for the provincial grids at the moment and the pricing for cross-province and cross-region

grids is still under review. The situation distorts the prices within provinces and those across the provinces and regions. It is not conducive to the electric power transactions within provinces and those across provinces and regions. Furthermore, the price reform of incremental distribution needs to be improved as soon as possible, too.

4. There is no effective solution to the issue of cross subsidy yet. At present, there are multi-level cross subsidy such as businesses subsidizing residents, cities subsidizing rural areas, and high voltage class subsidizing low voltage class. Although the basic principle of replacing hidden subsidy with explicit ones is set up, the actual amount of cross subsidy makes it difficult to come up with concrete measures to fix the issue, which becomes an major obstacle to the reform.
5. The financial accounting system of power grid enterprises cannot meet the requirements of supervision of transmission and distribution prices. The independent transmission and distribution price policy requires reforming the accounting system of power grid, which means that the cost accounting should be conducted by regions, business activities, asset types, and voltage classes. But the current accounting system cannot meet the requirements of supervision and the reform. The accounting items of power grid enterprises reflect single-dimensional information and the content of each accounting item of those enterprises is quite different from that in cost supervision and review. Those enterprises have taken the initiative in making adjustments, but the government has not come up with official policies on the reform of the financial accounting system of the power grid enterprises, which affects the reform of transmission and distribution prices and the progress of market reform.

ii. **Basic Principles on Reducing Energy Cost**

During the 13th Five-Year Plan period, the key to reducing the cost of energy use is to actively promote the implementation of the reform plan of the electric power system as well as that of the oil and gas system. Following principles should be firmly held in reducing the cost.

1. The reduction of energy-use cost should not be the last resort for backward enterprises. The purpose of deepening the reform of energy system is to correct the system arrangement that causes high energy cost and bring systematic interests to the national economy. The beneficiaries of the reduction should be screened in line with other aspects of the supply-side structural reform, which means "good steel should be used on the edge of the knife". For high energy consumption enterprises with backward capacity and technologies, mismanagement, and low efficiency, the cost reduction should not be their last resort. The cost reduced should be the real driver to the transformation of the enterprises.
2. Measures should be adopted properly in reducing the cost. The nature of deepening the reform of energy system and classification of energy back to commodities is to strike a balance between government and market. Before a sound market mechanism is well-established, a thorny issue for the government is how to balance market-based price reduction and government-led price reduction. The basic principle for the government to stick to is to be brave in exploring new ways of market-based price reduction and take proper intervention measures on the basis of respect for enterprises and scientific investigation before an effective market is set up.
3. The short-and long-term effects of the cost reduction should be balanced well. In the reform of energy system, some costs can be quickly reduced while some others require a long period of efforts. If the reduction is conducted for the goal of cost reduction, it may compromise the healthy development of the energy industry or even the national economy. Issues such as coordination cost between the upper & down streams of the energy industry and stranded cost due to inefficient and unreasonable investments need to be properly resolved in a relatively long period of reform and transition.
4. Cost reduction and sustainable development should be well-balanced too. A reasonable energy pricing mechanism should be the basis of deepening the reform and reducing the cost. Costs that are not reflected in the energy price under the conventional system, such as environment pollution and carbon emission, should be included in the energy price in the process of the reform. It is necessary for the sustainable economic development of China and

in line with the cost reduction in the short term. Only by establishing a proper energy pricing mechanism can China enjoy the bonus brought by economic growth and environment protection.

iii. **Policy Recommendations**

1. Strike a balance between the reform of electric power price mechanism and energy cost reduction. In order to build a reasonable market of electric power in a scientific way, it is important to understand the relationship between mechanism reform and cost reduction, which should be a benign cycle of mutual improvement. Attentions should be paid in preventing the stakeholders from making opportunist choices which may result in missing reform opportunities and dragging the reform progress.
2. Improve market oversight in developing the electric power market. It is important to pilot the spot market of electric power timely in places where conditions permit to set up an example of market transaction that can generate electric power price in a right way. In places where conditions do not permit, it is necessary to implement the policies set for electric power transaction, standardize the behaviors of local governments and relevant marker players, and improve the rule-setting beforehand as well as supervision during the course and afterward. Besides, the anti-monopoly case in Shanxi Province should be used to emphasize the role of anti-monopoly in ensuring the development of the electric power market and to pay special attention to all types of hidden monopoly behaviors such as conspiracy.
3. Continue to improve and implement the policy of independent transmission and distribution prices. On the basis of experiences of transmission and distribution cost supervision and review as well as electric power price determination, we should find out the problems and provide solutions in order to make our policies effective and transparent and come up with improved policies on transmission and distribution prices in the next regulatory cycle. At the same time, the reform of cost supervision and review system needs to be reinforced. The work on the supervision and review of the cost of transmission and distribution across provinces and regions should be advanced as soon as possible. The price of the electric power transmitted and distributed across provinces and regions also needs to be determined quickly and brought in line with that of the electric power transmitted and distributed within provinces, so as to

promote the electric power transactions within and across provinces and regions. Besides, same efforts need to be made for incremental distribution as soon as possible.

4. Tackle the thorny issue of cross subsidy. It is necessary to research in depth on the issue, make clear the sizes of different types of cross subsidy, come up with solutions, and finalize a systematic plan to fix the issue. The market development of different places needs to be taken into account while resolving the issue. The solutions should vary from place to place and a road map of stable transition is necessary, since risks may be generated if the one-size-fits-all solution is applied to all places.
5. Promote the reform of the financial accounting system of power grid enterprises. The government departments such as NDRC, SASAC, and the Ministry of Finance should join in promoting the reform. The reformed system will provide accurate information for the accounting of transmission and distribution prices and lay a foundation for making policies for the next step of the market reform.

9.3.3 Improving the Price Mechanism and Facilitating the Strategy of Green Development

Explore the price forming mechanism for the sake of environment. External costs need to be taken into account in the price forming process. The forming mechanism of multistep electric power and water prices needs to be improved and customized pricing mechanisms based on different demands need to be established so as to encourage enterprises and residents to save energy. The reform of the heating price forming mechanism needs to be conducted according to residents' living standard. The "coal-to-electricity" and "coal-to-gas" projects in northern China need to be further implemented. The ecological compensation mechanism needs to be gradually improved and so do the carbon emission trading and ecological products trading markets.

9.4 Pricing Reform for Key Commodities and Stabilizing CPI

9.4.1 *Optimize the Pricing Mechanism for Agricultural Products*

i. **Further Improve the Price Supporting System for Agricultural Products**

1. Accelerate the transformation of direct grain subsidy policy from "being inclusive" to "being incentivizing". At present, there is no reasonable and fixed standard for direct grain subsidy in China. The subsidy budget is mainly determined by government's fiscal payment capacity instead of the actual need for subsidy. China's direct grain subsidy policy has actually become an inclusive and fixed one which is not based on grain price and output, thus gradually failing to incentivize productivity. Therefore, to reverse this phenomenon, it is necessary to adjust the distribution standards and methods so that the subsidy will meet the policy objective of increasing farmers' income, and also achieve the policy effect of enhancing food productivity and output. To this end, the direct grain subsidy should be divided into two parts, namely, fixed subsidy and grain sales subsidy. Fixed subsidy which is based on the planting areas, regardless of the output, cost and food price in the market, is directly given to farmers via their bank accounts. As for the grain sales subsidy, the government should first set up a grain sales subsidy rate (RMB/ton) based on the current economic status, per capita income, market prices and other factors, and then calculate the subsidy on the formula: grain sales subsidy = the amount of food sold per year by each farmer * the grain sales subsidy rate, and finally deliver the subsidy to farmers. The rate should not be fixed but adjusted every three years. Fixed subsidy can remain at the current level. With additional grain sales subsidy, farmers who are actually engaged in grain production can obtain more income, which will realize the objectives of the policy. However, the rapidly rising expenditure on subsidy may impose extra burden on governments. In order to limit the subsidy expenditure to an appropriate range, the to-be-delivered fixed subsidy should be 90 percent of the amount of direct subsidy in 2012. And to fix the gap, grain sales subsidy will be paid to farmers who are actually engaged in grain production. In this way, the increase in government's expenditure on subsidy will be within an appropriate

range. At the same time, the government should formulate and promote the enactment of such laws and regulations as Agricultural Subsidy Regulation of China, which will legalize and institutionalize grain subsidy system, stabilize farmers' expectations, and increase their production enthusiasm.

2. Connect the comprehensive subsidy for agricultural materials with the fluctuating price index of producer goods for agriculture as soon as possible. Since 2006, China's comprehensive subsidy for agricultural materials has been growing at a rapid pace. By 2012, it had increased by 7.925 times over 2006, with an average annual growth rate of 132 percent. However, in 2016, China's fiscal revenue increased by only 4.5 percent over the previous year, continuing the downward trend of growth. In the future, with the current growth rate of fiscal revenue, it will be very difficult to maintain a rapid growth of comprehensive subsidy for agricultural materials. Moreover, due to the lasting impact of the European and American financial crisis, the prices of commodities such as crude oil have fallen significantly, and it is unlikely that the prices of producer goods for agriculture continue to rise significantly in the future. Therefore, starting from 2017, the annual comprehensive subsidy for agricultural materials should be related to the price index of the producer goods for agriculture on the basis of the subsidy in 2016. If the price index drops, the subsidy should remain at the current level; if the price index increases, the subsidy should be increased proportionately.
3. Stabilize the prices of producer goods for agriculture at a reasonable level. This will help alleviate the pressure on the producer goods and agricultural machinery subsidies. With China's agriculture being more modernized, the cost of producer goods for agriculture accounts for an increasingly large proportion of the total planting cost. The excessively rapid rise in prices of fertilizers, pesticides, and agricultural machinery has squeezed the profit of grain production, thus failing the policy's objective of benefiting farmers. At the same time, in order to make up for the increase of farmers' production costs, the government has correspondingly increased its expenditure on comprehensive subsidy for producer goods and agricultural machinery subsidy, which imposes a heavier financial burden. To solve this problem, the following major tasks should be done. First, improve the price monitoring system for

producer goods for agriculture. Close attention should be paid to the price dynamics and supply & demand in the market of producer goods as well as changes in production & operation costs. More researches and forecasts should be done on the price trends of the producer goods. Price warnings should be more accurate and on time. Farmers should appropriately purchase the producer goods and properly arrange production and operation in accordance with the market conditions so as to gain more profits. Second, fully implement the country's preferential policies on taxation and logistics for the enterprises engaged in producing producer goods for agriculture, and encourage them to enlarge the production scale, which will help reduce the price of producer goods thus reducing the cost of grain production and ensuring farmers' enthusiasm. Third, improve the national reserve system of producer goods for agriculture. Since the prices of the producer goods are relatively lower in the off-seasons, purchasing more producer goods at such time to increase the country's reserve can help curb the sharp fluctuation of prices between the off-peak seasons. Fourth, enhance the management of operations and price behaviors in the market of producer goods, strengthen the supervision and inspection over the implementation of the price regulations conducted by agricultural machinery companies, pesticide companies, and other related enterprises, and crack down on various price frauds, shoddy, counterfeited products, bidding up prices and other violations regarding pricing with quicker and heavier punishment in accordance with the *National Development and Reform Commission's Notice on Conducting Special Inspections on Fertilizer Prices and Agriculture-related Charges Nationwide* and other provisions, in order to stabilize the supply and demand and prices of producer goods, and protect farmers' interest.

4. Continue to improve the systems of certified seed subsidy, minimum purchase price, and crop insurance. First, make good use of the combination of certified seeds with subsidy. According to the rule of the market, certified seed subsidy can promote the selling of seeds of high quality. As more farmers buy certified seeds, the grain yields will thus be increased. Second, find the equilibrium price of agricultural commodities from the futures market, and adjust it correspondingly according to the changes of domestic prices, so that the minimum purchase price policy can be further improved.

Finally, since domestic agricultural insurance industry finds it hard to be commercialized due to low awareness of people and not-well-designed products, we should accelerate the establishment of a sound policy-based agricultural insurance system and promote, with China's financial support, a model of integrated management, standardized operation, together with government subsidy and commercialized operation. We should popularize the crop insurance policy in major grain-producing areas such as Shandong and Henan provinces, especially to large grain growers and large-scale farms, raise the agricultural insurance compensation standards, and expand its coverage, so that the agricultural insurance business can grow up in scale and gradually be commercialized.

ii. **Improve the Price Warning and Regulation Mechanism for Major Agricultural Products and Reduce the Net Loss of Social Welfare**

Currently, the prices of important agricultural products (such as live pigs), eggs, and some small trade agricultural goods (such as garlic and ginger) in China see violent fluctuations. For example, the price of live pigs hit a record high of RMB21.21/kg in June 2016. Then it began to fall until it bottomed at RMB13/kg in June 2017, below the break-even point. Egg price had continued to fall for 7 months since October 2016, until it dropped at RMB2/kg in late April 2017, the lowest in 10 years.

Big fluctuations, especially the plunge of prices of live pigs and eggs mean business loss for rural livestock and fowl growers and are a blow to their confidence in production, and they mean also welfare loss for the society. When the prices of live pigs and eggs rise, the producers can gain profits as the consumer surplus moves into the pockets of producers, which means there is no net loss of social welfare. However, if the price of pigs falls sharply, farmers usually sell them ahead of time or simply slaughter sows to reduce losses. Small-scale pig growers may go bankrupt due to excessive losses, while large-scale pig growers also have to suffer huge losses. This will result in the net loss of social welfare. But due to consumption bottlenecks and the elasticity of demands, the increase in consumption caused by dropping prices is small, and the increase in consumer surplus is not considerable. Livestock and fowl growers, especially those whose breeding scale is small, will have problems in making profits and surviving when the market prices fluctuate sharply. Pork and eggs are the main sources of meat and protein for the Chinese. They are important in terms of nutrition, public health, and social welfare. Concerned government departments should carry out timely control measures to minimize the net loss of social productivity and eliminate the adverse effect of excessive price fluctuations in the cobweb model when the risk is getting bigger and the market fails to function to some extent.

Statistics show that for more than a decade, the per capita pork purchase of urban households in China has remained stable, at around 20 kg per year, while that of rural residents has been lower. And the overall demand has changed little. Egg consumption sees a similar pattern. As the population grows stably, the annual consumption of live pigs and eggs changes little. In this case, the output plays a decisive role in determining the price. At the same time, from the output fluctuations in the decline stages of previous two cycles (i.e., from 2006 to 2010 and from 2010 to 2015), we can see that the sharp increase of pork output (up by 18.3 percent and 12.1 percent year-on-year respectively) is the most important factor for the rapid decline of live pig price. From 2014 to 2016, China's pork output was 56.71 million tons, 54.87 million tons, and 52.99 million tons respectively, declining year by year, which led to a rapid rise in live pig price after hitting the bottom in March 2015.

In order to improve the price warning and regulation mechanism, there are several recommendations. First, study in depth the current output and price changes of important agricultural products such as live pigs and eggs in China and set up reasonable target output range. If the actual output is expected to exceed the upper limit, the information of the output should be timely released to guide farmers in adjusting their excessive expectations and production capacity. Preferential measures such as production subsidy, health and epidemic prevention, and agricultural insurance will be given to farmers who follow the guidance. Second, live pig futures should be launched as soon as possible, so that their functions of price discovery and risk aversion can be fully leveraged. Farmers should be helped to optimize their breeding scales. Fluctuation range of live pig price should be sized down. At the same time, the hedging of live pig futures will help scale up the breeding and processing of live pigs.

9.4.2 *Suggestions on the Policy of Medicine Price Reform*

i. **Guarantee the Stable Supply of affordable Medicines**

Affordable medicines should be available to the public, and it falls on the government to guarantee ample supply. In terms of pricing, in order to give pharmaceutical companies the incentives to produce affordable medicines and reduce the burden on patients, in May 2014, the National Development and Reform Commission issued the *List of Affordable Drugs Within NDRC's Pricing Scope*, which stipulates that pharmaceutical companies can price independently under the premise that the daily average costs of Chinese patent drugs and western medicines do not exceed RMB5 and RMB3 respectively. It is recommended that the daily average costs of affordable drugs should be linked to CPI and adjusted every three years. The adjustment should be flat with the CPI growth rate and around 5 percent. This can ensure acceptable profit for the production of affordable drugs. In terms of drug selling, certain tax concessions and subsidy should be given to drug selling companies which have reached a certain amount of sales of affordable drugs. Regarding the use of affordable drugs, the government should clearly stipulate that the proportion of affordable drugs in the sales revenue of hospitals and pharmacies should not be less than a certain percentage. Specific measures in this regard must be further studied and properly designed in the light of the progress of reforms of the management systems of the medical care, medicines, and medical insurance.

ii. **Increase the Pricing Leverage of Medical Insurance Providers, Reducing Bargaining Power Disparity between Sellers and Buyers in the Pharmaceutical Market, and Achieving Drug Price Affordability and Stability**

In the drug market, due to information asymmetry between doctors and patients and a lack of effective constraints, doctors are the ones that decide what drugs to prescribe to patients. Doctors and hospitals as sellers have an absolute monopoly position in the drug market, or at least, they can choose drugs according to the discriminating price of secondary monopoly. But patients have almost no power to bargain. To solve this problem, the medical insurance authorities should, by fulfilling their role as the representative of buyers in the medical market and their duty of controlling prices, and leveraging their rights to choose designated hospitals and examine the medical expenses, regulate the medicine types used by doctors and hospitals and require the hospitals to adopt a comprehensive payment method that considers patients' disease types, treatment programs, and in-hospital length. As long as the treatment effect is guaranteed, the hospitals should use as many affordable drugs as possible to balance the power between patients on the one side and doctors and hospitals on the other. At the same time, direct participation of the medical insurance authorities in the negotiation of drug prices is recommended based on other countries' experiences, so that prices can be more stable, and unreasonable increases in medical costs can be better controlled.

iii. **E-Medicine: Cutting out the Middleman, Reducing Costs, and Improving Distribution Efficiency**

In China, drug sales have to go through many links and levels. The agents include general drug agents, regional agents, and municipal agents, below which there are many intermediate agents, such as the first-level, second-level, and third-level agents. Such a model makes the intermediate costs of drugs high, thus raising the final retail prices. At present, pharmacies in China can only sell over-the-counter (OTC) medicines. When purchasing OTC medicines, patients usually have a basic knowledge of the types, dosages, and manufacturer of medicines they need. When people purchase related medicines through the Internet, they can bypass many intermediary links. As a result, the costs of distribution decreases, and so do the prices. At the same time, the drug regulatory authorities should thoroughly inspect the qualifications of online pharmacies and encourage online distribution of drugs from cheap pharmacies.

9.4.3 Providing Institutional Guarantee for Price Stability and Assistance for Low-Income Residents

When the overall price level fluctuates frequently, relevant state departments will pay special attention to the protection of low-income groups. For example, in 2016, the National Development and Reform Commission, the Ministry of Civil Affairs, the Ministry of Finance, the Ministry of Human Resources and Social Security, and the National Bureau of

Statistics jointly issued the Notice on Further Improving the Interactive Mechanism of Linking Social Assistance and Guarantee Standards with Price Increases. It indicates that when monthly CPI rises by 3.5 percent year-on-year, or when the food price in the CPI rises by 6 percent year-on-year, the local governments should activate the interactive mechanism, and grant temporary subsidy to appropriate recipients. The notice suggests that we should proactively adapt to, grasp and lead the "new normal" in our economic development, effectively respond to the new features and changes of prices, and fully leverage the role of the interactive mechanism to ensure that the low-income earners' basic living standards will not be harmed by the rise of prices. In the future, corresponding rules should be promulgated as soon as possible, and specific measures should be formulated according to different local conditions. Plans to ensure low-income earners' basic living standards should be formulated through coordination of various policies concerning prices, finance, taxation, currency, and others. At the same time, a long-term mechanism for linking standards of social assistance and security with price increases should be established to protect the interest of low-income groups from being infringed.

CHAPTER 10

Consumption: Mainstay of the Economy and Key Driver of Growth

Shaohua Yi and Guiyang Xu

Consumption is a significant source to meet the demand of people for better life. The main task is to adapt to the transformation of our society's principal tension, expand consumption, and improve consumption quality. Consumption, investment, and net export are called the three engines driving the economic growth. Nevertheless, the functions of each engine are changing subtly. Consumption is surpassing investment in the contribution to economic growth. Therefore, it is becoming the most important force in driving the economic growth, and is playing the role of stabilizer and ballast of China's economic growth.

S. Yi (✉) · G. Xu
National Academy of Economic Strategy, Chinese Academy of Social Sciences, Beijing, China

D. He et al. (eds.), *Chinese Finance Policy for a New Era*,
https://doi.org/10.1007/978-981-33-4054-1_10

10.1 Changing Role of Consumption in Economic Growth

10.1.1 The Development of China's Consumer Market Since the 18th National Congress of the Communist Party of China

i. A Basic Review of the Consumer Market

Since the outbreak of the financial crisis in 2008, the export demand has slowed down dramatically. Against this background, China's consumer market showed a basic trend of continued increase in total consumption and gradual slowdown in consumption growth. In terms of total consumption, from 2012 to 2016, the total retail sales of consumer goods steadily increased from RMB 21.4433 trillion to RMB 33.2316 trillion, with an average annual growth rate of 11.5 percent, showing that the total sales were continuously growing. From the perspective of annual growth rate, the year-on-year growth rates of 13.2 percent, 12.0 percent, 10.7 percent, and 10.4 percent, respectively, presented a gradual growth slowdown. However, the trend of slowdown was weakening and the growth rate was tending to be stable.

In terms of geographic location of business, the retail sales of consumer goods in urban areas increased from RMB 18.2414 trillion in 2012 to RMB 28.5814 trillion in 2016, accounting for a slightly reduced proportion in the total retail sales of consumer goods, from 86.7 percent to 86.0 percent. The year-on-year growth rates were 12.9 percent, 11.8 percent, 10.5 percent, and 10.4 percent, respectively. The retail sales of consumer goods in rural areas rose from RMB 2.7893 trillion in 2012 to RMB 4.6503 trillion in 2016, accounting for an increasing proportion in the total retail sales of consumer goods, from 13.2 percent to 14.0 percent. The year-on-year growth rates were 14.6 percent, 12.9 percent, 11.8 percent, and 10.9 percent, respectively.

From the perspective of consumption type, the retail sales of commodities grew from RMB 18.6859 trillion in 2012 to RMB 29.6518 trillion in 2016. The percentage of the retail sales of commodities in the total retail sales of consumer goods increased from 88.8 percent to 89.2 percent. Its year-on-year growth rates were 13.6 percent, 12.2 percent, 10.6 percent, and 10.4 percent, respectively. The catering revenue increased from RMB 2.3448 trillion to 3.5799 trillion Yuan, accounting for a decreased proportion in the total retail sales of consumer goods from 11.1

percent to 10.7 percent. Its year-on-year growth rates were 9 percent, 9.7 percent, 11.7 percent, and 10.8 percent, respectively.

From January to October 2017, the retail sales of consumer goods totaled 29.7419 trillion Yuan across the country, with a nominal year-on-year growth rate of 10.3 percent, flat with the growth rate of the same period of the previous year. The retail sales of consumer goods in urban areas were RMB 25.5129 trillion, with a year-on-year growth rate of 10.0 percent, 0.3 percentage points lower than the average growth rate nationwide. The retail sales of consumer goods in rural areas were RMB 4.2290 trillion, up 12.0 percent, 2.0 percentage points higher than the growth rate in urban areas. The gap between the growth rates in urban areas and rural areas widened again after continued narrowing down till 2016. Furthermore, the proportion of rural consumption in the total retail sales of consumer goods constantly increased to 14.2 percent, indicating that rural residents' disposable income continuously grew and their consumption potential was further tapped.

ii. **Analysis of the Current Consumer Market**

Since the 18th CPC National Congress, the total retail sales of consumer goods in China have grown steadily, showing that domestic demand is still playing a vital role in driving the economic growth. Although the growth rate shows a trend of gradual slowdown, it has tended to be stable. It is believed that along with the sustained recovery of real economy and steady increase of residents' disposable income, the retail sales will continue to grow steadily in the future. From the perspective of geographic location of business, the retail sales of consumer goods in both urban and rural areas grew continuously. But there were slight differences. The growth rate of retail sales in urban areas was always slightly lower than that in rural areas. The gap between them was the largest in 2013, at 1.7 percentage points, before it gradually narrowed down to 0.5 percentage points in 2016. It started to widen again from 2017. From January to October 2017, this gap reached 2 percentage points. Therefore, it can be seen that in the context of retail sales growth in both urban and rural areas, the consumption in rural areas shows a stronger growth and a greater potential, mainly due to the consistent advancement of urbanization and the increase of farmers' disposable income. To promote consumption in rural areas, we should adopt measures to improve consumption environment, increase consumption channels, and provide convenience for consumption. To promote consumption in urban areas, we should take actions like expanding effective supply and improving product quality. In terms of consumption type, both commodity and catering sales have increased. The former accounted for a slightly increasing proportion in the total retail sales. The latter presented a steady rise, but the proportion in the total retail sales decreased a little. The main reason behind this phenomenon was the gradually improved management of government official activities, which resulted in limited growth of high-end catering revenue.

10.1.2 Consumption Plays an Increasingly Significant Role in Promoting Economic Growth

i. The Mechanism of Consumption's Impact on Economic Growth

The role of consumption in promoting economic growth is mainly reflected in the following two aspects.

First, the consumer demand directly stimulates the formation of autonomous growth mechanism of economy, fundamentally driving the economy to grow. At the present stage, comparative excessiveness is a normal state in China's economy operation, consumer demand is becoming accordingly the most important constraint factor for economic growth. If the consumer demand is large, the constraint of market capacity for economic growth will be weak. It is more likely for actual supply to be close to potential supply. On the contrary, the smaller the consumer demand is, the stronger the market capacity constraint for economic growth will be, and the more likely the actual supply will be less than potential supply. When actual supply is approaching potential supply, the economy will grow autonomously in a circle where investment is driven by consumption, which is increased due to profit growth. In such a circle, the economy will grow steadily and autonomously along with the optimization and upgrading of consumption structure. Therefore, given the role of demand in economy, it is no doubt that consumer demand is becoming the fundamental driving force for autonomous growth of economy, and insufficient consumer demand will directly influence the formation of autonomous growth mechanism of economy.

Second, consumption growth will drive investment growth. First of all, the premise for a producer to maximize its profits is that its products can be accepted by the market. If consumers come to buy the products, the products can be sold at satisfactory prices. As long as there is consumer demand in the commodity market, even if there is potential consumption, enterprises will invest and produce, since they know they can make a profit. It suggests that consumption obviously plays a guiding role in production and investment. Moreover, the increase of supply for both consumption and production must be achieved by the increase of investment. Since investment can accelerate the economic development, and market prosperity means a general balance of supply and demand and a coordinated production of producer goods and consumer goods, consumption can ensure a relatively fast development of economy through boosting investment. Such development will be long-lasting rather than temporary. Basically, investment serves consumption. Without consumption growth, investment circle cannot continue forever. Investment in infrastructure and basic industries can bring some benefits, but from the perspective of social reproduction, it is consumer demand that can drive real long-lasting economic growth.

ii. Measurement of the Contribution of Consumption to Economic Growth

The fact that consumption drives and contributes to the economy is obvious, but there should be a proper measurement. At present, there are three basic methods to calculate GDP in China, including production method, income method, and expenditure method. Among them, expenditure method is an approach reflecting the final output of production activities in a certain period from the perspective of final usage of products by residents. It can be seen that according to the final usage of products (including goods and services), GDP is composed of three parts: final consumption expenditure, gross capital formation, and net export of goods and services. As shown in Formula (1), Y stands for GDP, C is consumption, I is investment, G is government purchase, X is export, M is import, and (X − M) is net export.

It suggests that the aggregate size and development level of economy of a country can be represented by three major demands—final consumption expenditure, gross capital formation, and net export of goods and services. At present, when we measure the facilitation made by consumption for economic growth, we usually measure the contribution of the three major demands respectively. Such measurement plays a very significant role when we establish policies of consumption, investment, import and export, and coordinated macro-economic development. The specific measurement is as below.

The contribution of consumption to economic growth in every year since the 18th CPC National Congress can be calculated by using the above-mentioned measurement. On the whole, such contribution has been at a high level, reflecting that consumption is still playing a significant role of stabilizer and ballast of economic growth. The contribution of consumption to economic growth was 54.9 percent in 2012, and then slightly fell down to 47.0 percent and 48.8 percent respectively in the following two years. From 2015, the contribution has been at a high level. From January to September 2017, it was 64.5 percent. It can be predicted that in the next few years, consumption will continue to facilitate the economic growth stably and significantly.

10.2 Main Features of China's Consumer Market

10.2.1 The Gap of Consumption Growth Rate Between Urban and Rural Areas Widens Again, and the Potential of Rural Consumption Is Huge

When we look at urban and rural consumption growth, the total retail sales of consumer goods in urban areas were RMB 28.5814 trillion in 2016, with a year-on-year growth rate of 10.4 percent, while the total retail sales of consumer goods in rural areas were 4.6503 trillion Yuan, with a year-on-year growth rate of 10.9 percent. The total retail sales of consumer goods in urban areas were RMB 2.95366 trillion as of October 2017, with a year-on-year growth rate of 9.8 percent. The total retail sales of consumer goods in rural area were RMB 470.43 billion, with a year-on-year growth rate of 11.3 percent. The growth rate of total retail sales of consumer goods in rural areas had been higher than that in urban areas for 4 successive years, and the gap between them was more than 1 percentage point. In the second half of 2016, this gap continued narrowing to 0.3 percentage points. In 2017, the gap widened again and reached 2.3 percentage points in May. As of October 2017, the gap was 1.5 percentage points.

The fact that rural consumption growth rate outpaces the urban consumption growth rate has become a normal, which indicates a relatively huge potential for rural consumption market. In the future, we should further improve the circulation infrastructure in rural areas, encourage large distribution companies to advance "channel sinking", strengthen the layout in the third and fourth tier cities and subcounty areas, improve rural consumption environment, and provide convenience and security to rural residents, so as to promote fast and sustained growth of rural consumption.

10.2.2 The Scale of Online Retail Market Continues to Expand, and the Online and Offline Markets Integrate to Develop

The online retail market continues to expand, and its proportion in total retail sales of consumer goods continues to rise. In 2016, the online retail sales were RMB 5.1556 trillion, up 26.2 percent compared with the previous year. The growth rate of online retail sales was 7.1 percentage points lower than in 2015. The online retail sales of physical goods were RMB 4.1944 trillion, up 25.6 percent. The growth rate of the online retail sales of physical goods was 6 percentage points lower than the previous year. The proportion of online retail sales of physical goods in total retails sales of consumer goods continued to rise to 12.6 percent, up 1.8 percentage points compared with the previous year. The online retail sales of food, clothes, and other supplies increased by 28.5 percent, 18.1 percent, and 28.8 percent, respectively, indicating an obvious growth trend in the sales of goods for daily life. The online retail sales of nonphysical goods reached RMB 961.2 billion, with an increase of 51.4 percent, which was much higher than that of physical goods and indicated a huge potential. The growth rate was 9 percentage points higher than that of the previous year. From January to June 2017, China's online retail sales were RMB 3.1073 trillion, with a year-on-year growth rate of 33.4 percent. This growth rate was 5.2 percentage points higher compared with the same period of the previous year. Among that, the online retail sales of physical goods were RMB 2.3747 trillion, up 28.6 percent, which meant the growth rate was 2.0 percentage points higher than that of the same period of the previous year. It indicated a trend of growth acceleration again after January 2016, when the growth rate dropped to 25 percent. Its proportion in total retail sales of consumer goods was 13.8 percent, which was 2.2 percentage points higher than that of the same period of the previous year. The rapid growth of online retail market is mainly based on the further progress in the application of mobile payment, artificial intelligence, big data, Internet of things, VR, and other technologies, which has generated new consumption modes, such as social economy and sharing economy.

The consumption has transformed from pure offline consumption to online–offline integrated consumption, and omni-channel retailing has become a trend. With the development of e-commerce, traditional trading companies have actively launched online marketing and distribution, emerging e-business companies have continued to expand offline business. The online–offline integration has greatly promoted consumption. Along with the penetration of the internet into residents' lives, the e-commerce platforms have accelerated their paces to expand offline business. They open offline real stores and actively establish a partnership with giant physical retail companies. For example, Alibaba strategically invested in Suning in 2015, invested in Sanjiang Shopping in 2016, acquired 74 percent stocks of Intime Retail, started a strategic partnership of "New Retail" with Bailian Group, became a shareholder of Lianhua Supermarket and fully deployed offline real stores in 2017. JD Group purchased shares of Yonghui Supermarket in 2015, and then announced to launch one million JD convenience stores across the whole country to fully develop its offline market. While online enterprises actively expand their offline channels, traditional brick-and-mortar retail enterprises also gradually expand their online business. Walmart and JD Group reached a strategic cooperation agreement, under which Walmart's supermarkets, Sam's club stores, and cross-border e-commerce platforms all joined JD.com. Wumart launched Dmall App to guarantee "same quality same price" online and offline, as well as quick delivery within 2 hours, so as to combine offline physical experience with online convenience to realize new integration. The transformation of e-commerce platforms and physical retail enterprises shows that omni-channel retail is becoming a new model for retail enterprises, and the in-depth integration of online and offline business is becoming a general trend.

10.2.3 Consumption of Services Increases Significantly, and Goes Hand in Hand with Consumption of Goods

With the increase of consumer demand for services and experiences, high-quality and upgraded products have become hotspots. Consumption has shifted from being focused on goods to attaching equal importance to goods and services. At present, Chinese residents' consumption has entered the development stage from the subsistence stage, with the focus shifting from material consumption to spirit consumption. The demand for services has been increasing rapidly, with the proportion higher and higher. Taking Beijing as an example. In 2016, Beijing's services consumption accounted for 45 percent, and the year-on-year growth rate was 3.5 percentage points higher than that of physical goods consumption. Services and experiences consumption is reflected in many aspects such as tourism and catering industry. According to relevant data from the National Tourism Administration, the number of domestic tourist trips reached 4.44 billion in 2016, with a year-on-year increase of 11 percent. The total revenue of domestic tourism was 3.9 trillion Yuan, increasing by 14 percent compared with the previous year, which was much higher than the growth rate of total retail sales of consumer goods, and had become a "new driving force" for economic growth. In 2017, the tourism served a total of 134 million tourists during the Labor Day holiday, which meant a year-on-year increase of 14.4 percent. The total tourism revenue was RMB 79.1 billion, with an increase of 16.2 percent. During the National Day holiday, the domestic tourists reached 705 million, with the domestic tourism revenue of RMB 583.6 billion. Based on the calculation in comparable terms of the same 7 days in 2016, the number of domestic tourists and the domestic tourism revenue increased by 11.9 percent and 13.9 percent, respectively, which hit a new high. In terms of catering consumption, in the first half of 2017, the nationwide catering revenue was RMB 1.85 trillion, increasing by 11.2 percent year-on-year. The films' box-office revenue across the country increased by 10.5 percent year-on-year. In addition, the consumption of services such as housekeeping, health and old-age care developed rapidly, which suggested this type of consumption might grow faster than the others.

10.2.4 *Quality Consumption, Green Consumption, and Health Consumption Are Becoming Hot Spots*

The continuous upgrading of consumption structure leads to a shift of consumer demand from satisfying daily needs to pursuing high quality. The demand for individualized and intelligent products keeps growing. Quality consumption, green consumption, and health consumption are getting hot.

The tendency toward quality consumption is obvious. During Singles Day (11th November) in 2017, the total online sales revenue reached 253.97 billion Yuan, with 1.38 billion parcels generated. If we look at the sales revenue by product category, large appliances accounted for 15.2 percent, mobile phones 8.7 percent, personal care products 5.6 percent, mom and baby products 3.6 percent, household appliances 2.8 percent, and cosmetics 2.5 percent. The unit purchase price on that day was typically higher than ordinary days. Sports brands like Adidas and Nike ranked high. Among 3C products, sales volume of iPhones and Huawei phones was on the top, and sales volume of drones, smart toilets, and other high-end products was also remarkable. According to the data of 5000 major retailers specially monitored by the Ministry of Commerce, the sales volume of ultra-high-definition 4K televisions increased by 37 percent and 4G mobiles increased by 18.5 percent in 2016 compared with 2015. The replacement of old family sedans with new ones was significantly faster in 2016, and the sales volume of cars exceeded 28 million, with a year-on-year increase of 13.7 percent. Among them, the sales volume of pure electric cars increased by 65 percent and that of second-hand cars by nearly 20 percent with over 16 million cars sold. With the steady development of cross-border e-commerce in pilot cities, the penetration of e-commerce into rural areas, the popularity of mobile internet and continuous improvement of payment scenarios, the pattern of "Internet + lifestyle" has already penetrated into all scenarios of residents' consumption, which makes consumption more convenient, residents' consumption more frequent, people's individualized needs met and the quality of consumption improved.

Green consumption has become a hot spot in market. In the first half of 2017, the major retailers' sales volume of air-conditioners of Energy Efficiency Grade 1, refrigerators of Energy Efficiency Grade 1, and smart televisions grew 29.9, 15.4, and 20.7 percentage points faster than that of all the air-conditioners, refrigerators, and televisions, respectively. The automobile market continued to be hot. Both the production and sales volumes of cars hit record high, among which the sales volume of new energy cars grew by over 50 percent, ranking No. 1 in the world for 2 consecutive years. Sharing economy represented by sharing bicycles boomed. In 2016, the market transaction of sharing economy in China reached 3.4520 trillion Yuan, up 103 percent compared with 2015. In the next few years, sharing economy will still keep a high growth rate at an average annual rate of around 40 percent. The proportion of sharing economy transaction volume in GDP will be more than 10 percent by 2020 and around 20 percent by 2025.

The consumption of leisure and tourism develops rapidly. The tourism industry continues to integrate and evolve. Traditional tourism continues to reform itself and new types of tourism keep emerging and evolving. New tourism products, services, and models emerge one after another. There are groups of tourism programs which are diversified, serialized, and adapt to different levels of demands. Variously new types of tourism come to the frontier and a few of them are gradually known by the people. They provide high-end tourism products as well as middle-end and popular products to meet the demands of different levels, which is expected to be an important area for the promotion of tourism consumption. There are new forms of tourism born from the process of industry integration, such as industry tourism, countryside tourism, cultural tourism, tourism equipment manufacturing, tourism real estate, and so on. There are others based on new tourism resources, such as industrial heritage tourism, cruise tourism, Red Tourism, medical tourism, awarding and meeting tourism, adventure tourism, and so on. There are some derived from tourism reform, like road trip, RV trip, cruise and yacht tourism, senior citizen tourism, and so on. Another new way of tourism is quite comprehensive due to strong capital. Others include tour clubs based on new life philosophy and style and tourism e-commerce based on mobile communication and the internet. All the above-mentioned forms of tourism will be key to future tourism consumption. It is estimated that the average trips per person per year in China will be 4.5 by 2020. The number of domestic tourists will exceed 6 billion and the scale of tourism consumption will reach RMB 5.5 trillion by 2020. It is expected that China will be a huge market of tourism and the tourism consumption will be a significant pillar for domestic consumption expansion.

The potential of health consumption is huge. Advocating a new concept of healthy life and developing a market of health consumption are necessary to improve people's life and their physical health. They are also important measures to further expand consumption demand and promote the sustained development of the tertiary industry. The improvement of the quality of life makes people have higher requirements for health. The environmental deterioration and the increase of pressure in life have led to widespread concern about health issues. The improvement of health awareness and renewal of thinking have further promoted the development of the general health industry. Health consumption will drive China's economic growth for a long time. At present, China's smart medical devices are limited in variety and application, thus not widely used. With the development of top-notch technologies, there will be more types of smart medical devices with more functions in the future. Consumptions of more household health equipment will be generated. The sales of health products and small devices for health care, rehabilitation, and auxiliary treatment will grow significantly in household health consumption. In particular, the smart medical devices used at home such as the smart blood pressure monitor and smart glucometer have a bright future in the market. Data shows that the consumption of such products in developed countries including European countries and the US have accounted for more than 25 percent of total consumption. Nevertheless, the consumption of medical health products per person per year in China only accounts for 0.07 percent, which suggests huge potential to be tapped.

10.2.5 Residents Are Optimistic in Consumption and Consumers' Confidence Index Hits New High

Since the 18th National Congress of the Communist Party of China, the consumer confidence index, satisfaction index, and expectation index have shown a steadily rising trend. Since the second half of 2016, the three major indexes have shown strong growth. As of October 2017, the consumer confidence index, satisfaction index, and expectation index were 123.9, 118.4, and 127.6, respectively, reaching new high in the recent five years. It suggests that due to the policies for current supply-side structural reforms and modest expansion of aggregate demand, positive factors in the consumer market are increasing, that consumers are more willing to spend since they are optimistic about the economic trend, future income and employment, and that they are more positive in consumption.

10.3 Main Issues in Consumption Growth in China

10.3.1 Effective Supply Is Still Insufficient

Since the 18th National Congress of the Communist Party of China, with the continuous improvement of people's living standard, China's construction of socialism with Chinese characteristics has entered a new era. In the report of the 19th National Congress of the Communist Party of China, General Secretary Xi Jinping came to a major political conclusion that "as socialism with Chinese characteristics has entered a new era, the principal tension facing Chinese society has evolved. What we now face is the tension between uneven and under development and the people's ever-growing needs for a better life", which is of great realistic significance.

Specifically, in the field of consumption, the tension reflects itself as the fact that the excess supply and insufficient effective supply coexist due to the structural imbalance between supply and demand. There is a big difference between supply and effective supply after China entering the new era of socialism with Chinese characteristics. Supply is more of a one-way behavior of producers, while effective supply is a two-way behavior that can continuously match consumers' growing need for a better life. In view of China's current situation, on the one hand, China's economy still maintains a medium to high speed of growth. China's comprehensive national power and people's living standard have both been greatly improved, and its economic aggregate ranks the second in the world. In the following five years after the 18th National Congress of the CPC, China's GDP increased from RMB 54 trillion to 80 trillion, contributing more than 30 percent of the world's economic growth. Foreign trade, foreign investment, and foreign exchange reserves rank among the top in the world. The total retail sales of social consumer goods have steadily increased from RMB 21.4433 trillion to RMB 33.2316 trillion, with an average annual growth rate of 11.5 percent. The increasing retail sales suggest that the contribution of consumption to economic growth has been steadily increasing. Commodities are extremely abundant, and the shortage of commodities in the planned economy no longer exists. On the other hand, at present, the issues of insufficient effective supply and backward way of supply are hidden behind the facts of excessive production capacity and insufficient demand. Nowadays, China's demand structure has been upgraded, close to the level of developed countries, but the structure and way of supply still remain the same as those of the late 1990s and early twenty-first century. Advance in technologies and equipment has been slow and so is the adjustment of industrial structure. The product structure fails to adapt to the rapidly changing demand which is upgrading, which leads to the special tension of supply restraining demand. That is because the quality and efficiency of economic development need to be improved and consumers' demand for better quality has not been satisfied yet. They are also important constraints to satisfying the people's growing needs for better life.

Currently, the lack of effective supply is mainly reflected in the following two aspects.

First, issues like slow upgrading of supply structure and insufficient innovation capacity seriously restrain people's realistic demand for consumption, and also result in the "demand spillover". In 2016, the Engel coefficient of Chinese households decreased from 30 percent to 40 percent. Under the condition of increasing income and upgrading demand for consumption, although we have a lot of low-level excess production capacity and excess supply of products in China, a lot of realistic consumption needs are still restrained seriously, because the supply structure cannot adapt to the changes of consumers' demand structure, product innovation capacity is not enough, products are not marketable, sophisticated, and famous-brand products with high added value are limited, realistic demands for products and services cannot be satisfied, or the issues of low quality and insecurity exist—for example, when the order of market economy is not sound, fake and inferior commodities, like toxic milk powder, inferior food, and fake medicine, are abundant in the market. Consumers' needs for high-quality products have not been satisfied yet. It directly results in the "demand spillover", which can be reflected by a continuous growth of consumption abroad resulted from imbalance of domestic consumption structure. In 2016, in terms of the number of tourists going abroad and the total consumption abroad, Chinese mainland was far ahead of other countries and regions. The total consumption abroad of consumers from Chinese mainland was USD

261.0 billion, increasing by 12 percent year-on-year, accounting for 20.9 percent of total consumption. The number of tourists going abroad increased by 6 percent year-on-year to 135 million. Ever since 2004, the year-on-year growth rates of total consumption abroad of Chinese tourists have been two digit. Meanwhile, in recent years, along with the change of population structure in China, the supply of education, household services, old-age care, medical care, and basic life services in rural areas has also become increasingly inadequate. In the new era, we need to generate additional supply for consumption of culture, information, old-age care, tourism and quality based on the changes of consumers' needs.

Second, the backward way of supply and asymmetry of supply and demand fail to make hidden needs transformed into effective needs. Since the reform and opening up, Chinese residents' income and savings deposit have been growing fast and their capacity of consumption and willingness to improve the living conditions have been continuing to increase. This is especially true for the newly rich. However, due to factors like business model and asymmetry of information, there are a lot of hidden needs for consumption which cannot be transformed to realistic needs for consumption because of lack of supply. For example, in the rural areas, the single business model and the high cost of acquiring the latest information on products make it difficult to attract people to consume and therefore leave a lot of consumption potential untapped.

10.3.2 The Consumption Environment Needs to Be Improved

Although currently China's consumer market is continuously expanding, the issues on consumption environment are still very serious. The cases of infringement of consumers' rights and benefits caused by various problems of consumption environment come about one after another and are malicious in nature. They should not be ignored. In such a harsh consumption environment, consumers' confidence is deeply affected, and their spending power will also shrink. This is against the macro environment of transforming the mode of economic growth and stimulating consumption. Only by straightening out consumption order with sound rules, encouraging consumption motivation with quality products and creating a responsible and trustworthy consumption environment, can we increase consumers' confidence in consumption. The tough domestic consumption environment has driven a lot of consumers abroad. Chinese people become the major force to rescue European luxury industry. Especially in Spring Festival, Chinese tourists constitute a big group for Europe tourism and are regarded as a group saving Europe by shopping. It suggests from another aspect that it is important to expand domestic demand, tap the potential of consumption, and retaining the existing spending power.

At present, the main problems of China's consumption environment are as follows. First, food safety cases occur frequently. Food safety problems in China have made consumers nervous. Consumers are crazy about foreign products including milk powder, meat, rice, edible oil, and snacks, and even prefer imported fresh milk and honey. The market share of imported drinking water in China is also increasing. Foreign manufacturers are flooding into high-end bottled water market in China. Besides, the consumption environment in rural areas, where unbranded products are frequently sold, is even harsher. Second, tourism market is in chaos. The domestic tourism market is full of problems. High ticket prices, contracting out of temples, rebates to tour guides, and poor services are not uncommon. Third, poor medical services and inferior medicines are abundant in the market. As the improvement of living conditions, consumers' demand for health care is increasing apart from basic living needs. But the health and medical care consumption market is still not well-regulated, and the consumption environment needs to be improved.

10.3.3 The Consumption Infrastructure Is Still Inadequate

The supporting facilities for emerging consumption are insufficient. In the area of automobile consumption, it is the hardware defects like insufficient supporting facilities for new energy cars and the imperfect city traffic planning and management system, rather than soft environment like car purchasing concept or willingness that make potential consumers dissatisfied. Besides, there is still big room for improvement in parking lots for traditional cars and charging spots for electric bicycles. The insufficient infrastructure for consumption also restrains further release of the spending power.

In the process of consumption upgrading, the infrastructure for goods recycling is also weak. After consumption upgrading, old household appliances, mobile phones, and many other things can be recycled and reused. However, such system has not been industrialized or standardized. The recycling facilities are insufficient. Relevant companies can carry out reverse logistics and build up necessary infrastructure to make more things recycled and reused.

There is still huge room for improvement regarding rural consumption infrastructure. First, the internet penetration in rural areas is much lower than that in urban areas. In 2016, the internet penetration rate in China reached 53.2 percent, while the internet penetration rate in rural area was only 33.1 percent, showing a big gap between rural and urban areas. The internet infrastructure coverage in rural areas is still limited. Second, the construction of rural circulation facilities falls behind seriously. Currently, there are small number of supermarkets in rural areas. The farmers markets and wholesale markets in rural areas do not have special storage spaces. The selling sites are also simple and shabby. Among the wholesale agricultural product markets, only 41.7 percent have their own cold storages, 11.1 percent are equipped with cold storage trucks, 12.9 percent have displaying freezers. As a result, about 70 percent of meat, 80 percent of aquatic products, and most of milk and soy products cannot be included in the cold chain system.

The problem of insufficient consumption infrastructure needs to be solved through efforts of the entire society. From the perspective of government investment, we should increase supply of social infrastructure, improve residents' consumption power, optimize consumption conditions in urban and rural areas, and lower down the willingness to save. At the same time, we should increase public investment in the central and west regions and rural areas, including by issuing more national debt and reinforcing transfer payment. We should focus on the rural basic medical care system, country roads, clean drinking water project for human and animals, construction of facilities of disaster prevention and mitigation and construction of infrastructure of electricity and telecommunication, so as to make up for the gap in consumption conditions in these areas, stimulate the growth of consumption power and improve consumption environment in the central and west regions and rural areas.

10.4 Policy Recommendations

10.4.1 Expand Effective Supply

i. **Let Circulation Play an Important Role in Promoting Consumption**

As a bridge between production and consumption, circulation industry stands at the forefront of the market. It is the terminal sector that is most systematic, straightforward, and sensitive in receiving market information. It can capture the consumption needs directly, and play a significant and irreplaceable role in expanding domestic demand, releasing production capacity, digesting inventory, and facilitating industrial restructuring and upgrading. Therefore, we should strive to develop the circulation industry by improving circulation efficiency, accelerating capital turnover and product circulation, leveraging the market in guiding consumption needs to transform consumers' instant and potential needs into realistic consumption and signals for production, so as to further expand effective supply. Specific measures include: (1) promoting transformation of the development pattern of the circulation industry. We should push forward wide application of modern technologies like Internet of things and mobile technology in circulation, develop the supply chain management, create integrated circulation chains, improve systematization of the circulation industry, and enhance circulation efficiency; (2) Launching a nationwide commercial network planning. We should support in land use for convenient circulation facilities related to livelihood like commercial outlets and delivery centers, carry out reasonable planning and gradually solve the tension between excessive competition of commercial facilities and insufficient supply; (3) Regulating unreasonable charges like slotting allowance, sales rebate, festival fee, and so on by retail companies. We should improve the nationwide procurement system for circulation companies, so as to lower down the procurement cost; (4) Actively support construction and upgrading of a batch of circulation facilities of public welfare nature. Although the emerging consumption areas have great potential, they always lack infrastructure and service system. Development of public and quasi-public products will greatly improve the emerging consumption, and yield twice the result with half the effort.

ii. Expand Effective Supply by System Design and Adjustment

We should reform and adjust current institutional constraints which are affecting supply for consumption, reduce institutional transaction cost of enterprises by reforming the tax system, canceling unreasonable charges and reforming the financial system, and further improve the systems that encourage innovation, including by strengthening protection of intellectual property rights and punishing producing and marketing fake and inferior products on the internet. Then, with the market orientation, we should accelerate the industrial restructuring and upgrading and create new ways of supply for consumption. In particular, we should make comprehensive use of various policies and measures of finance, tax, subsidy, and government procurement to support faster application and commercialization of new technologies and new products. We should focus on the improvement of circulation for residents' consumption upgrading and on the innovation and transformation of the service industry like services for residents, encourage the introduction of social capital in industries with new sources of consumption growth, keep an eye on increasing and optimizing supply, and expand effective supply, especially the mid-to-high-end supply. Against the background that the total supply can meet people's basic needs, we should increase the proportion of effective supply and encourage increase in the supply of mid-to-high-end products and other high-quality products. We should encourage companies to boost R&D on technologies and inspire them to develop and produce new technical products with more added values that can improve life quality, so that we can ultimately strike a general balance between effective supply and people's need for high-quality products, fully stimulate internal consumption motivation and mitigate the "consumption spillover".

iii. Push Forward Expansion of the Effective Supply through Urbanization

The process of urbanization in developed countries shows that urbanization plays an important role in expanding domestic demand. An increase of one percentage point in urbanization will drive the final consumption to increase by about 1.6 percentage points. According to the international experiences, the urbanization rate is generally stable at 70 percent.

Current urbanization rate in China is only 51.3 percent, meaning that there is still room for growth of nearly 20 percentage points. Therefore, urbanization will become the new engine of economic growth in China. In order to accelerate urbanization and give full play to urbanization's positive role in expanding domestic demand, we should: (1) Actively and steadily promote urbanization process in China, and avoid possible "urban diseases" by scientific city planning. At the same time, we should pay more attention to the joint development of large, medium and small cities, promote industry integration and synergy, expand employment for urban residents and broaden residents' sources of income; (2) by optimizing urban industrial structure and on the basis of specific conditions like resource endowment, environmental conditions and human capital, seek the best industry to lead the breakthrough, develop modern service industry such as tourism, trade and logistics, and increase employment opportunities for residents; (3) actively tap the release effect of urbanization on residents' consumption, create market conditions that are conducive to the expansion of residents' consumption, and actively encourage manufacturing and trading companies to build chain stores and direct sales stores in emerging urban areas to provide the residents with various and high-quality products and improve the life services, so the residents in emerging urban areas can be better integrated into the modern city life.

10.4.2 Enhance the Quality of Consumption

i. **Accelerate Classification of Consumption, Provide Specific Suggestions, and Promote Consumption Upgrading through Multi Channels**

China's consumption structure is now experiencing an upgrade and the new growth drivers of consumption have become multi-layered and diversified. Given the difference in growth drivers for different types of consumption, the differentiated needs of consumer groups, and regional gaps in spending power, we should formulate targeted policies to foster new growth drivers for consumption. Take the rural market as an example. In view of such problems as poor management, rampant counterfeit and shoddy products, and limited variety of products, we can set up, on a trial basis, convenience stores and vending machines in those areas where agricultural activities are concentrated. Capitalizing on supermarkets operating in nearby cities or towns, regional chain businesses or distribution networks, and by consolidating small shops or building new ones, we can extend the retail network to the rural areas, allowing each village access to convenience stores, and each residential quarter access to vending machines. Store chains made up of franchises or subsidiaries are the preferred form of distribution networks as in this way inventory replenishment and delivery is effectively guaranteed. At the same time, we should explore an efficient delivery system that has carefully designed routes and narrowed price difference with urban outlets, and expand the scope of goods for delivery to include fresh or frozen products in addition to other daily necessities and packaged foods. We may also consider integrating the delivery systems for brick-and-mortar stores and for online stores, or have the delivery network run by independent and professional third-party operators. The government can provide low-interest or interest-free loans toward store construction or renovation, and offer incentives to newly established stores based on sales growth.

ii. **Fully Leverage the Market to Enhance the Quality of Consumption**

Quality consumption should be encouraged and promoted, resource allocation should be guided by and reflect consumers' rational choices, and manufacturers who have core technologies and high added values should be supported. We should import more consumer goods of high quality and high added value, improve consumption quality for the Chinese, and eliminate gap between their spending inside and outside the country. We should relax control over market access, attract renowned manufacturing and service companies to invest and develop in China, improve the transformation and upgrading of China's consumption and supply structure, and further expand the domestic consumption. We can let market competition play its role in guiding consumption. Social force can be made a powerful complement of consumption security regulation. Limited government regulation can be supplemented by extensive social force. It is necessary to improve people's awareness of participation and give full play to urban and rural residents in finding clues and reporting problems, so that the cost of government regulation can be reduced. At the same time, we should make full use of the favorable guidance of market competition and industrial transformation and upgrading, and encourage enterprises to establish associations of self-discipline. In some regions, there are restaurants taking the lead in establishing Liangde Association which encouraging to operate with conscience and make consumers feel confidence. The member companies not only commit themselves to using qualified good raw materials, but also report those unscrupulous companies who reduce costs by unfair methods and undermine competition. The standardized operation of enterprises is consistent with consumers' long-term interest in nature, and is also a virtuous cycle formed by market competition.

iii. Improve the Quality of Consumption by Leveraging Taxation and Consumer Education

First, under the guiding mechanism of taxation leverage, R&D and consumption resources can be channeled to new areas of growth in consumption through collecting and adjusting consumption tax, environmental tax, fuel tax, carbon tax, and so on. We should establish and optimize a long-term mechanism of consumption subsidy, use public resources properly to encourage consumption of new products, support consumption of new products and services that fit the trend of technology development and consumption upgrading. Second, we should improve the quality of consumption by "consumer education". Domestic and foreign studies have shown that "customer education" plays an important role in improving healthy consumption. The authorities should pay attention to problems and provide topics in the process of regulation, encourage authoritative and scientific professional media to disseminate knowledge through various modern information channels like WeChat and Weibo, grasp the direction of public opinions in a right way, and form joint force in regulating circulation and satisfying customers' demand. It is companies' spontaneous requirement to satisfying customers' demand, and it is the purpose of regulation to protect consumers' benefit. They are consistent with each other in nature. At the same time, regarding emerging consumption modes or products, we can adopt proper and moderate promotion measures to guide consumers to form a healthy and green consumption concept.

10.4.3 Improve Consumption Environment

i. **To Optimize the Ecological Environment for Commercial Circulation Industry, and Improve Consumption Environment**

Several factors, such as lack of awareness, backward theory, and deviation of policy implementation, result in ecological environment deterioration of China's circulation industry, and thus severely restrict the formation of a big market and circulation. We need to do a good job in top-level design of big circulation, improve the circulation system with Chinese characteristics, and plan for reform and development of the circulation industry from a strategic and overall perspective. On the one hand, we need to promote establishment of law-based business environment, push forward domestic trade legislation, improve the legal and regulatory system for domestic trade circulation, and encourage breakthroughs in local circulation regulations. On the other hand, we should further eliminate unfair competition and transaction phenomena in circulation like industry access barrier, regional protectionism, and regional market segmentation, break up sectoral monopoly and local protectionism, and establish a unified, open, orderly, and competitive big market, to realize free flows of resources and products. We should further deepen the reform of domestic trade integration by combining the Internet + with cross-border e-commerce, and establish a two-way interaction system between domestic and overseas markets.

ii. **Strengthen Consumer Market Oversight and Reinforce Legislation for Consumer Protection**

We need to strengthen market oversight in new consumption areas (such as information consumption, finance consumption, and medical and health consumption), new technologies and new products, and vigorously promote consumer education and information services. Regarding the formation and development of new growth drivers of consumption, the governments and relevant consumer organizations should reinforce consumer education, publicize right information of consumption and services through public information platforms and media, and provide necessary consulting services of consumption. We should also strengthen oversight of weaknesses in product circulation. The authorities of food and drug, industry and commerce, and quality inspection should use "regulatory priorities and responsibilities sinking" as an important way to strengthen the oversight of weaknesses. Priorities sinking is conducive to improving regulatory efficiency. But under the requirement of controlling of the total amount, it is inevitable that there will be a shortage of personnel if we adopt the measure of adding levels of regulation. Therefore, it is feasible to set up supervision teams at provincial or city level to conduct random inspection. While below district and county level, we should focus on establishing and optimizing a mode of finding clues in daily supervision and solving problems by centralized remediation, organize specific or routine inspections with wide coverage from time to time, and perform joint supervision and law enforcement on important holidays and in peak seasons of issues. At the same time, local oversight authorities should be responsible for follow-up corrections.

iii. Focus on Constructing and Improving New Consumption Infrastructure

On the basis of continuous improvement of infrastructures like traffic, energy, telecommunication, water, electricity, and gas, we should make efforts in promoting construction of infrastructure in information, the internet and big data, speed up broadband network upgrading and renovation, and make an overall plan to expand the coverage and improve the connection to the broadband network in urban and rural areas. We should focus on supporting establishment and optimization of modern product circulation and logistics service system, especially promoting construction of modern commercial facilities in emerging cities and the central and west areas and actively promoting construction of major nationwide circulation network and urban logistics delivery system. We should improve the rural consumption environment and infrastructure, strengthen the infrastructure construction of signals and routes, rectify economic order of the market, regulate rural transaction behaviors, improve rural network construction, and encourage large and powerful enterprises to develop in rural areas. We should also optimize the layout of network and push forward the construction of circulation facilities for public welfare. We should further implement the *Distribution Plan of National Circulation Node Cities (2015–2020)*, and promote and optimize the layout of circulation network on the basis of strategies including the Belt and Road, the Integrated Development of Beijing, Tianjin and Hebei Province, and the Yangtze River Economic Belt. We need to reinforce governments' responsibilities and functions in domestic trade, and push forward the construction of circulation facilities for public welfare, like wholesale agricultural product markets and cold chain logistics facilities, so as to provide more public products and services and facilitate people's basic life. In terms of the construction of agricultural product circulation system in particular, we need to first strengthen the urban delivery of agricultural products, improve delivery efficiency and effectively reduce the costs of "the last kilometer". Second, we need to reinforce the cold chain logistics to guarantee the quality of agricultural products. Third, we should establish more intermediaries in the agricultural product supply chain, especially agricultural cooperatives and family farms, to protect farmers' interests. Fourth, we should study new business models like connections between farms and wholesale markets, farms and supply-and-marketing cooperatives, farms and restaurants, as well as e-commerce of agricultural products, so that we can improve the circulation efficiency of agricultural products.

10.4.4 Building a Credit System and Improving Consumption by Making Use of Financial Tools

i. **Optimizing the Personal Credit System and Boosting Consumption**

We need to optimize basic policies on consumption, encourage reasonable consumption, establish the consumer credit system, expand effective demand, strengthen protection of consumers' rights and interests, improve *Law on the Protection of Consumer Rights and Interests* as soon as possible, accelerate establishment of the social credit system, advocate integrity and oppose fraud, and strengthen crackdown on counterfeiting. We should accelerate building of an integrity system by using the internet, to improve monitoring of consumer market by the whole society and protection of consumers. We should speed up building and exploring a credit system that can promote consumption innovation. We should also promote financial innovation such as online payment, consumer finance, and pension finance, so as to provide financial support for consumption innovation and building of the consumer credit system.

ii. Building the Enterprise Credit System and a Healthy Consumption Environment

Credit of enterprises is the foundation for the healthy development of market economy. Dishonesty of corporates will directly lead to imbalance of social credit and chaos in market transactions, severely disrupt the order of market economy, and harm consumers' legitimate rights and interests. By getting corporates' credit information, consumers, as important participants in market transactions, are able to transact in the market more smoothly and effectively protect their own legitimate rights and interests, thus effectively releasing their consumption demand. Specific suggestions are as follows: (1) introduce specific laws on commercial credit to penalize corporates for dishonesty strictly and award and praise honest enterprises, making integrity a social responsibility; (2) build up a joint supervision system to fill in gaps of management in market oversight and quality accreditation process and cut off the channel of dishonest products into the market from the source; (3) establish industry integrity alliances with unified standards developed by relevant business organizations, to severely punish the companies who violate the laws and regulations and even expel the severe violators out of the industries, making integrity a self-discipline behavior of corporates; (4) establish an independent business credit evaluation system, which can, by establishing business credit standards and business integrity archive database, reduce the information asymmetry between sellers and buyers, promote transparency of information, share information and lower consumers' searching costs.

iii. Utilizing Financial Tools to Improve Consumer Market

According to the life cycle theory, a full-fledged financial capital market plays a significant role in supporting residents to realize intertemporal smooth consumption. When consumers transact in the market, they may be short of funds sometimes. It is financial institutions that can meet their need for funds. But the development of China's capital market is not good enough and there are a lot of credit constraints in financial institution credit. Therefore, China's supply of consumer credit is not enough as a whole. The obstructed direct and indirect financing channels increase the liquidity constraints of residents. As a result, they are less willing and more prudent to consume. Against the current circumstances of expanding domestic demand, it is important to expand consumption through financial innovation. We should adopt the following measures. First, establish third-party evaluation institutions who are reliable and highly recognized by the market to properly evaluate mortgaged assets, increase categories of qualified mortgage assets, and improve mortgage rules of intangible assets, bonds, and commercial lands, facilitating residents' intertemporal consumption. Second, encourage cooperation between banks and retail companies to improve electronic settlement, expand application of bank cards, and develop new financial products like consumer finance. Third, support development of rural credit products and innovation of management models, including by exploring install payment system based on the features of rural residents' income to reduce the pressure of a lump-sum credit payment; expanding the coverage of small credit to provide rural residents sufficient funds for productive consumption, reduce the constraints on their liquidity and ensure intertemporal smooth consumption.

CHAPTER 11

Creating More and Better Jobs

Binbin Zhang

Employment is the cornerstone of people's well-being. Continuing to expand employment and achieve better quality of employment is the foundation for meeting people's demand for a better life. The burgeoning of new forms of business and new technologies brings both opportunities and challenges for employment. We should remain committed to the new development philosophy, give priority to continuing to expand employment and achieve better quality of employment and seek new ideas and strategies.

11.1 Employment as the Bedrock of Survival and Living Standard

General Secretary Xi Jinping reemphasized in his report to the 19th National Congress of the Communist Party of China that we should "improve the quality of employment and raise incomes" and pointed out that we should strive to achieve fuller employment and create better quality jobs and continue to improve the income distribution system while

B. Zhang (✉)
National Academy of Economic Strategy, Chinese Academy of Social Sciences, Beijing, China

D. He et al. (eds.), *Chinese Finance Policy for a New Era*,
https://doi.org/10.1007/978-981-33-4054-1_11

following the principle of distribution according to one's work. It can be predicted that employment and participation in labor work are still the major approaches of most of people to obtaining consumer goods and improving life quality at present and in a relatively long time in the future. And it is even more so in China, which is the world's largest developing country. Therefore, the statement "employment is pivotal to people's well-being" has focused on the principal tension of "ensuring and improving people's well-being". Besides, giving high priority to employment and pursuing a proactive employment policy have been key to improving people's well-being.

In recent years, the situation of employment in China is sound. In particular, the indicators of urban job creation keep rising at a high level. The number of new urban jobs each year maintains over 12 million, going beyond annual targets of job creation over the five years after the 18th National Congress of the CPC (see Table 11.1).

The employment status stays generally stable because the central government of China keeps including employment into the policies concerning people's well-being. On the one hand, China actively promotes the adjustment of the economic structure, achieves generally stable economic growth while making further progress, and encourages waves of innovation and entrepreneurship so as to increase jobs for the whole society; in the meantime, in terms of direct employment promotion, China makes a large number of special investments to continue to improve the quality of public employment services and provide strong

Table 11.1 Urban job creation in China from 2011 to 2016 (Unit: 10,000 people, RMB100 million)

Year	*Incremental urban workers*	*Reemployed*	*College graduates*	*National funding support for employment*
2011	1,221	553	660	369
2012	1,266	552	680	454
2013	1,310	566	699	413.46
2014	1,322	551	727	417.66
2015	1,312	567	749	438.76
2016	1,314	554	765	438.76

Source *Statistical Communique on Human Resources and Social Security Development* and *Statistical Communique on National Economic and Social Development* over the years support for reemployment of the unemployed, employment of college graduates and other groups having difficulty securing employment. In addition, other social policies are continuously improved to optimize the employment environment. On the other hand, the completion of the demographic transition, especially the decline of the working-age population has caused a shortage of labor supply, creating certain objective conditions for alleviating the tension in the total volume of employment. From a comprehensive perspective, China has roughly balanced and matched the quantity of labor supply and labor demand.

11.2 Optimizing Match Between Labor Supply and Demand and Improving Quality of Employment

Employment is essentially the matching of the working time and skill structure provided by the labor supply-side and those of the labor demand side so that labor supply and labor demand have become the two most basic concepts for researches concerning employment issues. In general, an economy can reach full employment if all labor supply in the economy can meet the labor demand and all workers can get jobs that are in line with their skills and pay expectation. In reality, due to barriers such as information asymmetry, insufficient information, and search costs, the matching method of "worker-job" that can satisfy all workers and employers in economic activities is not likely to be realized. Therefore, some workers who do not get expected jobs will abandon available jobs and continue to seek or give up seeking expected jobs so there will be voluntary unemployment in real economic activities. In addition, some jobs have certain seasonal characteristics and some workers will change jobs and then be in an alternating state of employment and unemployment, making it hard for any economy to achieve ideal full employment. In reality, voluntary unemployment is generally excluded from the analysis of employment conditions, but the degree of voluntary unemployment in an economy is actually closely related to the development of the labor market and the social security system. The matching quality of labor supply and demand and the quality of employment of the whole economy also reflect the efficiency of the labor market of an economy.

11.2.1 Labor Supply

In the analysis of modern economic theory, a typical consumer not only buys goods and services from the market, but also earns remuneration through labor to ensure sustainable consumption. Therefore, the micro subject of labor supply is the consumer. According to the theory of consumer behavior, a consumer will maximize the benefits between general goods and leisure as a special "consumer product" by purchasing general goods with remuneration earned through labor and "purchasing" leisure through giving up part of the remuneration. For a micro individual with working ability, his labor supply is essentially a decision of time allocation. Apart from the time ensuring normal physiological needs, the rest of his time can be divided into two parts—one for participation in labor to earn remuneration, the other for leisure enjoyment. There are many factors that affect one's labor supply time, the most important of which is the "price" of labor—wages. For a lower-income worker, he will increase labor supply as his wage increases due to higher marginal utility of income (consumer goods in the general sense); but the continued wage increase will lead to the decrease of marginal utility of income and the increase of marginal utility of leisure. As a result, when wages reach a certain level, a typical consumer will reduce his labor supply as his wage continues to increase. It is generally believed that for individual workers, changes in wages have both income effect and substitution effect, with the former reducing labor supply and the latter increasing labor supply. The labor supply decision of consumers depends on the comparison of the two effects. When the income is at a low level, the substitution effect outweighs the income effect and after the income reaches a higher level, the income effect outweighs the substitution effect. Therefore, for micro individuals, the relationship between labor supply and wage level can be presented by a "backward-bending" curve.

By summing up the labor supply of all individuals in an economy, we can understand the status of the overall labor supply of that economy. On the whole, the labor supply of the whole society is monotonically increasing function of the social level of wages. The curve of aggregate labor supply, different from that of micro individual labor supply, does not have a backward-bending part. The reason is that in an economy, the middle-income group of people are always the majority while high-income people who will reduce their labor supply with the increase of remuneration are only the minority. As a consequence, there is no economy now in which aggregate labor supply of the society decreases as wages increase. In an economy, the total labor supply is affected by the abundance of social labor resources. The number of working-age population directly determines the amount of potential labor resources which refer to those with working ability among the working-age population. But for the convenience of statistics, the working-age population is often approximated as potential labor resource in macroeconomics (Lu Ming and Liang Wenquan 2017). A larger proportion of the working-age population in a society represents more abundant labor force in this economy and a greater possible demographic dividend. But not all people in the working-age group constitute the actual labor force of the economy since the group includes people still receiving education in schools, people voluntarily giving up jobs and people having retired early. Therefore, the actual labor force includes only those who are employed and those who are looking for work (or starting a business). In general, the percentage of the actual labor force in the potential labor force is called labor participation rate, an important indicator of the labor supply in an economy.

Since the reform and opening up, China's working-age population aged from 16 to 59 has accounted for a large proportion of the total population for a long time, making China's potential labor resources rich and creating a demographic dividend for the country's economic and social development. However, with the completion of the demographic transition, China has gradually entered an aging society, accompanied by a decline in the proportion of the working-age population in the total population. In recent years, the absolute number of China's working-age population aged from 16 to 59 has been decreasing year by year. The era of "unlimited supply of labor" has already passed. According to the annual sample surveys by the National Bureau of Statistics, from 2013 to 2016, the number of the working-age population aged from 16 to 59 was 919.54 million, 915.83 million, 910.96 million, and 907.47 million, respectively, a decrease of 2.44 million, 3.71 million, 4.87 million and 3.49 million over the previous year. The working-age population accounted for 67.6 percent, 67.0 percent, 66.3 percent, and 65.6 percent of the total population, respectively, revealing a significant year by year downward trend. China's economy had a very obvious dual economic characteristics in the past, with rural and urban sectors being long separated from each other. Since the reform and opening up, especially since the 1990s, a large number of rural workers have flowed to the cities, providing cities with large supply of labor and thus becoming an important source of unskilled labor for urban areas. However, in recent years, especially after 2011, the number of rural migrant workers stopped accelerating year by year as it did at the turn of the twenty-first century. Although the total number of rural migrant workers has continued to increase, the growth rate has declined year by year. According to *2016 Migrant Workers Monitoring Survey Report* released by the National Bureau of Statistics in April 2017, the number of rural migrant workers in China in 2016 was 281.71 million, an increase of 4.24 million and a growth rate of 1.5 percent compared with 2015. The year-on-year increase in number and the year-on-year growth rate of 2016 are both slightly higher than the year-on-year increase in number (3.52 million) and the year-on-year growth rate (1.3 percent) of 2015, but are far lower than the growth rate between 2011 and 2014. Du Yang (2014) believed that the gradual reduction of rural surplus labor was the main reason for frequent occurrences of labor shortage in recent years.

In addition, labor participation rate reflects the proportion of actual labor force in the potential working-age population in economy. In recent years, China sees a decline of labor participation rate (Cai Fang 2017) which leads to a more severe labor shortage.

In fact, the working-age population and labor participation rate are just two important aspects in evaluating the labor supply status. Labor quality is another important aspect of labor supply. Labor quality determines labor output. When the amount of labor force decreases, the average output of each laborer will experience a significant increase if the labor quality is greatly promoted. Thus, economic and social development will not be constrained by labor shortage. Labor quality is reflected in the accumulation of human capital including a worker's knowledge, skills, and health condition in production and can be roughly equated with the education level of the worker. Table 11.2 shows the education level composition of employed people based on data from China's largest census (census, 1 percent population sample survey).

It can be seen from Table 11.2 that in the recent ten years, the average education level of workers has increased with the development of education undertakings, rapidly improving the quality of labor supply. With the economic and social development, the diversity of people's consumption demand pushes forward technological advances so that workers are required to be highly qualified to meet people's demand.

Table 11.2 Education level composition of employed people of China (Unit: percent)

Year	*Secondary school*	*High school/secondary vocational school*	*Junior college/higher vocational school*	*Bachelor degree*	*Master degree or above*
2005	44.1	12.1	4.5	2.1	0.18
2010	48.8	13.9	6.0	3.7	0.39
2015	43.3	17.3	10.6	7.5	0.7

Source Data from 1 percent population sample survey by National Bureau of Statistics (2005, 2015) and data from national census by National Bureau of Statistics (2010)

11.2.2 Labor Demand

Employment results from the demand of the economy and society for labor force so the prerequisite for employment is the demand for labor force. All producers and operators who provide the society with goods and services including enterprises, corporate groups, and individual operators require labor force for better meeting the market's needs for goods and services. Labor demand is a derived demand since the demand for labor force comes from a direct need of the economy for products and labor services. The consequence is that the first and foremost way to expand employment is market prosperity or the market's increasing demand for goods and services, which requires us to promote the economy to grow stably and orderly.

In the analysis of modern labor economics, labor demand is a kind of decision-making of a firm in running its business based on profit maximization or cost minimization. Labor and capital are regarded as two basic production factors that can replace each other and are actually put into production under certain technical conditions. The firm's demand for labor is decided by changes in the relative prices of capital and labor in the short term and in production scale in the long term. On the whole, under the premise that technology remains at certain level or the labor force does not show too many differences, the higher the proportion of wages to capital cost is, the more likely the firm will reduce its demand for labor. And as the firm expands its production scale or the number of such firms in an economy rises, the labor demand will increase. This theoretical basis implies that the wage growth mechanism will have an impact on labor demand, which in turn affects the level of employment of the society.

From the perspective of the firm, wages should not rise too fast because when wages exceed the marginal output of labor, expanding the scale of recruitment will lead to reduction of profits and employment opportunities. At the same time, this theory also shows that creating a good production and operating environment for enterprises, allowing existing firms to grow bigger and stronger in a healthy way and encouraging a wave of entrepreneurship will increase employment opportunities for the whole society.

However, due to the differences of human capital among workers, the assumption of labor homogeneity by the classical paradigm of modern economics has increasingly shown its inadequacy. Firms' demand for labor is not confined to pursuit of quantity but focuses on a certain kind of monopoly of their workers in market competition, that is, a possession of the skill level and structure that cannot be replaced by other workers. In the face of economic globalization, production technologies used by economies are affected by external factors to a considerable extent. If an economy employs a production technology far behind the world level, its products will be eliminated due to a lack of competitiveness and the economy itself will in turn lose jobs in the labor market. A country's technological edge and its workers' high skill level or even strong R&D and innovation capabilities will be reflected in the competitiveness of products or services, which will increase market share and in turn make firms demand for labor force with certain skill level in the labor market. The labor market will require higher quality of workers as the production technology advances along with the social and economic development.

With the decline of the total working-age population of China and the rise of the average wage level of workers, the demand structure of the economy and society has also changed. First, there remains a great demand for highly skilled labor force with rich knowledge who are good at practice. According to China Human Resources Market Information Monitoring Center's monitoring of public employment service agencies in some cities across the country, the demand for "senior technicians" and other talent has increased significantly in recent years. The fact that talents with advanced professional skills are in great demand and receive high salaries has been frequently reported in recent years. For example, a report in October 2017 on the demand for fresh graduates of 2018 showed that Microsoft, Tencent, Huawei, Baidu, and other well-known Internet companies mostly offered the fresh graduates with master's degree an entry level annual salary between RMB300,000 and RMB500,000 for technical jobs such as algorithm engineers, R&D engineers, and software engineers and pointed out that talents in these positions were in great demand but in short supply.[1] Second, a trend of capital and technology replacing labor has gradually emerged. In order to save labor costs, firms have used robots to do part of mechanically repetitive and operational jobs or cut the demand for general labor by improving production. However, most of the current production positions that can be replaced by robots are process-oriented and highly standardized and those positions that need full human initiative still have a strong demand for unskilled labor force. Third, against the backdrop of the economic "new normal", the process of industrial restructuring has also had a far-reaching impact on labor demand. On the one hand, actions such as eliminating outdated production facilities, reducing excess production capacity, and shutting down high-emission and high-polluting enterprises have greatly reduced the demand for labor. On the other hand, the rapid development of the service industry and the action of "mass entrepreneurship and innovation" have created a large number of new labor demands. For example, related researches have shown that at a constant price of 2015, every RMB1,000,000 added value of the tertiary industry of 2016 created 9.1 jobs, 1.6 jobs more than that in the secondary industry; in 2016, 16.51 million market entities were registered, an increase of 74.6 percent over 2012, among which 5.53 million were newly registered enterprises, which created more than 10 million jobs throughout the year (Zhang Juwei 2017).

At the macro level, labor demand reflects the development of the industrial structure. On the whole, if an industrial sector accounts for a larger proportion of the national economy, has a greater labor demand and experiences faster technological development, it will require a higher level of human capital accumulation of workers. At present, as the Internet becomes quite popular in the cities, an increasing number of people are trying to find jobs that are in line with their own expectation through the Internet. Therefore, we can understand the general situation of the labor market demand at the current stage of our country's economy by tracking and observing those representative and professional recruitment websites. Figures 11.1 and 11.2 show the daily job postings

[1] Refer to Low Annual Salary of RMB250,000! Graduates of These Majors Are Being Scrambled, IFENG.com, https://news.ifeng.com/a/20171020/52725024_0.shtml, date of visit: November 27, 2017.

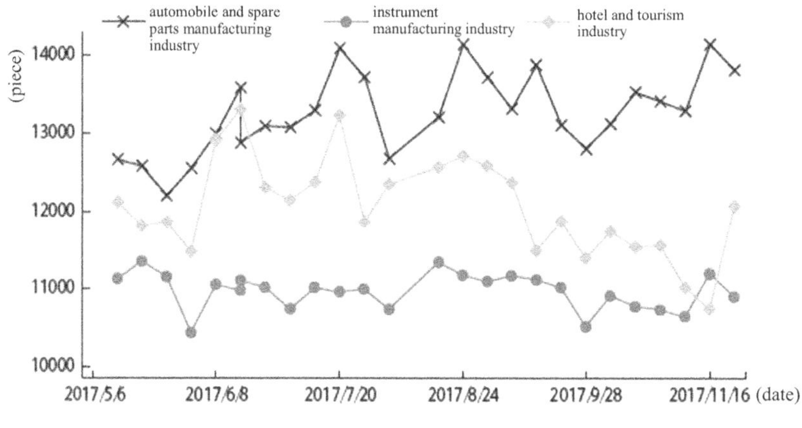

Fig. 11.1 Daily job postings of some industries (*Source* Data from 51job.com)

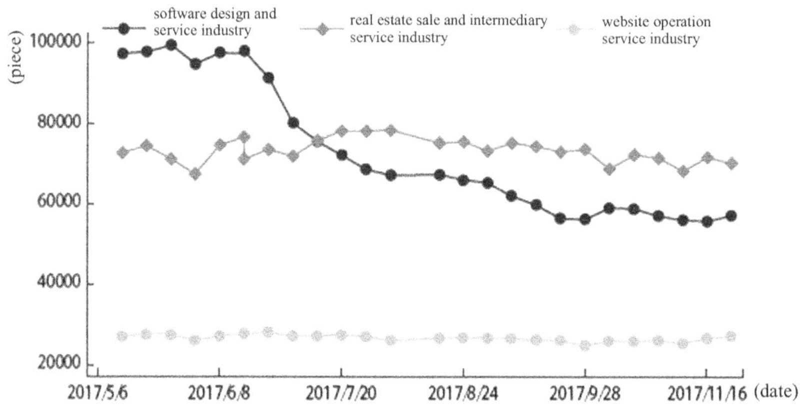

Fig. 11.2 Daily job postings of some industries (*Source* Data from 51job.com)

of some industries since May 2017 on the recruitment website 51job.com.

The number of job postings on the recruitment websites is related to the websites' efforts of market development. In the meantime, enterprises that post their recruitment information on recruitment websites will not necessarily remove it as soon as they find qualified people because those job postings have an advertising function. But keeping observing a certain recruitment website can help us understand the general characteristics of labor market demand. As can be seen from Figs. 11.1 and 11.2, on the whole, the labor demand of the surveyed industries was relatively stable in the second half of 2017 but the gap between industries was obvious. The instrument manufacturing industry, as the industry with the least demand fluctuation, published about 11,000 job postings per day and the daily fluctuation range was about 500 from May to November of 2017 and it also has the least labor demand among the six surveyed industries. However, what is not shown from the data is that the instrument manufacturing industry has relatively high requirements on applicants and offers generally high salaries but has a great salary gap among different positions. During the investigation period, the labor demand of the automobile and spare parts manufacturing industry increased slightly while experiencing fluctuation. The number of released daily job postings increased from about 12,500 in May to about 14,000 in mid-November of 2017. The labor demand of the hotel and tourism industry presents a non-standard parabolic curve, which might indicate that the labor demand of this industry has certain seasonal characteristics. The industry released over 13,000 new job postings per day during the summer peak season of tourism while 11,000–12,000 during the low season.

The website operation service industry, the software design and service industry, the real estate sale and intermediary service industry have greater labor demands than the instrument manufacturing industry, the automobile and spare parts manufacturing industry, and the hotel and tourism industry. For example, according to the website, the number of daily job postings of the software design and service industry is 6–10 times as many as that of the instrument manufacturing industry. The labor demand of the website operation service industry is relatively stable. During the investigation period, the industry published about 30,000 job postings daily and there was not a great difference between publishing days in terms of the number of postings. The real estate sales and intermediary service industry still has great labor demands, which is a reflection of continued prosperity of the Chinese property market. According to statistics, the number of job postings of the industry reached its peak in July 2017 with about 80,000 new daily postings and then slowly decreased. By mid-November, the number was about 76,000. Noticeably, in terms of the characteristics of the labor demand, the software design and service industry published up to about 100,000 job postings per day on the website from May to early June. The number started to decline dramatically from mid-June and dropped to about 60,000 by the end of September. After that, the decline slowed down, with the number remaining at 59,000–60,000. As can be seen from the industry tracking data obtained from this recruitment website, it is obvious that industries providing services and jobs requiring a lot of using of computers and the Internet have greater labor demands, reflecting a fact that the service industry has gradually become China's largest industry since 2012.

11.2.3 Labor Market Matching

Labor market matching refers to the fact that the labor supply-side and the labor demand side reach an agreement. A job seeker as the labor supply-side receives an acceptable reward for his labor and an enterprise (or employers of other forms) as the labor demand side is willing to offer this reward through search and "transaction".

The matching of job applicants and positions can be seen from two dimensions. From the perspective of labor demand, one is number matching: the number of job applicants equates to that of positions; the other is skill structure matching: workers can meet the requirements of the positions. From the perspective of labor supply, on the one hand, the supplier needs to consider whether the salary offered by the company can meet his expectation and on the other hand, he needs to evaluate whether he is qualified for the job. At the macro level, the labor market must match all the labor demand with qualified workers and match workers with different skills with suitable positions as many as possible.

11.2.3.1 Quantity Equilibrium

Figure 11.3 shows the quantity comparison between the supply-side and the demand side of the Chinese labor market in recent years. Quantity equilibrium is one of the prerequisites for realizing labor market matching. The demand ratio can roughly reflect the quantity comparison between the supply-side and the demand side. It is the ratio of job vacancies to job applicants: when the ratio is 1, the labor market achieves quantity equilibrium between supply and demand; when it exceeds 1, labor demand is greater than supply; and when it is smaller than 1, labor demand is less than supply.

As can be seen from Fig. 11.3, in the Chinese labor market, labor demand has exceeded supply since 2010 and such situation has continued

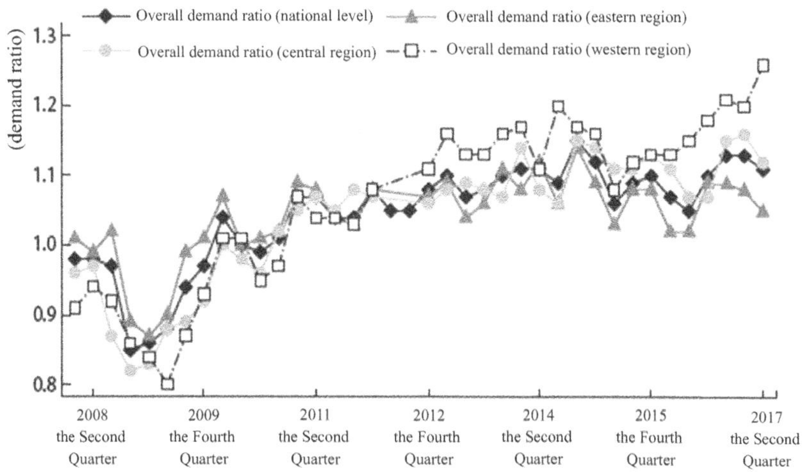

Fig. 11.3 Demand and supply of China's labor market by quarter (*Source* Data from China Human Resources Market Information Monitoring Center's monitoring data collected from about 100 Chinese public employment service agencies)

till now. The average demand ratio of sample cities fluctuated around 1.1 after 2014, indicating that across the country, every 100 job applicants could choose jobs from 110 vacant positions regardless of the matching of applicants' skill level and requirements of positions, leaving 10 positions still vacant. When we evaluate the issue with regard to regional differences (East China, Central China, West China): (1) on the one hand, the eastern region with the best economic status quo provides more jobs and higher wages so that the region attracts labor force from the central and western regions, making labor shortage not severe. On the other hand, the industrial structure upgrading of the eastern region will motivate some labor-intensive manufacturers to address the rising labor cost with more technological and capital invest in order to reduce part of the labor demand, alleviating the tension between labor supply and demand. (2) The quantity matching of jobs and applicants of the central region's labor market basically follows the national level. After 2010, labor demand started to slightly exceed supply and continued to be much greater until the first quarter of 2014. After the first quarter of 2014, the demand ratio fluctuated around 1.1. (3) The western region has suffered more severe labor shortage than the central and eastern regions, especially from the third quarter of 2012, the demand ratio of the labor market of each quarter became higher than the national average and it was 13.5 percent higher than the national average and 20 percent higher than that of the eastern region in the second quarter of 2017, reflecting a rapid increase of the labor demand relative to supply. It was because labor-intensive manufacturing industries in the eastern region have sped up removing to the central and western regions and new jobs have been created in the western region; on the other hand, a great number of labor force of the western region have flowed to the eastern region, worsening labor shortage of the western region.

11.2.3.2 Quality Improvement

Labor market matching requires not only quantity equilibrium but also a certain level of matching quality, i.e., the skills of labor supply and the skills of labor demand are roughly matched. Matching efficiency directly affects production efficiency, which in turn influences both the welfare of firms and workers and eventually the growth and development of the whole economy. Information asymmetry in the labor market leads to search costs for both job applicants and labor demanders so that the most efficient matching method is often difficult to come up. Even if the skill level of job applicants is consistent with the requirements of certain positions, there is still a coexistence of job vacancies and unemployment. It is an example of matching failure caused by search barrier. In addition, since corporate recruitment takes costs and suffers from some other unobservable constraints, even if replacing some employees with newly hired more productive workers can promote production efficiency, enterprises will not be likely to improve the quality of matching between workers and jobs by doing so in reality, which is already explained by the "insider–outsider" model of labor economics.

Under the same labor market development conditions, the matching status at the micro level is often closely related to the education level of workers. A more educated worker often has easier access to labor market information and then reduces his job search cost. Receiving more education and obtaining a diploma also have a certain signaling function, which makes employers tend to believe that workers with them have stronger ability to learn and master production skills. Thus, the agreement between these two parties is easier to reach. More importantly, in the context of technological progress, a more educated worker is more likely to adapt to new production technologies while a worker with insufficient human capital investment may overflow in the "creative destruction" of jobs. Unemployment is a matching failure between the supply-side and the demand side in the labor market. The unemployment rates of people with different education levels indicate that more human capital investment is conducive to improving the "worker-job" matching rate and then lower the unemployment rate (see Fig. 11.4).

As the Chinese labor market continues to develop and especially the obstacles to reasonable labor mobility are gradually removed, the overall matching quality of the labor market has been significantly improved. An effective indicator for observing labor matching efficiency from the macro level is labor productivity. Labor productivity increase means allocation of the labor force to more productive positions and skill improvement of workers. If the market manages to let every worker to do a job that gives full play to his or her ability, labor matching efficiency will be bound to be maximized. According to calculations based on official statistics by Cai Fang (2017), China's labor productivity (actual GDP/size of workforce) increased by 16.7 times from 1978 to 2015, of which 45 percent resulted

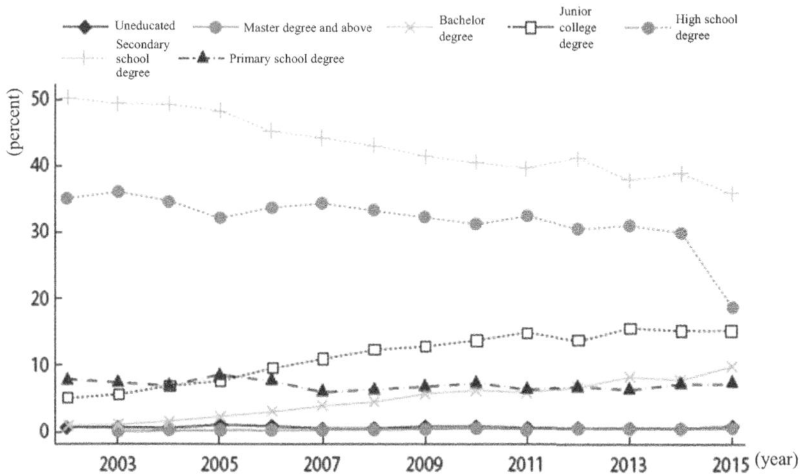

Fig. 11.4 Education of the urban-registered unemployed (*Source* Data from *China Labor Statistical Yearbook* and *China Population* and *Employment Statistics Yearbook*)

from labor relocation (i.e., labor flows to sectors with higher productivity or faster growth rate of productivity).

As a result, higher employment quality relies on human capital accumulation of workers and efficiency of human resource allocation of the labor market.

11.3 New Employment Trends

The adjustment of the industrial structure will bring about changes in the employment structure. In recent years, a typical feature of China's labor market is that the service industry has created the largest number of jobs with job creation increasing year by year. It can be seen from Fig. 11.5 that since the reform and opening up, the proportion of workers in the agricultural sector in the total employment of the society has declined rapidly, from 70.5 percent in 1978 to 52.2 percent in 1995 and has accelerated the decline since 2003 from 49.1 percent in 2003 to 27.7 percent in 2016 after a stable period from the late 1990s to the early twenty-first century. The employment portion of the agricultural sector has been less than that of the industrial sector since 2014, becoming the sector with the smallest number of jobs. The secondary industry mainly represented by the manufacturing industry, the construction industry and the mining

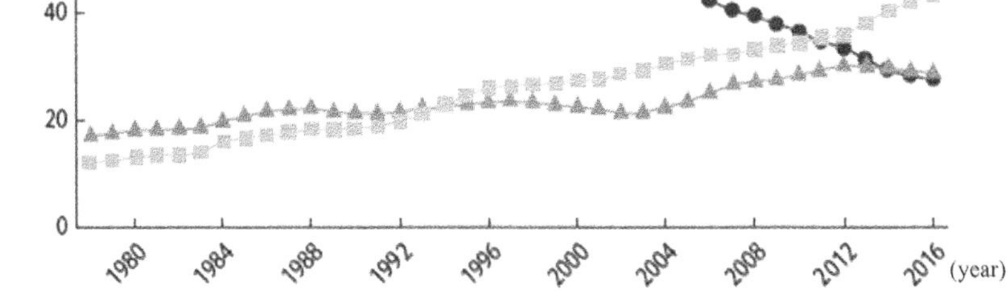

Fig. 11.5 Trends in worker composition of each industry (*Source* Data from *China Statistical Yearbook*)

industry experienced an undulating rise in terms of the proportion of the secondary industry workers in total workers after the reform and opening up, from 17.3 percent in 1978 to 28.8 percent at the end of 2016, during which the proportion saw a slight and steady decline after reaching its peak (30.3 percent) in 2012. The portion of the service sector in the total employment has increased steadily since the reform and opening up. As shown in Fig. 11.5, the portion of this sector experienced two periods of growth acceleration: one is 1992–1996, during which the number of the workers of this sector exceeded that of the industrial sector in 1994; it then exceeded that of the agricultural sector in 2011 after a steady increase, becoming an industry with the largest amount of employment. It started the second growth acceleration period from 2012. According to statistics, China is no longer a major agricultural country in terms of the industrial structure of employment. As the service industry develops, a more specialized division of labor will be formed within the industry and the technical structure will also change, which will adjust employment dynamically and raise new requirements for human capital accumulation of workers.

The emergence of "the new economy" has expanded employment. "The new economy" is a relatively vague concept which represents newer methods of production organization, distribution and consumption with "knowledge capital" playing a huge role in it. The term "the new economy" first appeared in the 2016 Chinese government work report. Premier Li Keqiang pointed out to the Chinese and foreign reporters at the Fourth Session of the 12th National People's Congress that "the new economy" had a wide coverage and connotation, involving the primary, secondary, and tertiary industries. And it referred to not only the emerging industries and business models of the tertiary industry, such as "Internet Plus", the Internet of Things, cloud computing, and e-commerce, but also intelligent manufacturing, mass customization, and so forth of the secondary industry and the family farm and the joint-stock cooperative system that were conducive to the promotion of appropriately scaled up farming of the primary industry.[2] Since the "new economy" emerged from the integration of new production methods, technologies and market thinking with the current economy, it is difficult to count the

[2] Connotation of the New Economy Explained by Li Keqiang, *21st Century Business Herald*, March 16, 2016.

contribution of the "new economy" to economic growth and employment. According to a survey by the National Bureau of Statistics, the new economy is estimated to have contributed about 70 percent to all new jobs of 2016 (Zhang Juwei 2017).

The wave of entrepreneurship brought about new job opportunities and working patterns. After the 18th National Congress of the CPC, a series of policies supporting innovation and entrepreneurship encouraged waves of entrepreneurship. For anyone with working ability, engagement in entrepreneurship is an employment and will help create new jobs. From 2012 to 2016, the number of newly registered market entities nationwide increased from 9.458 million to 16.51 million, an increase of 74.6 percent; the number of newly registered enterprises increased by 1.2 times, from 2.5 million to 5.53 million. In 2016, the average daily number of newly registered enterprises in the country reached 15,000 and newly registered enterprises altogether created more than 10 million jobs. Besides, other newly registered market entities brought far more job opportunities than the newly registered enterprises did. The ability of entrepreneurship to drive job creation is tremendous in terms of volume. In the context of "mass entrepreneurship", job opportunities brought by entrepreneurship have typical characteristics. First, entrepreneurs have a strong ability to collect market information so that they can provide goods or services that well meet the market demands. Second, entrepreneurship is becoming more and more "popular" and the society has taken a more open attitude toward the process of entrepreneurship. Among entrepreneurs, there are "veterans in the workplace" with years of working experience and graduates just leaving the campus, highly educated people and less educated ones, starters with a large capital and people starting "from scratch". At the same time, entrepreneurial directions are exceptionally diversified. Some startups focus on developing the most advanced global technology while some provide labor-intensive personalized services that facilitate people's daily lives, and many of them make use of the Internet and information communication. Third, the employment-driven positions are very flexible. With the instant communication technology, everyone can be an entrepreneur, an employer, and a labor supplier to some extent so that the general labor conditions, work leaves, and wage payment methods are not applicable to them anymore. Entrepreneurs face more risks and greater uncertainty because they are closely connected with the market and their returns rely largely on market recognition.

11.4 New Employment Challenges

In the context of Chinese economic slowdown and major economic restructuring, employment is also facing a series of new challenges that need to be addressed at present and in the future for continuing to expand employment and achieve better quality of employment.

11.4.1 Tension Between Employment Expansion and Uneven and Insufficient Economic Development

Employment, spawned by the labor market demand which derives from the demand of the goods and service markets, essentially comes from economic development. However, the economic development of China now still sees a great gap between cities and rural areas and between different regions. Job opportunities are abundant in economically developed eastern regions and major cities in the central and western regions but scarce in economically backward regions especially poor rural areas of central and western China. In addition to the difference of economic development, the gap in working environment, wages, and other interests that laborers concern most about further intensifies the imbalance in job opportunities.

11.4.2 Tension Between Institutional Obstacles of the Labor Market and Employment Expansion and Better Employment Quality Achievement

The institutional obstacles of the labor market has hindered labor allocation based on the market efficiency principle, leading to the coexistence of over-staffing and unemployment and of low efficiency with high wages and high efficiency with low wages, and to the loss of welfare and efficiency caused by some workers' early withdrawal from the labor market. Currently, the biggest institutional obstacle in the labor market is still the long-standing household registration system. Although the reform of this system is proceeding orderly, the differentiated treatment of labor from different sources becomes a big barrier to the employment of urban migrant workers and employment quality promotion through human capital investment.

11.4.3 Tension Between Job Opportunities and Employment Quality

The report to the 19th National Congress of the Communist Party of China emphasizes that when building a modernized economy, "we must put quality first and give priority to performance and we should pursue supply-side structural reform as our main task, and work hard for better quality, higher efficiency, and more robust drivers of economic growth through reform", and when speeding up reform of the system for developing an ecological civilization, we must "promote green development" and "solve prominent environmental problems". This series of reforms will require workers to improve their employability to meet the new requirements of economic structural changes. With the improvement of labor productivity and increase of working rewards, we should promote the "green development" of jobs in order to improve the overall employment quality. However, elimination of backward production methods will lead to a great loss of job opportunities, especially those jobs suiting low-skilled workers during the process of industrial restructuring, which will increase the number of people with employment difficulty.

11.4.4 Tension Between Diversified Approaches of Employment and Coverage of Social Security

On the one hand, the new employment approaches generated by the new economy have the highly flexible labor relations, which show a strong capability of "metabolism". In other words, some jobs can be replaced through new and more advanced production methods after lasting for a short period of time (such as shared bikes). And those workers who cannot adapt to this change need to find new jobs. When social security (such as unemployment insurance) fails to cover low-skilled workers who cannot immediately find new jobs, those workers will fall into poverty. On the other hand, in the context of "mass entrepreneurship", there are some "informal" workers who do not work in "formal" workplaces and are not covered by the current social security system. It is also a big problem to address issues including medical care and old-age care for these workers.

11.4.5 Tension Between a More Severe Labor Shortage and Human Capital Investment

In the context of labor shortage, the rapid wage rise, on the one hand, has increased the income of workers, which helps achieve better income distribution; on the other hand, implies an increase of opportunity cost of human capital investments including more education and training. The price signal may instigate the reappearance of a certain "useless education" theory so that workers will cut the time of education and other forms of human capital investment and enter the labor market too early. Families below the middle-income level are even more so. In addition, insufficient human capital investment will make it hard for workers to adapt to the future technological changes and industrial structure upgrading and may lead to new unemployment problems, changing the trend of continuous improvement of employment quality.

11.5 Policy Recommendations

11.5.1 Applying a New Vision of Development and Maintaining Coordinated and Steady Economic Growth

A close connection between economic growth and better quality employment lies in that the number of jobs and the average returns provided to the workers by jobs depend on a healthy and orderly economic system. Therefore, we should deepen the supply-side structural reform, focus on developing the real economy, promote the upgrading of traditional industries, and speed up developing the modern service industry to improve the overall quality of our national economy. We should make strong efforts in the coordinated regional development strategy and the rural revitalization strategy to achieve better balance in development between rural and urban areas and between regions.

11.5.2 Continuing Household Registration System Reform to Improve Urbanization

If the restriction of the household registration system on the flexibility of the labor market is not removed, goals including employment expansion, the "worker-job" matching improvement and employment quality promotion may not be well realized. For a long time, the hidden public benefits of hukou, or household registration vary greatly from region to region, making it difficult for Beijing, Shanghai, and other megacities to substantively relax restrictions on household registration in a short period of time. Therefore, buffer methods such as the points-based household registration system have been adopted. We now must speed up reform of the household registration system because restrictions of the system on the labor market, basic public services and so forth have not yet been relaxed on a large scale. The reform focuses on phasing out opportunity differences in aspects including education, medicine, employment, social security, housing and land between local and migrant residents, and urban and rural residents. We should ensure that urban migrants can gradually enjoy the same treatment in old-age care, medicine, education of children, housing and other aspects that the local urban residents have so as to make them feel a sense of occupational stability. Thus, they are willing to invest more in human capital, which can promote employment quality and labor productivity.

11.5.3 Combining Proactive and Remedial Labor Market Policies to Expand Employment and Improve Employment Quality

The proactive labor market policy focuses on encouraging and helping people with working ability to find jobs while the remedial labor market policy mainly aims to meet the most basic needs of people with employment difficulty. Industrial restructuring and especially actions promoting green production such as elimination of outdated production facilities and handling of environmental pollution will lead to a reduction in job opportunities during a certain period of time and may cause some unemployment. It is necessary to remove some workers to sectors that better accord with China's economic development direction by implementing more effective positive labor market policies. For the overflow of people who are unemployed and having difficulty in finding new jobs, on the one hand, we should provide them with various kinds of occupational training to help change their skill structure and encourage them to find jobs or engage in entrepreneurship. On the other hand, we should take advantage of the securing function of negative labor market policies to provide unemployed people with necessary security and buffer for reemployment. We should not hinder the process of economic restructuring just for keeping job opportunities, which will in turn hamper the improvement of the employment quality of the whole society.

11.5.4 Speeding Up Reform of the Social Security System Represented by Bringing the Pension Scheme Under National Unified Management

The current social security system of China is mostly operated independently with funding support from the local government and mainly serve the local residents, which will not facilitate the full and reasonable mobility of labor force and in turn will not help expand employment and improve employment quality. Urban workers still cannot transfer the share paid by employers in their pension accounts with them to other regions, which greatly hinders the cross-region mobility of ordinary workers. In the next-stage reform, we must further strengthen the achievements of bringing the basic pension scheme for urban employees under provincial unified management and speed up experimenting the central system for pension funds to be used inter-provincially in order to lay a solid foundation for bringing basic pension schemes under national unified management. At the same time, we should promote reforms in other aspects of social security systematically to ultimately realize the integrated development of national social security.

11.5.5 Creating a Talent Cultivation Mechanism and Further Strengthening Human Capital Investment

The report to the 19th National Congress of the Communist Party of China emphasizes that we should "build an educated, skilled, and innovative workforce, foster respect for model workers, promote quality workmanship, and see that taking pride in labor becomes a social norm and seeking excellence is valued as a good work ethic", to which talents and workers with greater human capital accumulation are key. We should provide reasonable returns for knowledge and technologies, form a model of respecting knowledge and talents and advocate in society that it is admirable to become a talent. We will give priority to the development of education by increasing the proportion of education investment in the gross national product and expanding the investment scale and especially increasing education investment in economically backward areas. We will also further improve the funding system for higher education and encourage the school-age population to receive more formal school education. We will continue to carry out various forms of on-the-job education and vocational training while promoting the quality of the courses, and improve the institutions or mechanisms for encouraging workers' participation in the on-the-job training and vocational skill training.

11.5.6 Promoting All-Round Employment Services

We should broaden the employment service net, encourage commercial employment service agencies to provide diversified employment services, and motivate public employment service agencies to improve their service quality so as to form an employment service market with the market-based system as the main body and government participation as the supplement. We will improve the standardized system of employment services and include employment services of broader dimensions into the system to provide workers all-round services including information consultancy concerning employment and entrepreneurship, vocational technological support, services for labor relations, and psychological counselling of employment.

References

Cai Fang (2017). Analysis of the Effect of Chinese Economic Reforms—From the Perspective of Labor Reallocation. *Economic Research Journal*, (7).

Du Yang (2014). Labor Market Changes and New Drives for Economic Growth. *China Opening Journal*, (3).

Lu Ming and Liang Wenquan (2017). *Labor Economics and Human Resource Economics—Economic System and Public Policy*, the 2nd ed. Truth & Wisdom Press, Shanghai SDX Joint Publishing Company, Shanghai Renmin Press.

Zhang Juwei (2017). The New Features of China's Employment and New Connotations of the Employment-Priority Strategy Since the 18th National Congress of the Communist Party of China. *Human Resources Development Journal*, (19).

CHAPTER 12

Facilitating Rural Rejuvenation by Addressing Key Sources of Tension

Zhixiong Du

The rural revitalization strategy features prominently in the report to the 19th National Congress of the Communist Party of China. The development of agriculture and rural areas is a weak link in China's social and economic development. To shore up this weak link, we must place the focus of our work on the principal tension in the development of agriculture and rural areas to better implement the rural revitalization strategy.

Z. Du (✉)
Chinese Academy of Social Sciences, National Academy of Economic Strategy, Beijing, China

D. He et al. (eds.), *Chinese Finance Policy for a New Era*,
https://doi.org/10.1007/978-981-33-4054-1_12

12.1 Problems and Challenges in Agricultural and Rural Development in the New Era

12.1.1 Principal Tension in the Development of Agriculture and Rural Areas in the New Era

The report to the 19th National Congress of the CPC notes that the principal tension of China has transitioned to the tension between the people's ever-growing needs for a better life and the inadequate and imbalanced development. The inadequacy and imbalance of development is quite obvious in the development of agriculture and rural areas as seen in the outstanding tensions in our socio-economic development such as the imbalance between the output of agriculture and other industries, between the income of rural residents and urban residents, between the sense of achievement of rural residents and urban residents, and in the gap between rural development and urban development. The central rural work conference pointed out that problems in rural areas are the heaviest burden we have to shoulder on our way to pursue the "Two Centennial Goals" in time, but the deepest foundation and greatest potential lie in rural areas. In this context, the rural revitalization strategy becomes a path we must take, if we want to address the tension between the people's ever-growing needs for a better life and the inadequate and imbalanced development. Why is the problem of inadequate and imbalanced development in agriculture and rural areas so prominent?

Farmers are still the vulnerable group in the structure of national income distribution. On one hand, the rural population accounts for a significant share of the total population and will continue to be so in a fairly long time. In 2016, China had over 590 million permanent rural residents, accounting for 42.6 percent of the total population. Even if we can reduce that percentage to 20 percent in the future by measures like speeding up the urbanization, there will still be more than 200 million people living in rural areas. The fact that a large number of farmers live in rural areas for a long time will remain the same. We should not leave rural residents, especially those disadvantaged groups in rural areas, out of the people-centered development concept. On the other hand, the increase of rural income lacks momentum and the long-term mechanism for rural income growth is still up in the air. In recent years, the urban–rural income gap keeps narrowing, but the per capita income ratio of urban residents to rural residents is still as high as 2.7:1. The structures of rural population and income suggest that there are 282 million migrant workers (close to half of the total rural population), whose income is 20 percent higher than that of the other rural residents. Income from wage and salary makes up the overwhelming majority of rural residents' total income. Due to high living costs in cities, unequal social security and anemic employment market, the number of migrant workers returning to villages is increasing. According to the statistics from the Ministry of Agriculture and Rural Affairs, in 2015, seven million people went to rural areas for entrepreneurship, of whom 68.5 percent were returned migrant workers.[1] Lastly, the overall supply of agricultural products exceeds market demand and higher price will not contribute much to the income growth of farmers. After several years of crop yields increasing in a row, the price of crops faces downward pressure, which will bring more negative impact on the income of rural households who live on farming, especially of the new types of agricultural businesses who have increased income and scaled up by growing grains in the past few years. It is a great challenge to guarantee a sustained and high growth of income for farmers in the future.

The insufficient economic returns in agricultural production and weak competitiveness of agricultural products are two problems that are holding back the transition toward modern agriculture. Three factors are accountable for the situation. First, we face an imbalance between the quantity and the quality of the supply of agricultural products. China boasts a huge demand for agricultural products and is home to a large population. The top priority of agricultural production is to ensure effective supply, especially food security. In recent years, thanks to the growing support for agricultural production and products by the central government, the major tension we face in agriculture has transitioned from insufficient total supply to imbalanced production structure as shown in the periodical concurrent of oversupply in quantity and undersupply in high quality. We have a large quantity of generic agricultural products, which cannot bring much economic returns because they are sold at a low price. The production of major crops is trapped in the "Three Highs" and faces "Double Pressures", and the current agricultural structure cannot satisfy consumers' needs for a better life and is holding back farmers'

[1] The Ministry of Agriculture and Rural Affairs, Seven Million People Have Gone to Rural Areas for Mass Entrepreneurship and Innovation, *Economic Daily*, September 15, 2017.

income increase. Second, farmers are not fully engaged in modern agricultural development. The competitiveness of agricultural products depends much on the scale of production. Currently, we have over 877,000 family farms and contracted arable land of 460 million mu (about 306,666.66 km^2) in transfer, accounting for over 1/3 of the total. In some of the coastal areas in East China, the contracted arable land in transfer makes up more than half of the total. But at the same time, the rural households that manage an arable land smaller than 10 mu (about 6666.67 m^2) remain more than 200 million, accounting for nearly 80 percent of the total of China.[2] In a word, individual rural households will still be the basic units of agricultural production and operation, the carrier of traditional farming culture and the stabilizer of our economy and society in a long time to come. Therefore, the problems facing these households, including small-scale and fragmented production, aging labor force and concurrent business, humble literacy of science and technology, and lack of modern production technologies and information, are holding back the overall development of modern agriculture in China. Third, the multiple functions and added value of agricultural production have yet to be unleashed. In the past, our aim of agricultural development was to pursue high yield by excessively increasing the use of fertilizer and pesticide. But today, as consumers' needs become more and more diverse, individualized and life-oriented, their demand for high-quality, nutritious, green, ecological, and efficient products is growing stronger, so is their demand for other functions of agriculture, including leisure, sightseeing, experience, science popularization, and processing. But due to the limit of natural resource, market and technology, the versatility, sustainability, and added value of agricultural production still wait to be unleashed.

We haven't established a mechanism for integrated development of urban and rural areas. First, the loss of factors of production in rural areas has not stopped. The Communist Party of China blazed in the practice a special trail for revolution—"Starting with cities and moving towards the countryside". Under its leadership, we finally realized nationwide peace and laid a solid foundation for the founding of the People's Republic of China. In the fairly long time between the founding of our republic and the launch of reform and opening up, the agricultural

[2] Vice Minister of the Ministry of Agriculture and Rural Affairs, With Over 200 Million Rural Households Managing a Land Smaller Than 10 Mu, Decentralized Small-Scale Agricultural Operation Is Hard to Change, *People's Daily*, December 25, 2016.

production provided primitive accumulation for the development of heavy industry, the rural areas supported the development of cities, and the price difference between agricultural products and industrial products provided agricultural surplus to the industrialization. These efforts provided significant support for China's industrialization and urbanization. However, the one-way flow of the factors of production from rural to urban areas has caused a series of side effects. The progress of agricultural modernization has been left behind by the other three aims (a new type of industrialization, informatization, and urbanization). Agriculture and rural areas have not fully benefited from economic development. Now, a large proportion of rural areas are going downwards because they are losing talents and are troubled by insufficient infrastructure investment. Second, the policy system of industry nurturing agriculture and urban areas driving rural areas has yet to be established. In 2003, we launched the strategy for balanced urban and rural development and many rural areas were transformed into industrial areas or urban areas. In other words, in the economic and social development, we didn't give the rural areas the attention that they deserve. Most of the existing policies are designed to promote urbanization. Some local governments expanded the coverage of urban areas by land finance, but in this process, rural areas could not make the best use of their own advantages, and the one-way flow of the factors of production was still going on, thus leading to larger development gap between the urban areas and rural areas. Third, a mutually beneficial mechanism for integrated and balanced urban and rural development hasn't come into being. International experience suggests that when the urbanization rate exceeds 50 percent in a country, the capital, technology, and management factors would flow to the agricultural sector. The US, Japan, and developed countries in Europe all went through such a stage.[3] A series of pro-agriculture policies introduced since the 18th National Congress of the CPC have boosted infrastructure construction, the application of information technology, and the development of education, health, and social insurance system in rural areas. But as our economic development enters the stage of "new normal", the economic growth is slowing down, the effect of demographic dividends is fading away, and big cities are plagued with many problems while rural areas lack momentum. More and more people have a strong desire for life in

[3]Wang Dongjing, My View on Rural Revitalization Strategy, *Study Times*, November 24, 2017.

villages. In 2016, the percentage of added value of the secondary industry and the tertiary industry reached 39.8 percent and 51.6 percent, respectively, while that of the primary industry dropped to 8.6 percent. The urbanization rate was up to 57.4 percent. Our per capita GDP will soon exceed USD 10,000 and the proportion of the population living in urban areas will exceed 60 percent.[4] We can say that the cities are well capable of nurturing the rural areas and the secondary industry and the tertiary industry are well capable of nurturing the primary industry. But we should first establish a mechanism for the integrated development of urban and rural areas.

12.1.2 Why "Rural Area" Not "Village"?

In the context of Chinese language, "rural area" is a dynamic concept that will change as time passes. In *Ci Hai*, the word "village" is defined as a compact community inhabited mostly by people who engage in agricultural production for a living. From the perspective of human development, an overwhelming majority of China's history was dominated by primitive villages, in which the labor force took farming as a living. In this sense, "village" and "rural area" have the same meaning. However, as modern sci-tech revolutions advance and as our economy and society develop, our industrial structure has changed. An increasing number of labor force in the rural area are giving up their work in agricultural production and taking up jobs in other sectors. In this process, cities and townships have been taking place of villages. Therefore, "village" and "rural area" come to diverge. Since the 1980s, the rapid development of enterprises in the rural area of south of Jiangsu has been accelerating the fall of the share of agriculture and the rise of the share of industry in the rural industrial structure. At the same time, small cities and townships have been springing up, and urbanization and industrialization are viewed increasingly as two signs of sound social and economic development. Then, the connotation of "rural area" changed significantly.

First, the material basis that underlies the development of rural area has seen profound changes. The rural area is no longer a place for agricultural production or a compact community inhabited mostly by people

[4] Minister of the Ministry of Agriculture and Rural Affairs, Rural Revitalization Is an Essential Step to Build an All-Round Well-Off Society, *People's Daily*, November 17, 2017.

who engage in agricultural production but a complexity with multiple functions covering production, life, and ecology. In addition to traditional agricultural industries, many material production and non-material production sectors have found their operations in the rural area, including handicraft industry, business and commerce, services and so on. The number of people engaged in other industries except agriculture production or concurrent business behavior is growing and has exceeded the number of labor force engaged in agricultural production. More surprisingly, in some economically developed areas, farming business has become a rare thing in the rural area.

Second, the functions and significance of the rural area are getting diverse. The rural area is both an economic entity and a complexity that encompasses multiple meanings of economy, politics, culture, society, and ecological environment. It is also a basic unit that constitutes the social and economic network. It is fair to say that the rural area is the origin of city and urban residents come from rural residents.

Third, the coverage of rural area keeps expanding. In the past, the rural area was more like a compact living place for labor force for the convenience of agricultural production. As the industrial structure in the rural area undergoes profound changes, the rural labor force keeps flowing to urban non-agricultural industries. The rural area and the urban area develop simultaneously. More and more villages choose to be built in areas closer to cities or towns where life is more convenient. Now, the rural area has grown into a general system that integrates the agriculture, villages, and rural residents. The subjects of rural revitalization include not only the rural area but also the agricultural industry and rural residents. Therefore, we can say that the rural revitalization strategy is a systematic project that has a broad meaning and coverage and it is essential to the overall development of China.

12.2 Rural Development: A Matter of National Interest

Since ancient times, China has been an agricultural society. Agriculture accounts for a high proportion, a large population is engaged in agricultural production, the rural areas are extensive and farmers always enjoy an important position in the social strata. Over the past 90 years since the founding of the Communist Party of China, the huge population of farmers have been resolutely defending the leadership of and unswervingly following the guidance of the Party and we embraced one victory after another. That's because we always found a proper way to handle the issue of farmers during the periods of revolutionary war, economic development and reform and opening up. In the new era, we must unite farmers around the Party, which is a fundamental experience of our Party, if we want to realize the "Two Centennial Goals" and the great rejuvenation of the Chinese nation. The rural revitalization strategy is a continuation and development of the policies and guidance on the three issues of agriculture, rural areas, and rural people. Throughout the development process of urban and rural areas since the founding of the People's Republic of China, the Central Committee of the Communist Party of China (the CPC Central Committee), according to the national conditions, had different strategy and policy priorities in the development of urban–rural relationship and the development of agriculture and rural areas in different periods.

12.2.1 Urban–Rural Dual System Established Since the Founding of the PRC

The years from 1949 to 1957 are the primary period for the urban–rural dual system to take shape. In March 1949, the 2nd Plenary Session of the 7th Central Committee of the CPC made two major decisions. First, the focus of the Party would be shifted from urban areas to rural areas. Second, attaching equal importance to urban areas and rural areas was established as the core principle in the development of urban–rural relationship. The CPC leadership team with Mao Zedong at its core realized that in the old semi-feudal and semi-colonial urban–rural relationship, the rural areas were ruled in politics and exploited in economy by the urban areas. This problematic relationship had caused one-sided prosperity in urban areas and overall poverty in rural areas. Without the support of rural areas, the cities are like water without a source or trees without roots. Therefore, we must attach equal importance to the urban areas and rural areas and strive for coordinated development.

Then, the socialist transformation of agriculture, handicraft industry and capitalist industry and commerce was completed and placing heavy industry first became a development guidance. Under this strategic background, we established a centralized purchasing and selling system for grains and other major agricultural and sideline products and a population management system. From then on, the urban–rural dual system began to take shape. These actions and systems laid down the institutional basis for the formal establishment and consolidation of the urban–rural dual system.

Although at that time, both urban residents and rural residents saw a sharp rise in their spending, the annual spending growth rate of urban residents far outweighed that of rural residents. And the growth rate of agriculture was much lower than that of industry. Some agricultural products such as cotton, oil plants, and sugar beet and sugar cane as raw materials for industrial production fell short of demand and the products of light industries also faced severe shortage. In his essays *On the Ten Major Relationships* and *On the Correct Handling of the Tensions Among the People*, Mao Zedong pointed out that we needed to strike a balance between agriculture and industry and handled the relationship between the government, the collectives, and the farmers properly.

The period from 1958 to 1978 marks the establishment and consolidation of the urban–rural separation system. A set of closely related and mutually reinforcing systems and policies were established during that period. First, the urban–rural dual household registration system was formally put into use so the flow of residents from rural areas to urban areas was strictly restricted by law. Instead, urban residents returned to rural areas as a result of political mobilization and policy impetus for many times. Second, the employment system and social welfare system separated the urban household registration and the rural household registration. The household registration system had two categories—agricultural registered permanent residence and non-agricultural registered permanent residence, and it gave rise to another dozen of dual systems, including employment system, the supply system of food, oil, non-staple food and fuel, medical insurance system, education system, social insurance system, labor protection system, housing system, and conscription system.

The centralized purchasing and selling system restricted fair trade of industrial products and agricultural products, and the tightened household registration system curbed the free flow of the factors of production between urban areas and rural areas. Urban residents and rural residents faced unequal development opportunities. The urban–rural dual separation system began to take shape. At the same time, in order to ensure the smooth implementation of the strategy, the central government adopted agricultural collectivization to improve agricultural productivity on the one hand. On the other hand, the government tried to cut the cost of the centralized purchasing and selling system through the dual household registration system, the People's commune system, and the price difference between industrial products and agricultural products in order to accumulate more funds for industrialization. Under the urban–rural dual system, China developed the urban–rural relationship marked by the feature of agriculture helping industry and rural areas supporting urban areas.

China's industrial gross output increased by 15 times from 1952 to 1978 but the gross output of agriculture grew merely by 1.3 times. Agriculture, rural areas, and farmers made enormous contribution to the establishment of the national industrial system and the rapid development of cities. Under this development model dominated by industrialization, agriculture was always dominated by traditional production methods and was trapped in the half self-sufficient production state. We made no progress in urbanization and were faced with many problems including imbalance of urban and rural development and between industry and agriculture.[5]

12.2.2 Flow of Factors Between Rural Areas and Urban Areas Under the Market Economy Since the Launch of Reform and Opening Up

The household contract responsibility system introduced since the launch of reform and opening up significantly stimulated farmers' production initiative and the supply of agricultural products reached a record high. In the mid 1980s, the central government abolished the centralized purchasing and selling system and gradually liberalized the trade of most agricultural products. Then most agricultural products began to be priced by the market. The extremely unreasonable price relationship between industrial products and agricultural products under the planned economy was readjusted and the price difference was gradually eliminated.

Our economic system gradually transitioned from planned economy to market economy. The rise of enterprises in rural areas or townships significantly boosted local development, which brought a huge impact to the traditional urban–rural relationship. In the past, our national economic structure was a dual structure consisting of agriculture in rural areas and

[5] Han Jun, Review and Outlook on the Evolution of China's Urban–Rural Relationship over the Past 60 Years, *Reform*, 2009 (11).

industry in urban areas. After the launch of reform and opening up, it became a ternary economic structure consisting of industry in urban areas, industry in rural areas, and agriculture in rural areas. The rapid urbanization of rural areas was the primary stage of urbanization and it also marked the transition of our industrial structure from agricultural to non-agricultural. In this period, a large quantity of resources including land, funds, and labor force flowed from rural areas to urban areas, especially the able-bodied labor force flowed from agriculture to non-agricultural industries in urban areas. The agricultural migrant labor force accounted for over half of the total.

In the new era, China has more material wealth and greater management capabilities to integrate the development of the urban areas and rural areas, to make industry nurture agriculture, and to let the urban areas drive the rural areas. We must stay true to our original aspiration and keep our mission firmly in mind. In addition, we must be fully aware that agriculture and rural areas are still faced with a series of problems, including weak infrastructure, large urban–rural income gap, and sharp difference in public services between urban and rural areas. The pattern of integrated development of urban areas and rural areas has yet to be established and the sustainability of agriculture and rural areas has to be strengthened. Although China is experiencing rapid urbanization, it still has 590 million rural permanent residents and 280 million migrant workers. Rural residents still make up the largest share of our population. Even if the urbanization rate reaches 80 percent or 90 percent in the future, there will still be hundreds of millions of people living in the rural areas. General Secretary Xi Jinping once said, "We must always attach great importance to agriculture, rural areas and rural residents". In 2017, the central rural work conference pointed out that "the Party, governments at all levels and the general public must make full efforts to promote all-round development of agriculture, rural areas and rural residents with greater resolution, clearer target and better measures".

12.3 Ten Relationships Crucial to Rural Development

The report to the 19th National Congress of the CPC and the central rural work conference pointed out that we will realize modernization of agriculture and rural areas in step with that of the whole nation, and the rural revitalization strategy will serve as the guidance for rural work in a rather long time in the future. The report also pointed out the principle of the rural revitalization strategy and targets at different stages. Rural areas in different regions have different foundations and different temporary tensions. There is no existing or fixed approach to implement the rural revitalization strategy. We must properly handle the following ten relationships in practice.

First, we need to maintain a sound relationship between agriculture, rural areas, and rural residents. The biggest concern of rural residents is to increase the income. The income growth comes from industrial growth. According to the report, the revitalization of rural areas must meet the overall requirements of prosperous industries, ecological and livable environment, civilized conduct, effective rural governance, and wealthy life. Prosperous industries are the material basis, because well-developed industries can bring enormous material gains and attract more talents. In addition to the production function, we need to explore many other functions of agriculture, promote the integrated development of the primary, secondary, and tertiary industry, and establish and improve three systems. An ecological and livable environment reflects the quality of development and we should not pursue industrial development at the cost of our environment. We should try to develop our industries on the basis of a favorable ecological environment and make our environment cleaner in the process of development so as to build a living environment in which human and nature live in harmony. Civilized conduct is the symbol of rural civilization and the soul of rural development. We should tap into our traditional cultural preserve and celebrate the best of our folk customs to show the diversity, inclusiveness and complexity. We should make the best use of modern technologies and management methods to better preserve our traditional culture and carry on our civilization. Effective rural governance ensures the safety and stability of rural areas in the long run. The basis of rural governance is the rule of law. We should make full use of the rural social network to help us improve rural governance and we should also practice the rule of virtue and the rule of man in the rural governance. A wealthy life is the natural result of thriving industries. It is a necessary condition to retain labor force and attract talents, two essential elements for rural development.

Second, we should keep a sound relationship between the market and the government. As a country develops from agrarian economy to industrial economy, especially during its rapid development of industrialization and modernization, cities and the secondary industry will benefit from preferential policies of the government and ardent support of the society. Under this circumstance, human and material resources in rural areas will flow to cities, causing concentration of a large number of development elements in cities. The profit-pursuing nature of the capital will direct investment to cities in the market economy, making rural areas a less attractive choice for investors. Hence, the decline of rural areas is an iron law. General Secretary Xi Jinping said, "We must always attach great importance to agriculture, rural areas and rural residents". China has a huge agricultural economy and is the largest socialist country in the world. Only by letting the large rural population work together with the CPC can we make socialism with Chinese characteristics better. The central rural work conference pointed out that we should strengthen and improve the Party's leadership in the rural work, thus providing a solid political guarantee for the three issues of agriculture, rural areas, and rural residents. To carry out the rural revitalization strategy, we should fully leverage the role of both the government and the market—the invisible hand. We should improve the system of rural property rights and the market-oriented allocation of the factors of production on the basis of the law of market economy and the change of market demand to energize the market players, all types of factors of production and the whole market. In the end, we will build a mechanism in which the government and the market work in mutually beneficial cooperation to form a development pattern of rural revitalization marked by both efficiency and equity.

Third, we should maintain a balanced relationship between the urban areas and the rural areas. The urban–rural relationship always features prominently in the modernization drive of socialist development. In the early years since the founding of the People's Republic of China, under the strategy of attaching equal importance to the urban areas and the rural areas, we developed a dual economic structure for urban areas and rural areas. Since the introduction of reform and opening up, we have been pursuing integrated urban and rural development and trying to improve the dual economic structure by re-optimizing the allocation of resources and making the urban areas support the rural areas. But in fact, the root of the long-established dual economic structure remains unchanged. Due to the lack of reliable systems and mutually beneficial mechanisms, the integrated urban–rural development leads the one-way flow of resources of land, labor force and capital from rural areas to urbanization. Urban areas and rural areas follow two different development paths. Finally, rural areas are left behind in the drive of urbanization and industrialization and it is impossible for rural areas to catch up with the steps of urbanization by themselves. Now, we are faced with the challenges of “Big City Diseases” and the decline of rural areas at the same time. On the one hand, to revitalize the rural areas does not mean we should regenerate all villages regardless of cost. To achieve that end, we should respect the law of rural development and let those unlivable villages naturally die away. On the other hand, rural revitalization does not mean de-urbanization. Urban development at a reasonable pace will not hold back the revitalization of rural areas. On the contrary, it can promote the development of rural areas by transferring the surplus rural labor force and promoting the productivity of agricultural production. In the end, we must reshape the urban–rural relationship, recover the value of agriculture and rural areas, and follow a path marked by integrated urban–rural development. We need to strengthen the policy support to make industry nurture agriculture and let the urban development drive the rural development. We need to develop rural infrastructure that is complementary to urban infrastructure and establish a unified social insurance system. We should also make full use of the advantages of rural areas including abundant natural resources, ecological environment, agricultural production, leisure and sightseeing, space layout, rural culture, and folk customs to promote the two-way flow of the factors of production between urban and rural areas in order to realize the integrated urban–rural development.

Fourth, we should strike a balance between the primary industry, the secondary industry, and the tertiary industry. China is one of the largest countries in the world in terms of population. Therefore, the most important mission of agricultural production is to ensure sufficient food supply. In the modernization drive across the world, the share of the added value of the primary industry in the GNP of most countries and overall employment rate of the primary industry keep falling. In the US, the value of its agricultural production only accounts for 1.2 percent of the economy and its population engage in agricultural production less than one percent of the total. In some modern big cities in China like Beijing and Shanghai, the value of agricultural production and the number of people who engage in agriculture have fallen to less than one percent. In 2016, the share of the added value of China’s primary industry is down to 8.6 percent. As the industrialization and urbanization push ahead, the share of its agriculture in the GDP will experience a sharper fall, but there will still be a large proportion of people living in the rural areas. Although economically, the status of agriculture is declining, its position as a fundamental industry is as important as before, so is its fundamental role as the source of food. We must first improve the overall benefits and competitiveness of agricultural products if we want to consolidate the fundamental status of agriculture. Then, we need to promote the integration of agriculture with the secondary and the tertiary industry and try to meet people's diverse and personalized needs. Last, we should tap into many other functions of agriculture and explore the historical, cultural, and ecological value of the rural areas so as to revitalize the overall value of the rural areas.

Fifth, we should maintain a sound relationship between the urban areas and the rural areas. In 2016, China had 590 million permanent rural residents and 280 million migrant workers who had lived in the urban areas for half a year or more. Together they accounted for 63 percent of the total population. Although the nominal urbanization rate reached 57.4 percent (all migrant workers included), the number of registered permanent urban residents only made up 41.2 percent of the population.[6] The number of rural residents still outweighs that of the urban residents. But the long-established household registration system has caused a huge gap between urban residents and rural residents in terms of the quality of basic public services and social security. To realize coordinated development of the urban areas and the rural areas we must maintain a good relationship between farmers, migrant workers, and urban residents. We should make it easier for rural residents who have transferred to non-agricultural sectors to get permanent urban residence registration and let those who meet certain requirements and are willing to settle down enjoy equal public services as urban residents. And we should unify the social security system for the urban areas and the rural areas, providing basic public services for those not eligible for or unwilling to apply for permanent urban residence, thus eliminating the discrimination caused by household registration. In addition, we should improve the rural infrastructure for agricultural production and the rural system for public services, providing the same public services for rural residents as those for urban residents. Farmers' income should be pegged to their labor. Through our efforts, we strive to make rural areas a home for innovators and entrepreneurs.

Sixth, we should maintain a sound relationship between small rural households and modern agriculture. In recent years, our agricultural

[6] Urbanization Rate of Residents with Household Registration Reached 41.2 percent Last Year, Xinhua News Agency, February 13, 2017.

production has been growing in scale and many new types of entities begin to engage in agricultural production activities, thus addressing the problem of "who should grow food for us" by many types of production relationship. With an annual growth rate of 3 percent of the rural land in transfer from 2007 to 2017, there will still be 170 million and 100 million small rural households in 2030 and 2050, respectively, who farm a land smaller than 50 mu (33,333.33 m^2), accounting for 80 percent and 70 percent of the total, respectively. In the process of rural revitalization and modernization of agriculture, we must help those small rural households better adapt to the development of modern agriculture. We should be fully aware of the fact that in a rather long period agricultural production has been undertaken by individual rural households and today, small rural households are still an integral part of rural economy. In addition, we should continue to absorb the surplus rural labor force as we strive to promote industrialization and urbanization and to create more jobs in non-agricultural sectors. We should also create an encouraging environment for business startups in rural areas and promote the productivity and per capita resources of rural residents in the agricultural sector. And we should foster large-scale agricultural production entities such as family farms through the separation of ownership right, contract right, and management right and let them set a role model for small individual rural households in production and operation. We should develop and improve a social service system to meet the needs of the entities in agricultural production, leverage the role of the market mechanism and the role of government in purchasing competitive services. On the one hand, we need to satisfy the requirements of large-scale production. On the other hand, we need to meet the needs of small individual rural households.

Seventh, we need to strike a balance between production, life and the ecological environment. The rural areas as a complex encompasses production, life and sustainable ecology. The traditional agricultural development model that aimed solely at higher yields at the cost of resources and environment made the problems in agricultural production increasingly serious. In many rural places, little attention was paid to ecological environment protection in the process of economic development. Some places even resorted to an approach that developed economy first at all costs and then tried to tackle the problem of pollution. As a result, some rural areas suffered severe ecological environment damage. The report to the 19th National Congress of the CPC pointed out that we should strive to build a modern China marked by harmony between human and nature, rich material wealth and spiritual wealth, and more quality ecological products. An ecological and livable environment requires us to keep the environment clean and beautiful, follow the path of green development, and build rural areas where man and nature coexist harmoniously. To that end, we must uphold the principle of green development with protection first and follow revitalization path marked by resource conservation and environment protection. We should also make the best use of local resources and advantages to set up a mechanism for sustainable development and strengthen lawmaking and policymaking to encourage green production and consumption. In this way, we can have both external restrictions against environment pollution and internal incentives for green development and reduce behaviors in life or production that may cause pollution.

Eighth, we need to keep a balance between food security and economic returns on food crops. Food security is the prerequisite of modern agriculture in China. The area of arable land in China is limited compared with its huge population. In order to ensure our national food security, a large proportion of our arable land must be used to grow food crops. Therefore, the economic returns on the production of food crops decide the stability of agricultural development and the initiative of farmers. At the same time, the macro regulation by the government and resources allocation by the market are very important for food security. We need to leverage the role of the food production area and the protected area for major agricultural products and improve the supporting system for agricultural development. In addition, we need to find a way to establish a complementary system for benefits of the two areas. We also need to improve the food purchasing and reserving system and the price forming mechanism for important agricultural products and gradually implement a food purchasing and reserving system that is marked by market-based pricing, separated price and subsidy and multiple market entities. Besides, we should develop specialized family farms for food production and forge a modern industrial system, production system, and trade system that are good for food production. We should guarantee the overall returns and risk-resisting capabilities of food production by ensuring farmers' income and providing insurance and services to them. We should promote the application of modern agricultural technologies and equipment in production and let social organizations provide multi-level and all-round services for the whole industry, thus improving the competitiveness of food production.

Ninth, we need to well balance the long-term and short-term development. The decision of the central CPC to revitalize the rural areas is good for now and will bring benefits in the future. The rural revitalization strategy is related to the welfare of hundreds of millions of rural people and to the realization of the "Two Centenary Goals". It is a complicated, systematic, and significant project and a historic task that cannot be finished overnight. To do a good job for the rural people and revitalize the rural areas, the key is the leadership of the CPC and the practice of the local officials. China's political structure and the promotion system for officials require us to properly handle the relationship between short-term development and long-term development. We should set the development targets, paths, and specific measures for rural revitalization through scientific planning with the overarching planning and introduce specific implementation plans and missions to carry out the rural revitalization strategy. We must value the quality over quantity and implement the strategy step-by-step, year by year, and generation after generation. We should also reform the assessment system for community-level government officials to attach more importance to the quality of their work and how they work rather than the number of targets and tasks accomplished. In addition, we should set up a responsibility system for rural revitalization to ensure that those who are responsible for the implementation of the strategy should be held accountable for any malpractice in a life time.

Tenth, we should maintain a balance between regions and the big picture. The situation of economic development differs from region to region. Different places have their own special conditions in terms of development basis, resource endowment, economic and social development, and internal and external market. Conditions may differ significantly even between villages within the same province (region or city). Therefore, there is a common goal for the strategy but no common method to carry out. We should first break all institutional barriers to rural revitalization and work hard to build up the institutional framework and policy system. We should energize the market players in the rural areas and the agricultural sector and revitalize key elements in rural development so as to stimulate the initiative of skilled people and encourage them to contribute to rural revitalization. In addition, we should make the best use of local resources of natural scenery, history, culture, and ecology and both traditional and modern advantages to explore multiple functions of agricultural production according to market demand and create an encouraging environment for rural development. We should also proactively encourage all kinds of skilled people and leverage all kinds of resources to contribute to rural revitalization. We should first develop several outstanding model villages and use their development experience to drive forward all-round development.

CHAPTER 13

Openness as the Cornerstone of the New Economic System

Jin Zhao, Xianliang Xia, and Ning Zhang

In the report to the 19th National Congress of the Communist Party of China, General Secretary Xi Jinping said, "Openness brings progress, while self-seclusion leaves one behind. China will not close its door to the world; we will only become more and more open. We hope to make new ground in opening China further through links running eastward and westward, across land and over sea". In the new era of socialism with Chinese characteristics, we must work harder to establish a new economic system that is open to the world, thus making our economy more and more open.

13.1 Framework and Approaches

The *Several Opinions of The Central Committee of the Communist Party of China (CPC) and the State Council on Establishing a New Systems for*

J. Zhao (✉) · X. Xia · N. Zhang
National Academy of Economic Strategy, Chinese Academy of Social Sciences, Beijing, China

D. He et al. (eds.), *Chinese Finance Policy for a New Era*,
https://doi.org/10.1007/978-981-33-4054-1_13

an Open Economy (referred to as the Opinions thereafter) set the overarching target for the system: to work harder to foster new advantages to embrace international cooperation and face international competition; to strike a balance between internal demand and external demand, between imports and exports, and between domestic and overseas investment; to achieve basic balance of international payments step-by-step; to forge an all-round open economic landscape; to develop open economic governance system and capabilities; to uphold a correct view of justice and interest as we open wider to the world; to effectively defend our national interests and national security; to promote the common development of our country and other countries in the world; and finally to set up a new economic system that is mutually beneficial, diverse, balanced, safe, and efficient. Guided by the general goal, in order to build an open economic system that is mutually beneficial, diverse, balanced, safe, and efficient, the Opinions outlined a general framework which places our emphasis on three sectors—trade, investment, and finance, expands the domestic and international space, and establishes the support mechanism and security mechanism as a guarantee.

13.1.1 Three Major Areas: Institutional Innovation Is the Key

i. Investment. In this area, our core mission is to promote the reform of the foreign investors management system and improve the overseas investment management system. In terms of bringing in, we need to innovate the foreign investors management system by adopting the pre-establishment national treatment plus a negative list. In a word, we should strengthen supervision while we strive to open wider to the world. Our work in this area can be summarized with the following keywords: an environment (institutional environment and market environment), two cores, and a carrier. "An environment" means that we need to unify the rules and regulations on domestic and foreign funds, and keep the foreign investment policies stable, transparent, and predictable, thereby creating a standard institutional environment and stable market environment. "Two cores" refers to: first, opening the manufacturing industry and the service industry, with the focus on relaxing the market access restrictions for foreign investment in the service industry and further liberalizing the general manufacturing industry; second, strengthening supervision by strengthening preregistration, in-process and post-event oversight and establishing a supervision system which covers the whole foreign investment process. "A carrier" means we will make the development zones the pioneers in building the open economic system by promoting their transformation, upgrading, and innovative development. In terms of going global, we should establish a new system to promote the strategy of going global and facilitate overseas investment, including improving the overseas investment management system which takes registration as the main approach and approval as a complement to increase facilitation, and strengthening service and guidance before and supervision and guarantee during and after overseas investment.

ii. Trade. The focus of our work in this area is to foster new advantages in the foreign trade competition and develop a new mechanism for foreign trade sustainable development. To foster new advantages in the foreign trade competition means shifting from the advantage of low cost due to the quantity of labor force to new advantages of human capital, technology, brand, quality, and service. We should strive to develop new forms of foreign trade like cross-border e-commerce. In addition, we will develop the new mechanism for sustainable foreign trade by promoting coordinated development of trade in goods and services and institutional innovation. In terms of trade of goods, our priority is to improve the management system of trade in goods. We should establish a management system for new forms of trade like cross-border e-commerce; explore the innovation of supervision modes of international exhibits, artworks, e-commerce express, and other special items; fully implement the "single-window system" for international trade and customs clearance integration to advance the trade facilitation reform; explore new models to regulate the operation of foreign trade, and so on. In terms of trade in services, our priority is to improve the management system of trade in services. We will establish and improve a system to promote facilitation and liberalization of trade in services and expand the scale of the trade; improve the statistical system for trade in services; improve the supervision model for trade in services by setting up a comprehensive supervision platform for trade in services.

iii. Finance. We need to build an open and safe financial system. As we open the financial sector to the world, we must build a safe financial system. The Opinions suggested that we should open the sector wider, promote orderly two-way opening of the capital market, build a support system for finance to go out, expand the use of RMB in cross-border trade and improve the exchange rate formation mechanism and the foreign exchange management system.

13.1.2 *Regional Landscape for Further Opening Up: Expand Domestic and International Space*

To expand our domestic opening up space means to improve the regional landscape of opening up. On the one hand, it put forward new tasks as to the existing opening up landscape, such as improving the inland opening up mechanism, developing new pivots and highlands for opening up along the border and coast, opening the Chinese Mainland wider to Hong Kong SAR, Macao SAR, and Taiwan. On the other hand, it includes establishing several pilot free trade zones in Shanghai, Tianjin, Guangdong, and Fujian Provinces and carrying out institutional innovation and stress tests in order to adapt to the international high-standard trade and investment rules.

To expand the international opening up space means to expand our regional landscape of opening up in the world. On the one hand, we should work harder to carry out the Belt and Road Initiative by promoting infrastructure interconnectivity, deepening economic and trade cooperation with countries along the routes, strengthening scientific and cultural exchanges, and promoting marine economic cooperation. We will also proactively construct the China–Pakistan Economic Corridor and the Bangladesh–China–India–Myanmar Economic Corridor. On the other hand, we will develop new international space for economic cooperation by adhering to the rules of the world trade system, building a high-standard network of free trade zones, proactively participating in global economic governance, building a new pattern of multilateral and bilateral all-round economic and trade cooperation, and establishing a new mechanism for international economic and trade negotiation.

13.1.3 *Guarantee Mechanism for Further Opening Up: Establish and Improve the Support and Security Mechanisms*

Today, China's economy has become an integral part of the global economy. We attach greater importance to our national economic security while raising the level of economic opening up in terms of scope, domain, and depth. The Opinions suggested that we should build and improve a security system for the open economy and establish two supporting mechanisms. On the one hand, we need to strengthen the supporting guarantee system by adopting more liberal talent policies, building a think tank for the opening up strategy, promoting the cultural exchanges and international publicity. On the other hand, we should establish and improve a security system for an open economy covering trade, investment, and finance, by improving the national security review mechanism for foreign investment, establishing a risk prevention system for going global, building an economic and trade security system, and improving the financial risk prevention system.

13.2 Pathway and Achievements

To speed up the building of new systems for an open economy, we have adopted the following 4 approaches: establishing 11 free trade zones including 1 in Shanghai, building a comprehensive pilot project in Beijing for further opening up the service industry, setting up a comprehensive pilot for developing new systems for an open economy, promoting the service trade liberalization in Guangdong, Hong Kong, and Macao. The aim of these pilot projects is to form a set of generalizable and replicable experiences.

13.2.1 The Shanghai and Other Pilot Free Trade Zones

To build open institutions and mechanisms that meet the requirements of international rules, we have established several pilot free trade zones in three batches since 2013. On September 29, 2013, the Shanghai Pilot Free Trade Zone was officially set up. In December 2014, the State Council decided to set up the China (Guangdong) Pilot Free Trade Zone, the China (Tianjin) Pilot Free Trade Zone, and the China (Fujian) Pilot Free Trade Zone. In August 2016, the State Council decided to set up 7 pilot free trade zones in Liaoning province, Zhejiang province, Henan province, Hubei province, Chongqing municipality, Sichuan province, and Shaanxi province.

The development of the pilot free trade zones has three stages covering many areas including the eastern coastal area, the central and western area, and the northeastern area. The construction of the 11 free trade zones is based on institutional innovation and complies with the basic requirement of "being replicable and generalizable". But these pilot zones have their different strategic positionings. The Shanghai Pilot Free Trade Zone is positioned as an important carrier for China to further integrate into the economic globalization, with the aim to upgrade China's economy. The Tianjin Pilot Free Trade Zone is to be a high-level opening up platform for Beijing–Tianjin–Hebei integrated development, a pilot of national reform and opening up, a test field for institutional innovation, and a high-level free trade zone open to the world. The Guangdong Pilot Free Trade Zone is a demonstration zone for in-depth cooperation between Guangdong, Hong Kong, and Macao, an important hub of the 21st Maritime Silk Road and the pilot of the new round of national reform and opening up. The Fujian Pilot Free Trade Zone is a demonstrative zone for cross-strait economic cooperation and a critical center for cooperation with countries and regions along the 21st Maritime Silk Road.

With 3-year experience in institutional innovation, the Shanghai Pilot Free Trade Zone has provided over 100 achievements for replication and generalization. In addition, on March 30, 2017, the State Council issued *Plan for Comprehensive Furthering the Efforts of Reform and Opening Up in the China (Shanghai) Pilot Free Trade Zone*, which outlined the goal as follows: by 2020, we should have taken the lead in establishing a system that is compatible with the international rules on investment and trade, building our pilot free trade zones to internationally high-standard ones featuring free trade and investment, transparent rules, fair and efficient supervision and an encouraging business environment, improving an investment management system that provides equal market access and orderly competition for all types of market players, a trade supervision and service system that can help promote trade transformation and upgrading and facilitate custom clearance, a financial service system that can further opening up and innovation of the financial sector and prevent risks, and a government administrative system that is consistent with the rules of the market economy and modernization of governance, and creating a law-based, international and enabling business environment and a fair, unified, and efficient market environment.

The Plan emphasized comprehensively furthering the reform and integrating all relevant systems. It also stressed the importance of more holistic, coordinated, harmonious, and systematic institutional innovation. We need to reform the system integration and build pilot regions combining opening up with an innovation for comprehensive reforms; make efforts to meet international rules by establishing risk stress test areas for an open economic system; further transform the government functions and build pilot areas for improving governance capability;

find innovative modes for cooperative development and make them the bridgehead of the Belt and Road to encourage market players to go global; serve the big picture of national reform and produce more institutional innovations that can be replicated and promoted.

13.2.2 *The Beijing Comprehensive Pilot Project for Further Opening Up the Service Industry*

The service industry is a critical link for maintaining steady growth, economic restructuring, advancing reform, and improving people's lives. It is also an important field for opening up during the 13th Five-Year Plan. In order to implement the *Decision of the CPC Central Committee on Major Issues about Deepening All-round Reform* and the *Several Opinions of The Central Committee of the CPC and the State Council on Establishing New Systems for an Open Economy*, establish and improve new institutions and mechanisms with Chinese characteristics and capital features in line with the trend of the times, and build a basic framework consistent with international rules for further opening up the service industry, the State Council approved the comprehensive pilot project in Beijing for further opening up the service industry on May 5, 2015, to contribute to the exploration of new systems for an open economy.

According to the approval of the State Council, the Beijing municipal government released *Overall Plan* consisting of the "6+1" further opening up landscape and 5 supporting systems. In the plan, "6" refers to 6 key service fields—science and technology, internet and information, culture and education, finance, commerce and tourism, and health care, which we should further open up by leveraging Beijing's advantages in development of the service industry; "1" refers to overseas investment, which requires us to deepen the reform of the overseas investment management system to encourage Chinese enterprises to go global. We will forge a basic landscape for opening up the service industry that supports "bringing in" and "going global" by establishing the 5 supporting systems in improving the social credit environment, reforming the market supervision model, innovating the mechanism for attracting high-end talents, strengthening financial security, and streamlining the process of customs clearance.

Different from the Shanghai and other free trade zones, the Beijing comprehensive pilot project for further opening up the service industry is the only one designated for industrial opening up, the service industry opening up in particular in China. The Beijing municipal government faithfully implemented the key spirit of General Secretary Xi Jinping's keynote speeches delivered during his visit in Beijing. The pilot measures focus on realizing the functions of Beijing as the political center, cultural center, international communication center, and technological innovation center and promoting integrated development of Beijing, Tianjin, and Hebei by further opening the service industry and deepening the supply-side structural reform. Over the past two years, the four-phased pilot project has made the following achievements: (1) the new service-led development landscape in line with the supply-side structural reform has been established; (2) the new path for the development of the service industry that is conductive to the integrated development of Beijing, Tianjin, and Hebei has been continuously expanded, with the number of local offices in Tianjin and Hebei set up by service outsourcing companies in Beijing over 20; (3) the new drivers for the development of the service industry that match the functional positioning of Beijing as China's capital have been accumulating; (4) the service trade facilitation mechanism in line with the features of the development of the service industry has been established gradually; and (5) the during- and after-event supervision system that is consistent with the requirement of regulating the behaviors of market players has been established gradually and significantly improved the government supervision service.[1]

13.2.3 Comprehensive Pilot Projects of Establishing New Systems for an Open Economy

In order to implement the *Several Opinions of The Central Committee of the CPC and the State Council on Establishing New Systems for an Open Economy*, the central government decided in May 2016 to conduct a 2-year comprehensive pilot trial of establishing new systems for an open economy (referred to as the pilot trial thereafter) in 6 cities (Jinan, Nanchang, Tangshan, Zhangzhou, Dongguan, and Fangchenggang) and 6 areas (Pudong New Area in Shanghai, Liangjiang New Area

[1] Speech made by the Vice Minister of Commerce Mr. Wang Shouwen at the press conference hold by the State Council Information Office of the PRC on "Information about the Beijing Comprehensive Pilot Project for Further Opening Up the Service Industry", china.com.cn, July 27, 2017.

in Chongqing, Xixian New Area in Shaanxi, Jinpu New Area in Dalian, Wuhan Metropolitan Area, and Suzhou Industrial Park).

The overall goal of the pilot trial is, by conducting the pilot trial in the 12 cities and areas, to produce a set of replicable and generalizable experiences and models in developing a new mechanism of market-based resource allocation, a new model of economic operation and management, a new landscape of all-round opening up and new advantages in international cooperation and competition, and to further the breadth and depth of our opening up, thereby laying down a solid foundation for basically establishing new systems for an open economy during the 13th Five-Year Plan and creating a new situation of all-round opening up.

13.2.4 Service Trade Liberalization in Guangdong, Hong Kong, and Macao

In 2013, the *Decision of the CPC Central Committee on Major Issues about Deepening All-round Reform* said that we should expand the opening up to and cooperation with Hong Kong Special Administrative Region, Macao Special Administrative Region, and Taiwan in terms of building new systems for an open economy. In May 2015, to open wider to Hong Kong, Macao, and Taiwan, *Several Opinions of The Central Committee of the CPC and the State Council on Establishing New Systems for an Open Economy* further pointed out that we should better leverage the role of Hong Kong and Macao as open platforms and demonstration areas, strengthen the economic and trade relationship between Chinese Mainland and Hong Kong SAR and Macao SAR, and speed up the liberalization of service trade with Hong Kong and Macao.

In order to realize the liberalization of service trade between the Chinese mainland and Hong Kong and Macao, on December 18, 2014, the agreement between Guangdong, Hong Kong, and Macao on basically realizing the liberalization of service trade, which officially announce the beginning of the service trade liberalization in Guangdong, Hong Kong, and Macao, was signed and then took effect on March 1, 2015. On November 27, 2015, the Agreement on Trade in Services under CEPA between the Mainland and Hong Kong was signed. On November 28, 2015, the Agreement on Trade in Services under CEPA between the Mainland and Macao was signed. The two agreements took effect on June 1, 2016. They are the first free trade agreements signed in the form of pre-establishment national treatment plus a negative list in accordance with the international standards.

13.3 Future Directions and Reform Measures

13.3.1 Approaches to Building an Open Government

i. **Facilitating the Transformation of Government Functions by Advancing the Reform to Streamline Administration, Delegating Power, and Optimize Government Services**

The government should continue to advance the reform to streamline administration, delegate power, and optimize government services, which should be seen as a priority in the supply-side structural reform to energize the supply-side, improve the quality of our supply, and adapt to the market demand, in order to stimulate the vitality of the supply-side. It should further reduce the number of licenses and separate permits and licenses, especially the industrial licenses; promote the power list system; effectively cut taxes and fees to reduce the burden of companies; eliminate, reduce, or delegate preliminary approvals to shift from "strict access, lax supervision" to "easy access, stringent supervision", thereby establishing a fair market environment. On the one hand, the government should energize the market and reduce market extortion. On the other hand, the government should energize the market and avoid market distortion as much as possible. It should create and develop new markets and nurture and support their emergence, growth, and maturity. The government should delegate its approval right as soon as possible and try to eliminate the items that require government approval if possible, thereby sizing down the amount of delegation greatly. It should resolutely uphold the principles of open and transparent market, non-discrimination, national treatment, and fair competition and pursue the policies of free trade and investment to create a national united market and unify the policies of trade and investment across the country, including by prohibiting local protection, barriers, and economic silos.

ii. **Proactively Exploring a Democratic and Open Government Operation System Uniquely Suited to China's National Conditions**

Exploring an effective democratic institutional framework and rule of law system is the prerequisite for building an open government system. Without an effective democracy, we cannot build an open government system. At the same time, an open government is necessary for people to exercise their democratic rights. Currently, the defects in our democratic supervision system and the rigid and closed government operation system leave some institutional loopholes for corrupt officials and a breeding ground for the abuse of public power. We lack an institutional cage to stop and prevent corruption. Therefore, the work of anti-corruption should be based on a reliable institution, reform and innovation of the institution and mechanisms, and people's oversight, so as to make the work and public affairs of government officials open and transparent. To make progress in our anti-corruption, we must make our government more and more open, and hand state power back to the people by engaging people directly in our national governance and democratic supervision. The national governance system that is centered on people's interests will not come into being by itself. Therefore, we must make the civil servants and government officials and leaders keep people's interests in mind by a tight institutional system and a democratic supervision mechanism. We should work hard to establish an effective democratic system, safeguard people's democracy, make our government open, clean, and transparent, and ensure people's political, financial, and decision-making supervision over government officials and leaders. We should conduct assessments and hearings on the government officials' performance, and hold them accountable, thereby implementing the people's democratic dictatorship. Except for issues that cannot be open to the public, the governments and government departments must allow certain percentage of people's representatives from all walks of life to participate in the decision-making of major issues related to people's interest and the whole decision-making process must be open to the public in the form of video recording.

iii. Building an Open Government Organizational System and Developing a Flexible Cadre Placement System

The reform, adjustment, and improvement of the government organization must meet the requirements of the market economy, the new systems for an open economy, open global economy, and the trend of globalization. We should transform government functions, advance the reform to streamline administration, delegate power and optimize government services, simplify and standardize the functions of the government, and significantly reduce the government affairs. We should also promote the pilot trial of the overhaul of ministry system, improve the allocation of government functions, the setup of government departments and the work process, clarify the list of powers and boundaries of powers, cut redundant institutions, shore up weak links, make clear governments' functions, powers and responsibilities, and performance assessment targets, and improve the administration mechanism in which the power of decision-making, enforcement and supervision check and coordinate with each other, to form a government organization marked by corresponding responsibility, power, and interest. Therefore, it is necessary for the State Council to review and verify the functions, duties, and powers of each ministry under the new systems for an open economy, make clear the allocation of their functions, powers, and tasks. It should also specify the exact number of staff on the payroll, reduce redundant organizations and the headcounts of leadership, and set an annual target of organization streamlining.

iv. Building a Technical Support System to Facilitate Open Government

Technological innovation is critical to make the government more and more open. It is not so hard to develop relevant technologies. The problem is that whether or not the government is willing and determined to develop a technology system for an open government. The existing government information disclosure, government reports, and online government services only provide less than 10 percent of all the government information. In the future, we should ensure the work, words, and behaviors of all civil servants and government officials and leaders are kept on file in the form of video recording as a part of a lifelong e-record, and make these records available to the public without violating the privacy and the confidential terms. Governments at all levels and every official must keep a standard record of their work for review. Annual performance evaluation should be based on the work records on file and other unrecorded work should not be included in the process.

13.3.2 *Approaches to Building a New System for an Open Trade*

i. **Building a New Export-Oriented Open System**

Our priority in building a new export-oriented open system is to accelerate the transformation of our export from speed and scale to quality and returns. We should take the following approaches. First, we should change our export from consisting mainly of goods to including goods, services, technologies, and capital. Second, we should shift the export advantage of lower price to a comprehensive competition advantage of technology, brand, quality, and services. Third, we should transform the factor-driven export growth to the innovation-driven export growth. Fourth, we should develop the trade in services. Fifth, we should take an active part in making the international trade and economic rules instead of sticking and adapting to the existing ones in global economic governance.

We should work hard to adjust the mix of export commodities, maintain and improve the development of labor-intensive industries, accelerate the export of technology-intensive products, enhance the share of technical content in the export commodities, promote the structural adjustment of the international export market, and continue to implement the market diversification strategy. We should enhance the role of service trade in promoting the development of our foreign trade, continue to adjust the internal structure of service trade, and increase the share of the productive service trade and emerging service trade in the service trade. At the same time, we should strengthen the interaction between the service trade and the goods trade to foster new growth drivers for our foreign trade development. We will constantly increase the export of labor-intensive products to countries along the Belt and Road and boost the export of large machinery and equipment and technologies by taking the great opportunity of expanding infrastructure construction. We should increase the export of conventional mechanical and electrical products and the export of new high-tech products. In addition, we should work hard to open our market wider to the countries along the routes and promote the development of new export-oriented open system by making use of the opportunities provided by the Belt and Road Initiative. China will play a more proactive role in participating or even leading in the formulation of new rules of international trade so as to gain more benefits rather than being excluded from the new system again due to self-seclusion.

We should make great efforts to develop foreign trade and foster new forms and models of trade to enhance our national strength by trade. We should also improve the technological value of our export products. In addition, we should use modern technologies to transform traditional industries, promote the quality and technological value of labor-intensive products, and push our traditional industries toward medium to high level. We should work hard to develop famous brands in foreign trade by guiding enterprises to strengthen brand building and encouraging eligible regions, industries, and companies to establish their own brand promotion centers for the brand products with core technologies. We also encourage companies to apply for trademarks and patents in foreign countries to better protect their rights. We will adopt multiple approaches to promote Chinese brands in the international market and increase the influence of home-grown brands through overseas merger and acquisition, self-development, and so on.

ii. **Building a New Import-Oriented Open System**

The new import-oriented open system should be open, balanced, moderate, and diverse. It should help us achieve the following goals: to optimize the allocation of resources; to promote domestic technological progress; to increase effective supply in order to meet the needs of domestic production and life; to improve the quality of our products; to encourage entrepreneurship, innovation, and upgrade of economic structure; to make good use of the foreign exchange reserves; to improve the balance of international payment; and to strengthen cooperation and opening up.

We will mainly import technology innovative products and technologies that will promote industrial upgrading. We will speed up improving the tax policy on the imports of education products and equipment for technological research and development. We will strengthen the protection mechanism for intellectual property including by encouraging governments at all levels to strengthen the intellectual property protection mechanism through the improvement of market environment and by encouraging companies to increase their investment in research and development so as to build a system of technological innovation of products and technological upgrading of industries that is led by companies and driven by the market.

We need to build a dynamic phased import system to guarantee the security of energy and resources. We will properly expand the imports of non-food products on the basis of well ensuring food security, to bring more benefits to domestic consumers. We will expand the imports of medium- and high-end consumer goods especially the foreign high-quality food on the basis of well ensuring food security. We will increase the imports of common consumer goods reasonably and reduce the import tariffs on consumer goods. We will strive to develop the import of service trade, enlarge its scale, improve its structure, increase the percentage and scale of import of financial insurance services, information services, and other services. We will also increase the import of patent services, personal services, cultural and creative services and the import of tourism services and technology-intensive services. We will continue to enhance the facilitation of import trade, develop the import promotion platforms, and strengthen the management of nontraditional imports to encourage people to spend in the domestic market.

iii. **Building a New Open System for Cross-Border E-Commerce**

We need to improve the management of e-commerce payment. On the one hand, we should support the healthy and orderly development of the cross-border e-commerce payment platforms. On the other hand, we should gradually improve the management and supervision of e-commerce payment in order to let e-commerce payment fully support and guarantee the rapid development of cross-border e-commerce and lay a solid foundation for the new system of cross-border e-commerce.

We need to improve customs supervision. We will enact laws on customs enforcement in cross-border e-commerce to provide legal basis for customs supervision, build a new model of import and export inspection and supervision in cross-border e-commerce, accelerate developing a comprehensive e-commerce service platform for cross-border trade that is connected to the customs' network, and strengthen the information statistical work, analysis, and management about cross-border e-commerce by the customs.

We need to improve the credit system. We will speed up setting up a cross-border e-commerce accreditation system to verify all the companies in cross-border e-commerce and complete their credit registration in order to manage them based on the credit information provided by their customers and ensure the identity authenticity of both sides of the cross-border trade. We will also connect the credit rating of small and medium e-commerce businesses with their financing so as to raise their credit awareness and prevent fraud.

We need to build a comprehensive service system. We will work hard to build overseas warehouses, improve financing services for the cross-border e-commerce platforms, and small and medium businesses engaged in cross-border e-commerce. We will also build and improve a reliable public service platform for mobile finance and develop relevant policies for related application services.

iv. Giving Greater Autonomy to the Pilot Free Trade Zones and Explore in Construction of Free Trade Ports

We will give greater autonomy in deepening reform and opening up to the pilot free trade zones set up in 11 provinces (regions/cities) in 3 batches and take further steps to reform our trade management system, the customs management system and the health and quarantine system, the foreign investment management model of pre-establishment national treatment plus a negative list, the commercial system, the intellectual property protection system, the government service system, and the during- and after-event supervision system. Our aim is to produce replicable and generalizable institutions and mechanisms that can be applied in different regions nationwide for further opening up.

As we accumulate more and more reform experiences from the building of these pilot free trade zones, the central government will set up more pilot free trade ports. Shanghai Port, Tianjin Port, Guangzhou Port, Qingdao Port, Dalian Port, Ningbo Port, Haikou Port, and Fangchenggang Port may be included in the scope of the exploration. In the pilot free trade ports, the level of opening up and trade liberalization and facilitation is higher, the restrictions by the government on international trade and investment are less, the public services for trade and investment and the business environment are better, and the market rules and laws are closer to international high-standard ones. In a word, they will set a model of the modern and open economic system. Exploration of pilot free trade zones and ports must be in line with our realities and development interest. We should bear in mind not to be conservative or radical in opening up.

v. Creating a Comprehensive Landscape of Opening Up that Links Eastern and Western China and Coordinates the Inland the Coastal Areas Under the Belt and Road Initiative

Under the guiding principles of the Belt and Road Initiative (BRI) and the principle of achieving shared growth through discussion and collaboration, we will work hard to implement the strategy of free trade zones, improve the regional opening up landscape, further open the west region, facilitate the coordinated development of opening up internally and externally, in inland areas and coastal areas and of the east region and the west region, thus forging a new and harmonious landscape of regional opening up.

Based on the BRI, we will promote in-depth integration of China's economy with the global economy. We should uphold the new idea of open development and the idea of amity, sincerity, mutual benefit, and inclusiveness, adhere to the principle of achieving shared growth through discussion and collaboration, jointly promote strategic mutual trust, trade cooperation, and cultural exchanges, strive to develop mutually beneficial cooperation marked by in-depth integration. We will promote two-way opening up, orderly flow of international and domestic production factors, efficient allocation of resources, and in-depth integration of the domestic market with the international market, to open wider to the world and improve the bilateral and multilateral cooperation mechanisms. We should let companies play as the main players and give full play to the functions of the market. We will also develop pragmatic cooperation with other countries and regions to bring benefits to both sides and create a comprehensive landscape of opening up links the east and the west and coordinates the inland and coastal areas. We will develop a scientific plan for opening up, strike a balance between all-round opening up and key areas' opening up, keep a fine rhythm and order, and make the best use of the advantages of our regime and comparative advantages. We need to be fully aware of the principles, content, directions, major tasks of cooperation both at home and abroad. We should prevent the risks in the process of opening up and strive to blaze a new trail, new landscape, and new model for opening up. We will let the BRI play a leading role in the establishment of a new and open economic system and make the system to be more open, cooperative, inclusive, balanced, and sustainable. We will promote the ideas of innovation, coordination, openness, green development, and sharing. We should improve the relationship between efficiency and equity by leveraging the basic role of market in resource allocation and the important functions of government, promote people-centered economic development, and strive to achieve the target of common prosperity through common growth, to bring the benefits of development to the people, thus bringing our people and the government closer.

13.3.3 Approaches to Building a New System for an Open Investment and Finance

i. **Further Promoting the Liberalization and Facilitation of Foreign Investment and Creating a Supportive Environment for Foreign Investment**

We will reform and innovate our policies on the utilization of foreign investment with the new idea of development, take high-level policies to promote the liberalization and facilitation of trade and investment, comprehensively implement the pre-establishment national treatment plus a negative list system, expand market access, and open the service industry wider. We will also provide greater right to marketization, liberalization, and facilitation to foreign investors and work to protect their legitimate rights and interests. We should treat all the companies registered in China equally.

We will reduce items of inspection and fines and make a list of charges for businesses. We will improve the laws and regulations on the protection of intellectual property and make more efforts to crack down on the infringement of them. In addition, we will strive to improve the environment for business operation and innovation to make it stable, fair, transparent, and predictable, lower the cost, and improve the efficiency of market operation so as to enhance our international competitiveness. We will improve our public services for foreign-invested companies, making China the best investment destination for foreign investors where the encouraging business environment can provide convenience for foreign companies, organizations, and people to engage in exchange and cooperation with their Chinese counterparts. The government should provide better public services and an encouraging business environment for foreign-invested companies. It should adjust the *Catalog for the Guidance of Industries for Foreign Investment* in time to guide the foreign investors to adjust the distribution structure of foreign investment in line with the regional development structure in the 13th Five-Year Plan, and to channel more foreign funds to the central and west regions. We will also promote the revision and update of laws and regulations on foreign investment in keeping with the times. The management of foreign funds will gradually shift from the pre-approval to the high-quality services and the during- and after-event supervision. Foreign investment policies should encourage foreign-funded companies to proactively undertake social responsibilities as multinational companies which can bring benefits to society, environment, and their employees, and prevent serious offenses or misconducts.

The utilization of foreign investment should follow the steps of regional economic development and be in line with the overall development strategies and major functions of different regions across China. We will make full use of the comparative advantages of coastal areas, inland areas, and border areas and promote them to complement each other with advantages in opening up. We will promote the structural transformation and upgrading of foreign-funded companies in the east area and coastal areas and expand our participation in the international division of labor so as to take the lead in moving our industries to the medium and high end. In this way, we aim to shift the focus of using foreign funds from larger quantity to higher quality. In addition, we will work hard to make the middle and west regions and the border provinces and areas more attractive, to drive forward the industrial development and urbanization of backward areas.

We will improve the structure of foreign investment and increase indirect foreign investment in securities, bonds, and credit. We will also ease the investment restrictions on eligible foreign institutional investors and ease the restrictions on the merger and acquisition of Chinese companies or businesses by foreign companies. We will allow or encourage foreign companies to participate in the reform and reorganization of state-owned companies and encourage state-owned companies to become multinational companies. We will take the reform and reorganization of state-owned companies as a major approach to expand opening up and attract foreign investment, especially attracting foreign investment to merger and reorganize the zombie companies with too heavy debt to be energized, on condition that the state assets won't be lost.

ii. **Deepening the Reform of the Overseas Investment Systems, Establishing Global Presence, and Promoting International Cooperation in Production Capacity**

We should attach equal importance to "bringing in" and "going global", proactively negotiate investment protection agreement with the major investors, improve the bilateral protection mechanism and risk alert system, and promote further opening up by two-way investment. We will implement the approval system instead of the registration system for overseas investment, further streamline the approval of overseas investment, administer the overseas investment and international cooperation in a unified and centralized manner, delegate the power of examination and approval, provide better services, and enhance the mutual reinforcement between the financial services, fiscal services, legal services, consultation services, and security services on the one hand and the development of overseas investment on the other hand. We will establish and improve the laws and regulations on the management, supervision, insurance, tax, and other services for overseas investment. We will further improve the income tax policies for overseas investment companies, strengthen cooperation and coordination in international taxation, give more fiscal and tax support to overseas investment in key fields, enhance the level of tax administration and service for overseas investment companies. In addition, we will innovate our way of overseas investment, promote cooperation in international production capability, build a network of trade, investment and finance, production and service that is open to the world and foster new advantages in international economic cooperation and competition.

iii. **Accelerating the Opening Up of the Financial Industry**

The government needs to strengthen the top-level design of the system, work hard to reform the state-owned financial institutions, proactively promote the development of capital investment, financial market, and foreign exchange market, encourage orderly and effective competition in the financial, foreign exchange, and capital markets, and allow all types of eligible capital to join in investing in and financing of the service industry. We will provide more open and fair services for both investment and financing to ensure equal financial services for all types of market players, promote the development of real economy with the support from the financial sector, and prevent financial risks and debt risks. We will also proactively encourage our financial companies and institutions to expand their operation to the international market, strengthen the international cooperation, promote the international capital flows, drive forward the development of international financial businesses and financial network by cooperating with the Asian Infrastructure Investment Bank, the BRICS New Development Bank, and other multilateral financial institutions, enhance cooperation in the financial sector and in investment and financing practices under the Belt and Road Initiative, maintain a stable regional financial market, and prevent international financial risks and their spreading across the world.

iv. Deepening the Reform of the Foreign Exchange Management System and Promote Worldwide Adoption of the Renminbi

We will proactively promote the RMB to the world, gradually liberalize the capital account and promote two-way flows of the indirect investment of foreign investors and domestic investors. We will work hard to build international financial centers in Beijing, Shanghai, Shenzhen, and Hong Kong, strengthen the financial cooperation between the Chinese Mainland and Hong Kong, relax restrictions on the RMB QFII and QDII, open the domestic RMB market step-by-step, continue to promote the use of RMB in settlement, pricing, transaction, exchange, repatriation and reserve in international trade, investment and credit, and gradually extend the use of RMB in international settlement to commodity trade, international investment, international credit, international procurement, external aid, and international production capability cooperation. While striving to crack down on the international money laundering crime, we will loosen the amount limits on cross-border RMB settlement, RMB flow, and RMB cash carrying to facilitate the cross-border circulation of RMB and support the development of China Union Pay, Alipay, and Wechat finance in the international financial and currency markets.

13.3.4 *Approaches to Building a New System for an Open Social Governance*

i. **Reforming Our Social Administration System and Building a New Open Social Governance System in Which the Government Is Responsible**

The reform and opening up are important tools for the government to develop the social economy. The society today faces many problems and disadvantages due to the unilateral government administration system. The government should resolutely reform the systems, policies, and measures of social regulation, work harder to improve our social governance system and institutions and mechanisms, transform the way of social governance and the traditional single administration, promote the reform and opening up of social undertakings, and establish a law-based social governance system allowing the public to participate and requiring all members of the society to cooperate, in which the Party committees exercise the leadership and the governments assume responsibilities. It is a new open social governance system with multiple ways coexisting which aims to form a social governance landscape of co-building, co-governing, and sharing.

To build the new open social governance system in which the government is responsible, we need to proactively promote the development of basic public services, shore up the weak links in people's life and promote the full coverage of the social security system to improve people's livelihood. We will also improve the way the government provides public services, promote the development of the community-level social management and service system, and enhance public services in communities in urban and rural areas. We will also improve and innovate the services for the migrant population and special groups. We should be always open to public opinions and ensure people's rights to express their concerns, protect and coordinate their basic rights and interests, hold the government officials and Party leaders who curb people's voices accountable. We will properly handle the tensions among the people, improve the mechanism led by the Party and government to protect people's rights, upgrade the petition system, and optimize the coordination of people's mediation, administrative mediation, and judicial mediation. In addition, we will improve the risk assessment mechanism of major decisions to social stability, strengthen the public security system and enterprise safe production infrastructure, and prevent serious and major accidents.

ii. Developing Social Organizations, Cultivating Talents for Social Governance, and Fully Leveraging the Role of All Participants in Social Governance

As an important component of national development, the development of social organizations is as important as that of economic organizations and political organizations. To build a modern social governance system, we need to first clarify the status of social organizations. And then we should make the best use of these organizations. Last but not the least, we should strengthen the management and regulation of these organizations, stimulate their vitality, and build a new open social governance system with diverse participants.

We must pay much attention to the development of social organizations and stimulate their vitality. On the one hand, we need to work hard to reform our administrative system including by separating the government from social organizations; promoting the social organizations to make clear their rights and responsibilities, practicing law-based self-governance and make good use of their functions; separating the trade associations and commercial chambers from the administrative departments; giving priority to the development of trade associations in commerce, science and technology, philanthropy, and community services in urban and rural areas; supporting the development of volunteer organizations and other new social organizations in legislation, policy, and services. We will also cultivate specialized talents for the development of social organizations and social governance, create an good environment for the social activists and the social organizations to participate in social governance. We will also delegate relevant public services and affairs to social organizations so as to let them make a greater contributions to social governance. In addition, the government should enhance the management of social organizations and foreign non-government organizations in China, have them registered and guide their activities according to law and let them play a positive role.

iii. **Promoting the Development of Closer People-to-People Ties and Social Undertakings and Realizing the Socialist Core Values in Social Governance Practice**

The policies and the social governance plans developed by the government must demonstrate the value of the socialist culture and the socialist system and must meet the requirements of the new open economic system, the open global economy, and the trend of globalization. Our social governance will gradually transit from regulatory to open one, thus building an open socialist social governance system, and promote the development of social undertakings such as education, health care, culture, sports, old-age care, social security, social safety, social intermediation, social aid, social welfare, and social organizations in the open society and open economy. We will bring in social capital and foreign capital to develop social undertakings and proactively develop public welfare institutions, social aid institutions, social service institutions, and other social organization institutions. We will also work hard to promote the closer people-to-people ties, enhance the efforts of targeted poverty reduction and alleviation, and combine traditional administration of social governance with the rule of law, rule of virtue, self-governance and multiparty consultation to promote inclusive and coordinated development, gradually narrow the gaps between urban and rural areas, between regions and between industries in terms of social status, social income, social treatment, and social security, increase the mobility of social strata, the interaction of the poor and the rich, the integration of ethnic groups and the easiness of entry and exit, thereby ensuring the freedom of housing, transportation, employment, entrepreneurship, and building an open, transparent, mobile, inclusive, democratic, law-based, fair, orderly, harmonious, stable, and secure society.

iv. **Implementing the Comprehensive Strategic Layout of Rule of Law and Building an Equitable, Just, Open, and Harmonious Society**

We must implement the comprehensive strategy of rule of law in social governance and establish full-fledged legislative, judicial, law enforcement systems, and policies. We will transform the social governance mechanism and approaches. While encouraging all social members to address social tensions and disputes through consultation and self-governance, we will attach great importance to law-based social governance and work hard to build the public service, public affairs management, and public security systems. We will strengthen the legal protection for national security and social security to build peace in China. We will crack down on crimes including pornography, gambling, drug abuse, gangdom crime, and abducting, protect people's rights and interests, and develop and regulate the social undertakings and social organizations. We will enhance the social cohesion, maintain the social stability and peace, prevent risks in social governance, and promote harmonious development of the society.

v. Using Modern Technologies to Innovate Social Governance

The modernization of our social governance faces many problems, including outdated ideas, poor governance capability, and backward governance level, especially insufficient application of modern technologies. Today, to maintain social safety, we are adopting more technologies like image collection, security checks, and GPS. In the future, we will apply the modern high-tech means including the internet information technology, Internet of Things, mobile communication technology, big data technology, cloud computing technology, remote sensing technology, AI technology, and technology of medicopsychology in the practices of social governance in order to improve the social governance capability and level, thus forming a more socialized, legalized, intelligentialized, and professional social governance. We will also proactively use modern technologies to establish an open social governance system, including accelerating dealing with online petitions, obtaining appeals, opinions, and plans about social governance on the internet, and publicizing the administrative, judicial, and law enforcement activities in social governance. We will work hard to address social tensions and disputes and enhance the effectiveness and efficiency of social governance to build an open, transparent, fair, civilized, and harmonious society.

CHAPTER 14

Digital Trade: Strategic Significance and Policy Recommendations

Jiechang Xia

The concept of digital trade derives from digital economy. Digital trade takes the form of e-commerce in its early days and it is the natural result of globalization and digital economy.[1] Currently, the academic community has not reached a consensus on the definition of the concept. One generally acknowledged definition is "domestic business and international trade activities on the basis of the internet and the internet technologies; the internet and the internet-based technologies play a significant role in coordination, production, delivery of products and services in those

[1] In 2016, the digital economy accounted for around 50 percent of the GDP of developed countries (the US, Japan, Germany, and the UK). The value of digital trade in the US ranked the top of the world, exceeding USD10 trillion, accounting for over 58 percent of the GDP. In major countries, the value of integrated digital economy largely accounted for over 70 percent of their total GDP and even close to 90 percent in some of the countries. Refer to *White Paper on the Development of China's Digital Economy 2017*, http://www.xinhuanet.com/2017-07/17/c_1121331237.htm.

J. Xia (✉)
National Academy of Economic Strategy, Chinese Academy of Social Sciences, Beijing, China

D. He et al. (eds.), *Chinese Finance Policy for a New Era*,
https://doi.org/10.1007/978-981-33-4054-1_14

activities".[2] The digital trade industry includes four categories: digital content services, digital search engine services, internet social media, and cloud-based internet service providers.

14.1 If Not Now, When?

14.1.1 Technological Advances Are Changing Traditional Trade Models

According to the traditional theories on international trade, the differences of the demand for products and services in different countries (or regions) gave rise to activities of trade. In *An Inquiry into the Nature and Causes of the Wealth of Nations*, Adam Smith, the father of the science of economics said that the most significant improvement in the productive force comes from the division of labor, which is always followed by the exchange. We can infer from this straightforward logic chain that the progress of productive force is another important condition for the emergence of the division of labor and exchange. In his fundamental thesis on the theory of endogenous economic growth, Romer (1990) emphasized the importance of technology. He thought the technology plays a key role in economic growth and the new products and processes produced by the research and development departments enlarge the range of products produced by the intermediate product production departments. In fact, from the perspective of the history of economic thought, be it the classical economic school, the neoclassical growth theory or the endogenous growth theory, all hold the technology advance in high regard. And throughout the history of humanity, it was the technological innovations that made the industrial revolution in the eighteenth century generate historical changes in people's way of life and mode of production.

Since the 3rd industrial revolution, the new mode of production as represented by computer has brought profound changes to people's way of life and production. In the trade area, from the perspective of technological innovation, the internet technology has penetrated into all aspects of production and life since 1990s. Today, the life without computer technology and the internet is unimaginable. Under this circumstances,

[2] Jeff Horowitz, "U.S. International Trade Commission's Digital Trade Roundtable: Discussion Summary", *Journal of International Commerce and Economics*, October 2015, https://www.usitc.gov/.

a new economic model—digital economy, has gradually taken shape.[3] Based on that, big data technology, cloud computing, Internet of Things, new ways of information collection and storage, and new business models have significantly changed the traditional ways of trade. For example, thanks to the progress in the internet-related technologies, we can trade products and services like financial remittance transaction and translation service with people across the Pacific Ocean at home. The burgeoning e-commerce industry based on the digital technologies and the cross-border e-commerce platforms have kicked off a new revolution that will completely transform the traditional ways of trade.

Joseph Alois Schumpeter, a famous scholar has a similar view. He thought that original production factors can be rearranged through technological innovation and a new mode of production may lead to monopoly by increasing productivity, thus producing the excess return. A sign of the newly arranged production factors is that technological innovation will create a new market. In fact, the digital trade originates from the R&D and production based on the digital technologies, the exchange based on the digital information and the whole industrial chain of digital economy generated by those activities.

From the supply-side perspective, the changes that the digital technologies brought to business models can be seen in the de-platform and disintermediation trends and in the simplification of trade process base on the information collection. Take digital service for example. The businesses can analyze the customers' spending habits and future tendency using the big data technology to realize targeted advertisement placement, thus reducing costs and increasing efficiency. From the demand-side perspective, the digital products are wielding a significant influence over people's way of life in daily transportation, entertainment, and social networking. People's increasing reliance on these products is leading to growing market demands.

[3] In the *G20 Leaders' Communique* at G20 Hangzhou Summit (2016), the digital economy was defined as a series of economic activities powered by the digital knowledge and information as a key production factor, based on the modern information technology as a key vehicle and driven by the effective use of the information and communication technology as an important force for promoting efficiency and optimizing economic structure.

14.1.2 *Social and Economic Development in the New Era Provides Favorable Conditions for Digital Trade*

Throughout the past 40 years since the launch of reform and opening up, we have made impressive achievements in economic development. We have seen significant changes in the economic structure, people's livelihood, and spending habits. All these have laid down a solid foundation for the development of the digital trade.

First, the market structure has fundamentally changed. The burgeoning development of the service industry and the upcoming era of service economy are driving forward the development of service trade. From the perspective of industrial division of the digital trade, digital service, search engine, social media, and cloud computing service all have prominent features of the age of service economy. As our economy enters the age of "new normal", the servitization of the manufacturing industry, the service-oriented manufacturing, and the integration and interaction of the digital industry with other industries have become a major sign of the economic transformation and upgrading and of the transition from high-speed development to high-quality development in China. It is against such a background that the digital trade has emerged, developed, and grown prosperous.

Second, people's spending habits have changed significantly. We have made significant progress in social and economic development since the launch of reform and opening up. People's lifestyles, especially their spending habits, are changing as their purchasing power is growing. They bring no cash as they go out, claim their express deliveries as they go home, pay by scanning QR codes, and buy things on the cross-border online platforms. High-speed railway, payment by scanning QR codes, sharing bikes, and online shopping are nicknamed as the new Four Great Inventions of China by overseas netizens. As the mobile internet computing and smartphones develop, the forms and content of the digital trade are increasingly recognized by the public. People have unconsciously accepted the products and services of the digital trade. This is the mass base for the development of China's digital trade.

Third, people's demand for high-quality products is growing. As people's spending capability and lifestyles change, their demand for high-quality products and leisure time is also growing. Compared with products in the traditional trade, products in the digital trade mainly focus on satisfying people's demand for a better life. For example, the Smart

Home and Smart City based on smartphones, tablet computers, wearable equipment, and telemedicine have made people's life much easier. Digital products like online games, VoD, digital music, and digital publications have greatly diversified people's cultural life. The global online retail networks on the basis of B2B model and B2C model provide convenient purchasing service, fast logistics service, and multiple product choices so that people can buy products or services across the world without going out, thus satisfying people's growing demand for a better material life. The strong demand of people is the market foundation for the development of the digital trade.

Four, the Belt and Road Initiative (BRI) has expanded our market. Since the launch of the BRI, our trade relationship with countries and regions along the routes is getting closer. According to the comparison of our economic structure with that of those countries and regions, we almost have an absolute comparative advantage in the digital trade. For example, Alibaba, a Chinese e-commerce platform, has become a role model for countries and regions along the routes. And our telecommunications infrastructure and mobile internet technology are also badly needed by these countries and regions. In this sense, the digital trade in China has a broad international market.

14.1.3 Transition to High-Quality Development Entail New Objectives for Digital Trade Development

To develop the digital trade is an urgent requirement as we strive to build a modern economic system and complete the development transformation as well as an important measure to realize the strategic development goals in the new era. On October 18, 2017, President Xi Jinping mentioned "build a modern economic system" for the first time in the report to the 19th National Congress of the CPC and said that China's economy has been transitioning from a phase of rapid growth to a stage of high-quality development. As we all know, we have followed a path of rapid growth marked by quantity expansion since the launch of reform and opening up. After the 40-year rapid development, we have largely meet the basic needs. In the new era marked by the demand for higher quality and returns, the focus of our work is to enhance the quality of the supply.

In the field of foreign trade, the momentum of our rapid development came mostly from the fast growth of exports. For a rather long time, the advantages of our exports concentrated on the labor-intensive industries, which rely on the low-cost human resources and raw materials to develop the processing industry with products exported to the developed countries in Europe and North America and acquire the tiny price difference in the division of global value chain. But as more and more countries participate in the global value chain, China's traditional advantage of lower price for the means of production is overtaken by some southeastern Asian countries like Vietnam. The high-polluting, high-consumption, and low added value model driven by traditional development methods cannot be sustained any longer. China has a pressing need to transform its foreign trade.

Therefore, with the transition from high-speed development to high-quality development of China's economy, in the new era, we should first fully leverage the role of investment, consumption, and export to drive forward the economic development in foreign trade. Judging from the characteristics of the digital trade, it has unparalleled advantages over the traditional trade in logistics, business model, and market recognition. The developed countries represented by those in North America and Europe, have promoted the digital trade as their national strategies. Therefore, at the critical stage, to attach greater importance to the digital trade in line with the changes of the economic situation at home and abroad is an objective requirement for us to maintain and improve our competitiveness in foreign trade.

To our delight, in the trend of business model transformation brought by the digital technology revolution in the twenty-first century, China's companies are showing increasingly strong growth momentum in the international arena.[4] The internet companies represented by BAT (Baidu, Alibaba, and Tencent) and many emerging online business platforms have grown as the main carriers of foreign trade in the age of digital economy as well as an important force in the international competition with the developed countries.

[4] According to Bloomberg News, by June 2017, Alibaba Group has leaped to the sixth of the world's Top 10 companies. Among the Top 5 companies, only Alphabet and Amazon were internet companies. In other words, among the Top 6 companies, only Alibaba and Amazon are internet companies. According to the definition by the U.S. International Trade Commission, that is an important sign of digital trade.

14.2 Problems and Challenges

14.2.1 The Statistics System Is Not in Line with International Standards

Compared with the detailed categorization of statistics in digital trade and the sophisticated work in data tracking by the developed countries, especially the US, the importance we attach to the data collection work in digital trade is insignificant as seen in the incomplete data collection in the sector, the lack of a corresponding statistical mechanism in the National Bureau of Statistics and the lack of categorized collection of data of the four categories of digital trade. In the digital trade, most of the economic activities occur in the service industry including the information technology and cross-border e-commerce. The Ministry of Commerce, which is in charge of China's trade and commerce, also has some problems in this aspect. It fails to develop a systematic and chronical database with the numbers scattering in very few reports. Data collection in the digital trade faces problems of ambiguous categorization and incontinuity in time. Therefore, it is hard to analyze China's digital trade accurately at the micro level.

14.2.2 Weak Voice in the International Rule-Making

A global regime for digital trade has yet to be established. But some developed countries in the west attempt to impose their domestic standards to the world so as to have a say in the world. Currently, the US and the major economies in the European Union have signed some bilateral or multilateral trade agreements in digital trade. Take the European Union for example. The international standards on digital trade were provided in the European Union–Vietnam Free Trade Agreement (December 2015) and the EU–Canada Comprehensive Economic Trade Agreement (February 2017). But in many free trade agreements signed by China, we have not attached enough importance to digital trade-related topics. The US, in contrast, is the first country in the west to define, describe, and regulate the digital trade. The US strongly proposed, in many WTO negotiations, that the GATT principles and zero tariff principle should be applied to digital products. But those proposals were opposed by some other countries like EU who stood for the GATS standards which were good for the domestic markets of developing countries that could hardly compete with developed countries. Afterward, the US tried hard to spread its digital trade standards through a series of free trade agreements. In contrast, what China is doing is to accept the international standards. A lot more work needs to be done in promoting China's domestic standards to the world.

14.2.3 Insufficient Telecommunications Infrastructure

Although we have proposed the Broadband China Strategy as early as 2013 and proposed the strategic goals including "optical fiber in every urban household and broadband in every rural household" and a schedule, more work needs to be done to promote the construction of telecommunications infrastructure in China in terms of the actual implementation effect. For example, the connection speed of broadband in urban areas is still low. In many rural areas, especially the old revolutionary base areas, areas with concentration of ethnic minorities, border areas, and poor areas, the penetration rate of the internet remains low. Even in some urban areas, more work needs to be done to improve the speed and stability of the mobile internet and the coverage of the signals. In addition, though we have eased the restrictions on market access, since the huge amount of early investment in building telecommunications infrastructure has already been made, the private capital has not been deeply or widely involved in this area, which to a large extent leads to monopoly of state-owned companies and notoriously high charges. The gap in the global flow of data between China and the developed countries is obvious. We rank the 38th in the global link of data, lagging far behind big economies like the US, Germany, the UK, France, and Japan.

14.2.4 Supervision Is Not in Line with the Development of Digital Trade

Digital products are intangible, virtual, and transmittable in nature. People can easily trade digital products and services via the internet. But we have not come up with appropriate approaches to strengthen the supervision. For example, there is no specific articles in the Customs Law to regulate the digital copies of movies transmitted through the internet across borders. In this sense, it is difficult to regulate things like tax collection, customs supervision, and property rights protection. We can say that there is in fact a blank in the laws and regulations on digital trade. In some extreme cases, the local law enforcement authorities even have no laws to refer to.

14.3 Experiences of Other Major Economies

14.3.1 Development of Digital Trade Among APEC Members

Among the APEC members, the top 3 in the 2016 digital trade index ranking are the US, Australia, and Canada and the last 3 are Peru, the Philippines, and Vietnam. Obviously, within APEC, it is still the developed countries that have comparative advantages over other members and the digital trade indices of developing countries remain low.

14.3.2 Digital Trade in the US, the UK, and Japan

i. **The United States**

The US is the first to get an insight into the secrets of digital trade and to start to make rules and regulations on relevant issues. In as early as 1997, the US released *A Framework for Global Electronic Commerce*, an analysis of emerging online retail. Then in 1998, the US Department of Commerce released *The Emerging Digital Economy*, another analysis report. The report outlined the framework of the trend from the industrial economy to the digital economy, making a stir across the world. In 2013, the U.S. International Trade Commission released the first *Digital Trade Report* which studied and predicted the development trend of digital trade, considered the digital trade an important factor to promote other trade, and introduced a method to calculate the potential influence of digital trade on the US economy. Since 2011, as for the cloud computing, platform service, digital products, and so on, the US has released a series of strategic plans including the *Big Data Research and Development Initiative, Federal Cloud Computing Strategy*, and *Technology and Policy to Support Data-driven Innovation.*

The US also leads the world in making international rules on digital trade. For example, the U.S. International Trade Commission is the first professional organization to define and categorize the digital trade. Although it has certain disagreements with some countries including EU in this sense,[5] the US government has imposed its own standards on digital trade as important binding conditions onto a series of bilateral and multilateral trade negotiations led by it. By 2015, it has signed 15 free trade agreements with 20 countries. Almost all these agreements have separate chapters or articles on e-commerce to regulate the cross-border digital trade, except the *US–Israel Free Trade Agreement* and *North America Free Trade Agreement* which were signed earlier.

ii. **The United Kingdom**

As one of the earliest capitalist powers, the UK has also shown significant interest in the digital economy and digital trade. In 2015, the UK government released the *Digital Economy Strategy 2015–2018*, making digital economy the national strategy. In March 2017, it issued 7 strategies in the *Digital UK Strategy 2017*, including infrastructure connectivity, technological training, industrial development, integration of industries, cybersecurity, digital government, and open data. Specifically, the UK aimed to build the world-class digital connection infrastructure, make digital skills accessible to everyone, make the UK the best place to start and develop digital economy, help every UK company develop digital businesses, foster the most secure online environment for work and life, maintain the leading role of the UK government, and unleash the potential of data to boost the UK economy.[6]

In terms of implementation of the strategies, in order to promote the development of digital trade, the UK government made great efforts in another two aspects. First, it established a supporting system for exports, including establishing a smart database (GREAT.gov.uk) with the help of digital technologies thus connecting itself with Alibaba (China) and Amazon (US) to promote online business. Second, it improved the customs service system, including establishing a new digital technology-based customs declaration system (CDS) that is more flexible and efficient

[5] The US suggested on many occasions that the free transmission and the cross-border flow of data via the internet should not be limited. But it faced strong opposition, even in the TPP negotiations. Therefore, restrictive covenants on the free online transmission of data were not included in the text.

[6] https://www.gov.uk/government/publications/uk-digital-strategy/uk-digital-strategy.

to replace the old one so as to better adapt to the new trend of trade development.[7]

iii. **Japan**

The Japanese government once tried to mitigate the influence of the financial crisis and to shore up the insufficient domestic innovation capability by developing the digital economy. In as early as 2009, Japan released the *Innovation Plan of Digital Japan* (*ICT Hatoyama Plan*) in response to the global financial crisis. The plan consisted of 9 actions including the digital industry and cloud computing. In order to promote the development of digital economy, the Japanese government then released a series of strategies such as the *e-Japan Strategy, u-Japan Strategy*, and *i-Japan Strategy* which focused on the application of digital technologies in the manufacturing industry, the development of digital government (the data and services of government departments are available to the public in all places at all time) and cybersecurity. In particular, all the political parties of Japan followed the US steps in terms of the international rules of digital trade. There was almost no big voice against the US. In the failed TPP negotiations, the opposite voice in Japan was only limited in aspects such as the international arbitration terms, government procurement, food security and opening up in health care, and so on.

14.3.3 Digital Trade in the European Union

In order to adapt to the influence of digital trade that keeps growing, the European Parliament's Committee on International Trade approved the report *Digital Trade Strategy* on November 23, 2017. The report made suggestions on several issues such as e-commerce, internet neutral, and online consumer protection. For example, the report said the EU should set a standard for international rules and agreements on digital trade, ensure that other countries open their digital products and services to the world and that these rules bring more benefits to the people across

[7] *Report on the Digital Trade Strategy Adopted by the European Parliament's Committee on International Trade*, the Economic and Commercial Counselor's Office of the Mission of the PRC to the European Union, http://eu.mofcom.gov.cn/article/jmxw/201711/20171102677442.shtml.

the world, thus making the digital trade respect the fundamental rights of consumers. The report also said that the EU should increase the number of "certificate of sufficiency" for its trading partners. So far, only 5 countries obtained that certificates. At the same time, the report urged the EU to include a chapter about data flow in trade agreements to put a ban on mandatory requirement of localization of data.[8]

In terms of digital trade barriers, as one of the major economies in the world, the EU has certain differences with the US in digital trade in addition to their big differences in personal data protection and cross-border data transmission.[9] In terms of digital single market (DSM), the European Commission released on September 14, 2016 a series of proposals to update and revise the copyright-related rules in digital context. For example, these proposals suggested the rights of new publishers and that we reopen the contracts between authors, producers, and publishers, allow limited exceptions of the copyright of texts and data mining, establish a new copyright license mechanism for online radio transmission, impose obligations on the online platforms with a large amount of content uploaded by users and require them to work together with content owners to take effective measures to prevent infringements.[10]

To facilitate the digital trade, the EU signed EU–ROK Free Trade Agreement (FTA) with South Korea in Brussels on October 6, 2010. In October 2013, the EU reached a political agreement on key terms of Comprehensive Economic and Trade Agreement (CETA). On December 2, 2015, it signed the EU–Vietnam Free Trade Agreement with Vietnam.

[8] *Report on the Digital Trade Strategy Adopted by the European Parliament's Committee on International Trade*, the Economic and Commercial Counselor's Office of the Mission of the PRC to the European Union, http://eu.mofcom.gov.cn/article/jmxw/201711/20171102677442.shtml.

[9] The digital industries in the EU members can not compete with their US counterparts. In the traditional European culture, people value privacy very much. In 2013, the Snowden event triggered the EU's concern on privacy and national information security. On October 6, 2015, the European Court of Justice ruled that the Safe Harbor Agreement, a transatlantic data transmission agreement signed by the US Department of Commerce and the EU in 2000, was invalid and must be revoked. According to the ruling, large US technological companies can no longer transfer the information of their clients in Europe to the US, but it can set up data centers in Europe.

[10] *The US Digital Trade Working Group Pays Attention to Emerging Digital Trade Barriers*, China Council for the Promotion of International Trade Electronics and Information Industry Sub-council, http://www.ccpitecc.com/article.asp?id=7215.

Currently, the EU is negotiating with another two ASEAN members—Malaysia and Thailand as well as Japan from Asia, aiming at reaching similar agreements. All these already signed agreements have separated terms on the digital trade such as tariff reduction and information protection.

14.4 Conclusions and Development Strategies

14.4.1 Basic Conclusions

First, the digital economy is the foundation for the development of digital trade. The direct cause of the emergence of digital trade is the development of digital economy, and the root cause is the in-depth changes of production pattern triggered by the technological innovation. With the development of communications technologies represented by the computer, electric technologies are transforming the traditional way of life and production profoundly. As the digital technology develops, the manufacturing industry is making use of the internet, digital technologies, and AI increasingly. In the services sector, the cloud computing, big data, Internet of Things, 3D, and VR based on the digital technologies are playing an increasingly important role in every corner of the national economy such as government institutions, education, medical care, and tourism. This has laid a solid foundation for the transition from the traditional trade to the digital trade. In other words, to develop the digital trade is not only an objective requirement of the all-round development of digital economy but also a practical requirement for China's foreign trade to achieve high-quality development.

Second, the development of digital trade is necessary and urgent. On the one hand, on the basis of digital technologies such as the internet, the digital trade provides interactive digital information for both the supply-side and the demand side. The subject matter of such trade is the digital information product. Therefore, the digital trade has unique advantages in cost and speed. The arrival of the "new normal", the transition from high speed to high-quality development and the rapid development of digital economy have brought profound changes to the traditional trade, which in turn requires us to promote the development of digital trade and to pursue new comparative advantages to take the initiative in the international competition. On the other hand, compared with the developed countries in the West, although we started early in this sector, we do not have a great say in making relevant international rules. Currently, the developed countries led by the US have made their domestic rules the international ones by signing a series of bilateral or multilateral free trade agreements. Therefore, it is very important for China in the middle of rising up to develop the digital trade and strive for a greater say in making the international rules.

Third, we lag far behind developed countries in the digital trade. Compared with the developed countries, our digital infrastructure cannot keep up with the market demand of digital trade, the supervision is insufficient, and the attention paid is not enough. Specifically, we have a lot of work to do in improving our telecommunications infrastructure, in particular in the penetration rate of the internet and the speed of internet connection and in lowering the internet charges. At the same time, the new problems brought by the digital trade such as the customs supervision and tariffs collection still have no legal solutions. We have not had a dedicated functional department to track the data of digital trade of developed countries. In a whole, we lag far behind the developed countries in the west in terms of top-level design and coordination in digital trade.

14.4.2 Development Strategies

First, we should attach great importance to the development of digital economy. The digital economy is the source and foundation of the digital trade. At the second collective learning about the implementation of national big data strategy, the Political Bureau of the CPC Central Committee suggested that we should develop the digital economy that is centered on data and promote the integrated development of the real economy and the digital economy. Researches suggest that every 10 percent of digital growth will bring 0.5–0.62 percent increase in per capita GDP.[11] Therefore, we should strive to develop the digital economy, develop highly competitive digital industries, promote the integration and interaction of digital economy with businesses in the manufacturing industry and the service industry, and gradually promote the application of digital technologies at the same time. On the one hand, we should

[11] Zhang Xinxin, The Digital Economy Is Changing China—Analysing China's New Economic Heights from the Digital Economy, Xinhuanet.com, http://news.xinhua-net.com/politics/2017-12/17/c_1122122520.htm, 17 December.

encourage the development of new forms of digital businesses, establish a negative list in the digital economy, and encourage innovations based on the market demand. On the other hand, we should speed up the digital transformation of traditional industries and make use of new ways of production and organization based on the digital technologies to improve productivity and production. The aim of all these steps is to consolidate the foundation of the digital trade.

Second, we should improve the digital infrastructure. The broadband is the root of as well as the fundamental technology for the burgeoning development of our digital trade. The speed, penetration rate, and cost of broadband directly determine the depth and width of digital trade development. On the basis of the Broadband China Strategy, we should promote our work in the following three aspects: first, we should attach greater importance to the digital infrastructure. Strategically, we should place the digital infrastructure construction in a position as important as water supply, electricity supply, and road network construction and try to improve the connection speed in urban areas and expand the broadband coverage in rural areas; second, we should expand the market access to digital infrastructure and make full use of the "Catfish Effect" of the private capital to promote technological research and development and introduce advanced technologies from abroad, while leveraging the leading role of the state-owned companies in infrastructure investment so as to improve our digital infrastructure; third, we should continue to strengthen the research and development of new technologies, especially to improve the speed and stability of the mobile internet and provide tax and fee cuts and fiscal support for companies to promote the application of digital technologies and integration with other industries.

Third, we should build digital free trade zones. In November 2017, Alibaba Group together with the Malaysian government established the first digital free trade zone (DFTZ) in the world. The DFTZ is a platform based on the internet that provides trade opportunities for small and medium-sized companies in countries across the world. If a company keeps good credit records in trade, it will receive preferential treatment in the future. On that platform, we can narrow the geographical boundaries and expand the market. We can learn from this practice when we try to develop the digital trade. As we promote the Belt and Road Initiative, we can work together with the customs and immigration inspection authorities on the basis of our e-commerce platform to build a global digital free trade zone network that is supported by major cities and accessible to all the countries and regions along the routes of the Belt and Road, and finally cover the whole world in the future.

Four, we should gradually improve the government supervision. The biggest challenge facing the government in supervision over the digital trade is that the process of digital trade can be finished in virtual environment easily without any taxes paid. The US opposed taxation on the digital trade on many occasions, which has significantly improved the development of digital trade in the US. Due to our national reality, the one-size-fits-all tax deduction policy is not practical. We should strengthen our work in the following two aspects: first, we should include the digital trade in the customs supervision and strengthen supervision over the digital trade by making relevant laws and making use of technologies. In the current *Customs Law*, there are no rules regulating the digital trade. Therefore, we need to revise the law in time according to the new changes of the era. In addition, we should cooperate with the internet supervision authorities and cross-border e-commerce platforms in sharing and supervising data regularly, thus acquiring an understanding of the situation of digital trade in China; second, we should provide better services for the export of digital products. For example, we should offer tax refund to eligible companies to enhance the competitiveness of our digital products in the international market.

Fifth, we should become actively involved in the making of international rules. Currently, the major international rules on digital trade concentrate on three super large free trade agreements: TPP, TTIP, and TISA. The WTO agreements like GATT and GATS have digital trade-related rules. And negotiations under TISA have not made any progress because related countries have many disputes. From the already failed TPP led by the US and a series of bilateral and multilateral agreements, it can be seen that a framework of international rules and regulations on digital trade has taken shape. In fact, according to the texts of these agreements,the rules and regulations in TPP are the international versions of the domestic ones in the US. Therefore, we need to conduct an in-depth research in the US proposals and have a precise judgment of their strategic intention. On the one hand, we should proactively participate in the negotiations on the international service trade agreements, making China's voice heard in the international arena and offering China's wisdom. On the other hand, in the current and future bilateral or multilateral agreements, especially in the negotiations with countries or regions along the routes of the Belt and Road on trade agreements, we should include terms on digital trade that we stand for in order to take initiative.

Sixth, we should strive to develop some flagship companies in the digital trade. From the perspective of the division of the global value chain, large multinational corporations in the world take firm hold of the production link which has higher added value by the advantages of technology, capital, and large-scale operation. Actually, in the field of digital trade, such unicorn companies are commonly seen in the world. In the US, apart from Amazon and eBay, there are StubHub, Classifieds, Etsy of C2C and Steam, an e-game, and software platform. These flagship companies serve as an important platform for the US to improve its international competitiveness in digital trade and formulate international rules that are favorable to the US itself. In China, although Alibaba Group ranks among the Top 10 companies across the world, we have not built a team of internationally competitive companies in the industry subdivision compared with these world leaders. This makes China lose competitiveness and voice in the global arena. Therefore, on the one hand, we should continue to increase our support for the development of internationally competitive companies such as BAT (Baidu, Alibaba, and Tencent), and on the other hand, we should develop some digital trade companies in the subdivision of industries by means of fiscal and tax policies and talent attraction. For example, we should improve the services in manufacturing industries and promote the digitalization of companies in the service industry in order to foster some large-scale comprehensive companies as drivers in the digital trade and some other flagship companies in industry subdivisions that are quite profitable.

Reference

P. M. Romer. (1990). "Endogenous Technological Change". *Journal of Political Economy*, 98, S71–S102.

CHAPTER 15

Tourism in China: Fresh Aspiration in a New Era

Rui Song

At the 19th National Congress of the Communist Party of China, General Secretary Xi Jinping delivered a report *Secure a Decisive Victory in Building a Moderately Prosperous Society in All Respects and Strive for the Great Success of Socialism with Chinese Characteristics for a New Era*. This report depicts a blueprint of the great rejuvenation of the Chinese nation and outlines a series of new thoughts, new conclusions, new targets, and new plans and decisions. In the report, the judgments that our socialism with Chinese characteristics has entered a new era and that the principal tension facing Chinese society has evolved are of great importance. These judgments have a profound influence on many areas of our social and economic development, including tourism.

R. Song (✉)
Chinese Academy of Social Sciences, National Academy of Economic Strategy, Beijing, China

D. He et al. (eds.), *Chinese Finance Policy for a New Era*,
https://doi.org/10.1007/978-981-33-4054-1_15

15.1 A New Historical Phase

Over the past 40 years since the launch of reform and opening up, our tourism has made impressive progress from taking-off, high-speed development to high-quality development. Currently, we are at the key stage of the process of expanding overall influence, transforming our growth model, improving the quality of our development, and shifting to new growth drivers. We face an urgent need to achieve further development by finding a new strategic positioning and conducting new reforms.

15.1.1 Take Off Stage: Opening Up and Early Reform

From the founding of the People's Republic of China till 1978, the tourism mainly focused on dealing with foreign affairs. At that time, it did not have any feature of an established industry. The reform and opening up initiative started the development of modern tourism in China. From 1978 until early 1990s, our tourism industry started to take off.

In 1979, Deng Xiaoping said that since tourism had great potential, we must attach great importance to it and speed up its development. That was the first time we thought about treating tourism as an economic industry. In 1981, the State Council held the first national conference on tourism and pointed out that tourism was a comprehensive economic undertaking, an integral part of our national economy and an undertaking essential to our national development and people's livelihood. That conference defined tourism as an industry in economy.

Due to the lack of foreign currency reserves, the tourism development at that time aimed at earning more foreign currency. We took a series of measures to expand inbound tourism but did not encourage, publicize, or oppose domestic tourism. Faced with the problem of poor tourism infrastructure and an inadequate tourism supply system, we encouraged all social members including the central government, local governments, government departments, social groups, and individuals to contribute to the development of tourism and to make the best use of foreign funds so as to attract investment to the catering industry, travel agencies, and the transportation industry. In 1979, the earliest three of the first batch of joint venture projects approved were related to the tourism industry. In 1984, the first joint venture business—Jianguo Hotel, which is managed by a foreign group, was established.

In that stage, one of the core tasks of reform was to promote the transition of tourism management from government-oriented to market-oriented and from direct management to indirect management. In 1985, the State Council forwarded the *Report on the Issues in the Reform of Tourism System* submitted by the National Tourism Administration. It proposed that the management system for tourism should be characterized by "separation from government, centralized leadership, tiered management with separated business operations and open to the international market as a whole". In the same year, the State Council issued the first administrative regulation in the history of the tourism industry, the *Provisional Regulations on the Management of Travel Agencies*. In 1987, as a standard for the industry, the *Rating of Stars for Foreign Related Hotels* was issued, which marked the beginning of the standard development of the tourism industry.

As we strived to develop inbound tourism, the *Report on the Issues in the Reform of Tourism System* stressed that we should attach equal importance to international and domestic tourism. In 1990, we lifted the restrictions on individual travels to Singapore, Malaysia, and Thailand as a pilot trial for the opening up of outbound tourism.

15.1.2 High-Speed Development: Opening Internally and Deepening Reform

From the 1990s till the 2000s, our tourism industry was in a process of high-speed development, in which we focused on expanding the supply of tourist products and diversifying the forms of travel to satisfy people's fast-growing need for travel.

In terms of industrial positioning, in 1992, the State Council released the *Decision on Accelerating the Development of the Tertiary Industry*, stating that tourism is a key link in the tertiary industry. In 1998, tourism was defined as a new growth area in our national economy at the Central Economic Work Conference. In 2006, the Outline for China's Tourism During the 11th Five-Year Plan stated that we should develop tourism into a major industry in our national economy. In 2009, in the *Opinions on Accelerating the Development of the Tourism Industry*, the State Council mentioned for the first time that tourism would be developed to be a pillar of our national economy and be part of modern services to satisfy the people's needs.

In the three markets, inbound tourism registered stable growth with only slight fall in a few years. The domestic tourism market kept a high growth rate and the growth momentum in outbound tourism was even higher. In 1993, the State Council forwarded the *Opinions on Proactively Developing Domestic Tourism* submitted by the National Tourism Administration and proposed that we should energize the market, follow the right leadership, strengthen the management, and improve the development quality. In 1995, we started the two-day weekend system. In 1997, we proposed the guideline that we should vigorously develop inbound tourism, proactively develop domestic tourism, and moderately develop outbound tourism, and held a work conference on outbound tourism. In the same year, on the basis of pilot projects of Hong Kong and Macao tourism and border tourism, we lifted the restrictions on self-supported outbound travels. In 1999, the establishment of the "golden week" holiday boosted domestic tourism and a series of activities, such as quality rating of tourist resorts and selection of tourist cities, improved the quality of tourist products. In 2005, we proposed the guideline that we should vigorously develop inbound tourism, standardize the development of outbound tourism, and promote the overall development of domestic tourism. In 2009, the guideline was revised as that we should vigorously develop domestic tourism, proactively develop inbound tourism and develop outbound tourism in an orderly way.

15.1.3 High-Quality Development: Two-Way Opening Up and Deepening of Reform

In recent years, our tourism entered the stage of high-quality development. The development of tourism mainly focuses on improving the quality of tourist products to meet the people's ever-growing needs for diversified, personalized, and high-quality tourist products.

In terms of awareness of the industry, in 2016, the General Office of the State Council issued the *Opinions on Further Expanding Spending on Tourism, Culture, Sports, Health Care, Old-Age Care, Education, and Training*, proposing that we should develop industries for people's happiness and ranking tourism the top of these industries.

In terms of the industrial structure, modern technologies have a wide application in tourism. Different forms of tourism have registered rapid growth. The integration of tourism with other industries is accelerating.

The industry's structure is getting more and more diverse and sophisticated. For example, innovation in the catering industry is increasing fast. The development of shared accommodation and guesthouses is picking up in speed. Tourism and entertainment attach more importance to leisure and quality. The tourist products have more cultural attributes. Online travel agencies and their offline counterparts speed up the integration with each other. Online tourism and custom-made tourism are in full swing. New forms of tourism keep emerging, such as cruising, self-driving tour, sports tour, low altitude tour, and health care tour.

In terms of driving force of the industry, tourism is increasingly market-oriented and law-based. Tourism has attracted capital from different sources. In 2013, we developed and issued the *Tourism Law*. As the deepening of reform speeds up, problems that restrict the development of tourism such as land use, financing, taxation, and planning have been resolved to some extent.

As the report to the 19th National Congress of the CPC said, our socialism with Chinese characteristics has entered a new era. As we strive to secure a decisive victory in building a moderately prosperous society in all respects and move on with our all-out efforts to build a great modern socialist country, the tension between the people's ever-growing needs for a better life and the inadequate and imbalanced development is becoming prominent. China is playing an increasingly important role in the international arena and is making more and more contribution to humanity and therefore, the international community harbors a higher expectation for China in addressing global issues. Against the background of the new era, in the face of new tension of our society and our new role on the international platform, tourism will have to shoulder a new mission and adapt its functions, industry positioning, and international exchanges accordingly.

15.2 Two Basic Principles

In the new era, the development of China's tourism should follow two major principles: domestically, we should leverage the supporting role of tourism in addressing the basic social tension, building a moderately prosperous society in all respects, and developing modern socialism; internationally, we should better leverage its unique role in building new international relations, participating in the global governance system, and building a community with a shared future for humanity.

15.2.1 The Supporting Role of Tourism in Building a Moderately Prosperous Society in All Respects and Socialist Modernization

Now and in the future, we should start from the goal of developing modern socialism and realizing the great rejuvenation of the Chinese nation, center on building a moderately prosperous society in all respects, and pay more attention to the role of tourism in improving people's well-being, realizing social harmony, balancing regional development, improving cultural development, protecting ecological environment, and improving our national image. Especially when we face the tension between the people's ever-growing needs for a better life and the inadequate and imbalanced development, we should pay great attention to social equity and people's well-being in tourism development. We should let our people get a sense of achievement, equity, and happiness through the development of tourism so as to support the building of a moderately prosperous society in all respects and provide support for developing modern socialism.

15.2.2 Unique Role of Tourism in Participating in Global Governance and Building a Community with a Shared Future for Humanity

Tourism is an important channel for promoting cultural exchanges between different countries and promoting economic development of different countries. It is also an important vehicle for China to participate in the global development and governance, establishing a new type of international relationship and building a community with a shared future for humanity. As the largest source of outbound tourists and the fourth largest destination in terms of inbound tourism revenue, China is playing an increasingly important role in the global tourist economy. Looking into the future, we should try to improve our national image as a big country and participate in the global governance system through the tourism development. We should, based on our resource and market advantages, with the joint efforts of the government, international organizations, trade unions, tourism companies, and the general public, improve the international influence of our tourism in the world. In addition, we will develop tourism as an important channel for China to participate in the global development and public governance.

15.3 Maxmizing the Contribution of Tourism Toward National Development and Socialist Modernization

The report to the 19th National Congress of the CPC makes clear that the overarching task of upholding and developing socialism with Chinese characteristics is to realize socialist modernization and national rejuvenation, and that on the basis of finishing the building of a moderately prosperous society in all respects, a two-step approach should be taken to build China into a great modern socialist country that is prosperous, strong, democratic, culturally advanced, harmonious, and beautiful by the middle of the twenty-first century. That is to say, we will achieve the goal of building a moderately prosperous society in all aspects by 2020 and build China into a great modern socialist country that is prosperous, strong, democratic, culturally advanced, harmonious, and beautiful by 2050. Therefore, we should adjust the functions and positioning of tourism development to align the goals.

15.3.1 From Economic Functions to Comprehensive Functions

Our understanding of the functions of tourism is deepening as we develop the industry in practice. In the early years of the reform and opening up, we attached more importance to the inbound tourism market and to earning more foreign currency. After the domestic tourism started to take off in the 1990s, our major task became expanding domestic consumption to drive forward the economic growth. Currently, we have launched a series of new thoughts and new strategies including the "five-sphere integrated plan" to promote economic, political, cultural, social, and ecological advancement, the "Four Comprehensives" including comprehensively building a moderately prosperous society, comprehensively deepening reform, comprehensively implementing the rule of law, and comprehensively strengthening Party discipline, and the "Five Development Concepts" of innovation, harmonizaiton, green, openness, and sharing. Our focus of the development of tourism should be shifted from its economic functions such as earning more foreign currency, stimulating domestic demand, and driving economic development to noneconomic functions such as improving people's livelihood, realizing social harmony, promoting cultural development, balancing regional development, protecting ecological environment, and improving our national image. As we strive to achieve the Two Centennial Goals, the transition of our focus in tourism from its economic functions to comprehensive functions has become natural. We need to strengthen our work in the following three aspects.

15.3.1.1 Affirming the Dual Role of Tourism

Since the founding of the People's Republic of China, our tourism has been transformed from a public utility to an industry. At present and even in the future, we should start from the goal of developing socialist modernization and realizing the great rejuvenation of the Chinese nation, center on building a moderately prosperous society in all respects and reiterate the dual attributes of tourism as an industry and a public utility. Apart from its economic benefits, we need to pay more attention to its role in improving people's well-being, realizing social harmony, balancing regional development, promoting cultural development, protecting ecological environment, and improving our national image. Apart from letting the market play a decisive role in allocating resources in competitive sectors, we should attach more importance to the significant role of government in ensuring people's rights of enjoying public holidays and traveling. Apart from providing diverse commercial services, we should also improve the public facilities and services. Apart from paying attention to efficiency, we should also attach equal importance to equity in the development of tourism.

15.3.1.2 Identifying Major Tasks in the Development of Tourism

In a rather long time, the principal tension facing our society was the tension between the people's ever-growing material and cultural needs and the backward productive force. According to the report to the 19th National Congress of the CPC, what we face now is the tension between the people's ever-growing needs for a better life and the imbalanced and under development. Travel represents people's longing for a better life. Now we have relatively adequate material supply, and more and more people regard travel as a rigid demand which is important for people's mental health. But from the perspective of regional differences, the urban–rural gap, traveling groups, time–space distribution, consumption levels, and service supply, issues of inadequacy and imbalance are still commonly seen in the development of tourism. Our major task is to address the tension between the people's ever-growing needs for better traveling and the inadequate and imbalanced development of tourism, which will then help us deal with the principal tension between the people's ever-growing needs for a better life and the imbalanced and under development in China.

15.3.1.3 Adjusting Tourism Development Approach

Over the past 30 years, our tourism has expanded in its industrial scale and economic influence. However, compared with the stunning development speed and rapid expansion, the industrial structure, service quality, and operational efficiency of the industry need further improvement. Currently, China's economy is in a pivotal period in the transformation of its growth model, its structural improvement, and its shift to new growth drivers. Accordingly, our way of tourism development should be shifted from pursuing speed and quantity to pursuing efficiency and quality. We should adjust the performance assessment system for tourism development, the government evaluation system, and the focus of industrial policies so as to change the situation that the tourism development is mainly powered by heavy input of resources, labor force, and capital, and improve the quality and efficiency of China's tourism through system innovation.

15.3.2 From the Pillar Industry of Strategic Significance to the Propeller of Socialist Modernization

We should adjust the positioning of tourism according to its function changes. In the past, tourism was seen as a pillar industry of strategic significance to the national economy and a modern service industry to satisfy the people in a better way. Now, it serves as a propeller for building a moderately prosperous society in all respects and for achieving socialist modernization.

The positioning of tourism is a dynamic process adjusted according to social and economic development and changes in tourism development. In the new era, we should fully leverage the comprehensive leading role of tourism in building a moderately prosperous society in all aspects and in achieving socialist modernization. On the one hand, we should further expand the scale of tourism, improve its industrial structure, increase its efficiency, and improve its quality of growth so as to support our national economy strategically. On the other hand, we should pay more attention to its comprehensive leading role in improving people's livelihood, realizing social harmony, balancing regional development, promoting

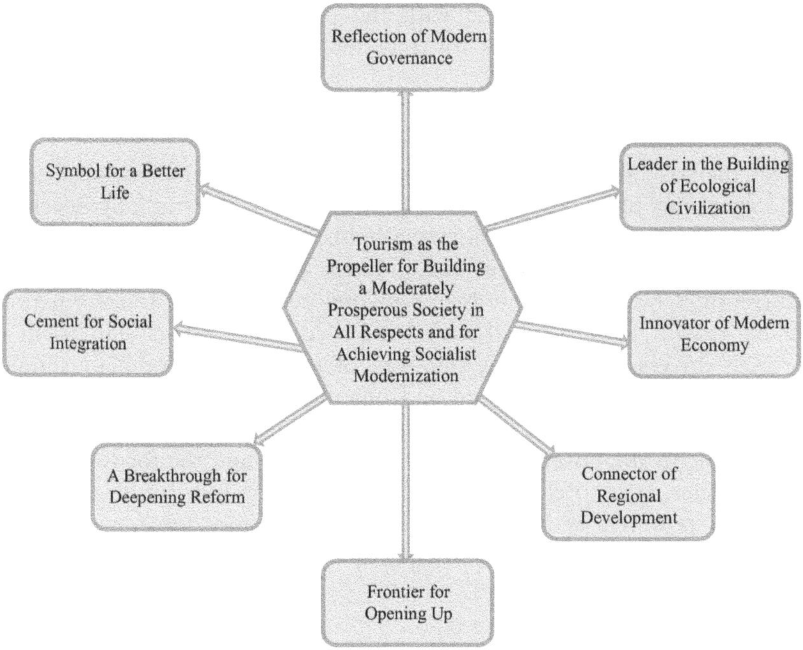

Fig. 15.1 Tourism—the propeller for building a moderately prosperous society in all respects and for achieving socialist modernization

ecological advancement, building modern economy, and realizing modern governance, and make it the propeller for building a moderately prosperous society in all respects and for achieving socialist modernization (see Fig. 15.1).

15.3.2.1 Symbol for a Better Life

At the press conference of the 18th National Congress of the CPC, General Secretary Xi Jinping said, "our goal is to strive for a better life for our people". The report to the 19th National Congress of the CPC said that the principal tension facing Chinese society now is the tension between the people's ever-growing needs for a better life and the inadequate and imbalanced development.

Today, tourism has become an integral part of Chinese people's life and an important sign of better life. It is also a way to gain a sense of happiness. But China's tourism also faces many problems such as inadequate and imbalanced development. Of all these problems, inequality and time limit in travel are the sharpest ones. On the one hand, tourism has not become a social activity for all. Due to many subjective and objective factors, there is still a large proportion of people who cannot enjoy traveling. The ever-widening gap between the rich and the poor and the resulting consumption gap have led to a sharp difference in exercising the right to travel among different groups of people. On the other hand, people cannot arrange their travels at their will. The paid leave system has not been established nationwide, so people have to travel during statutory holidays, especially during long holidays such as the National Day holiday. During these holidays, famous tourist attractions, transportation, hotels, ecological environment are faced with tremendous pressure and people's travel experience falls below their expectations.

As we work hard to build a moderately prosperous society in all respects, we should give high priority to people's right to vacation and travel, promote the nationwide application of paid leave and provide travel assistance to ensure more people's right to travel. Our aim is to let people enjoy their travels more freely and make tourism a real symbol of a better life.

15.3.2.2 Cement for Social Integration

In the process of all-round social transformation and rapid economic development, the anxiety, insecurity, and untrustworthiness spread across the society as a result of differences in thinking, diverse concerns and needs, complicated social environment, and widening social gap. Particularly, the disadvantaged groups may experience a sense of disappointment and imbalance. To strive for social consensus and promote social integration has become a major task in building a moderately prosperous society in all respects and building a great modern socialist country.

Tourism has a unique role in promoting social integration. On the one hand, tourism is essential in satisfying the people's increasing needs for a better life. Tourism can not only make people feel relaxed and happy, but also broaden people's horizons and enhance their understanding. For the disadvantaged groups, tourism plays a greater role in eliminating their bad mood, stimulating their enthusiasm in joining social affairs, and improving their initiatives, if they are given more opportunities to go out of the usual living environment. On the other hand, domestic and foreign researches have suggested that tourism can promote social integration through economic development, political development, and social culture. Economically, tourism can provide opportunities for more people to participate in the economic development, increase economic returns, improve their skills, and promote employment. Politically, tourism can stimulate people's enthusiasm in participating in social affairs and policymaking and improve their capability of social participation. Socially, tourism can foster an agreement on values, social recognition, participation, and integration.

In the process of building a moderately prosperous society in all respects and building a great modern socialist country that is prosperous, strong, democratic, culturally advanced, harmonious, and beautiful, we should improve all types of systems, encourage participation of all people in tourist activities (as travelers) and in tourism business (as businessmen). We should also leverage the cement role of tourism in connecting different social groups and enhancing social integration, thus providing a sense of achievement, equity, and happiness for more people.

15.3.2.3 A Breakthrough for Deepening Reform

Reform is the most characteristic trait of China in the new era. Since the 18th National Congress of the CPC, the CPC Central Committee with Xi Jinping at its core made an overall, systematic, integrated, and integral advancing plan for deepening reform in all aspects in the new era on the basis of the overarching goal of improving and developing socialism with Chinese characteristics and promoting the modernization of national governance system and capability. By August 2017, the central leading team for "comprehensively deepening reform" had held 38 conferences and issued over 1200 plans, policies, and documents.

Tourism is a comprehensive industry that has a connection with many other industries. In recent years, tourism is increasingly integrated with other industries and its influence in social, economic, cultural, and ecological development is growing stronger. Therefore, it is often seen as a breakthrough for deepening reform in all respects. In recent years, the reforms of land management, tax collection, financing, PPP, the management system for natural resources with national parks as the main part and the "1 plus 3" comprehensive management system including tourism development commissions, tourism policemen, and tourist circuit courts have shown the important role of tourism in driving and even forcing the reforms in relevant sectors.

In the future, tourism will continue to integrate with other industries like transportation, sports, education, medical care, finance, public security, diplomacy, science and technology, and aviation and promote their development and reforms. At the same time, tourism should deepen its own reforms and make greater progress in the reforms of tourism governance system, tourism market supervision, management system for tourist guides, travel agency system, management system for tourist resorts, tourism statistics system, and state-owned tourist enterprises.

15.3.2.4 Frontier For Opening Up

According to the report to the 19th National Congress, China will not close its door to the world; we will only open wider and wider; we should make new ground in pursuing opening up on all fronts; we should pursue the Belt and Road Initiative as a priority, give equal emphasis to "bringing in" and "going global", follow the principle of achieving shared growth through discussion and collaboration and enhance openness and cooperation in building innovation capacity. With these efforts, we hope to make new ground in opening China further through links running from east to west, across the land and over the sea.

Tourism is among the first industries that we open to the world. In the early years of reform and opening up, tourism was the most popular industry for foreign investment. From the first foreign-funded restaurant in 1984 to the first foreign-funded travel agency in 1998, tourism had always been a hotspot for foreign direct investment (FDI) and the most open sector in the opening up of the service industry.

In the future, we need to further promote the opening up of tourism on all fronts. For example, we should promote travel cooperation and exchange under the Belt and Road Initiative, establish a mechanism for friendly cooperation with countries and regions along the BRI routes, facilitate the visa application process, liberalize the traffic rights, promote mutual recognition of licenses and certificates and enhance cooperation in vehicle towing and travel insurance. We will deepen our cooperation in tourism with big countries, neighboring countries, and central and eastern European countries, enhance exchanges with countries friendly with us and developing countries, and promote the building of cross-border tourist cooperation zones and pilot border tourist zones with neighboring countries.

15.3.2.5 Connector of Regional Development

Due to natural, historical, and policy reasons, there is a big social and economic gap between the west (high level) and the east (low level). The differentiated resource allocation and the separated development model of rural and urban areas have aggravated the urban–rural dual economic structure. Narrowing the regional gap and urban–rural gap is a major task in addressing our inadequate and imbalanced development.

The development of tourism can direct the consumption and investment from wealthy areas to poor areas, thus realizing the transfer of wealth from economically developed areas to backward areas and promote positive interaction between different regions and between rural areas and urban areas. In addition, tourism is an important vehicle for regional cooperation. As we work hard to develop our high-speed railway network and air routes, the landscape of regional tourism development is increasingly diverse and balanced.

In the future, with the implementation of three new and major regional strategies namely the Belt and Road Initiative, the integrated development of Beijing–Tianjin–Hebei, the Yangtze River Economic Belt, we will establish a tourism pattern in which the eastern, middle, and western areas interact with each other, give play to complementary advantages, and seek common development. The implementation of the rural revitalization strategy and the building of small towns with unique features will play a more significant role in developing a new urban–rural relationship and promoting integrated urban–rural development.

15.3.2.6 Innovator of Modern Economy

We have passed the stage at which our economic development was driven by input and investment and entered the "new normal". Now, our economic development is increasingly driven by innovation. According to the report to the 19th National Congress of the CPC, innovation is the strategic support for building a modern economic system. We should strengthen research on innovation, strengthen the building of national innovation system, deepen reform of the science and technology system, advocate the culture of innovation, work hard to nurture talents, and make China an innovation-oriented country.

China's tourism is in the process of shifting growth drivers. Over the past 40 years, the growth rate of tourism was much higher than that of the national economy and that of the average of global tourism. The core driver of tourism has undergone two stages. At the first stage, tourism was powered by opening up practices, including opening our tourist destination to international travelers and allowing all types of capital invested in tourism. At the second stage, it was driven by consumption. Chinese people's growing spending in tourism not only boosted the development of domestic tourism but also changed the international landscape of tourism. Now and in the future, the driver of China's tourism development must be shifted to innovation, which can improve the efficiency and quality of tourism.

In the future, we should attach extra attention to innovation in tourism such as the innovation in product/service, management, process, technology, and marketing at company-level, the innovation in competition at industry-level, and the institutional innovation, policy innovation, governance innovation at government-level, and to the combination, integration, and coordination of all the above-mentioned innovations. We should make strategies for innovation in China's tourism development, develop national-level tourism innovation platform, and high-level innovation decision consulting mechanism, conduct systematic researches on the innovation status quo in China's tourism, problems of businesses in making innovations and innovation policies, and issue relevant policies to support nationwide mass entrepreneurship and innovation in tourism.

15.3.2.7 Leader in Ecological Civilization Development

According to the report to the 19th National Congress of the CPC, man and nature form a community of life. We should speed up reform of the system for developing an ecological civilization and build a beautiful China. We should develop a nature reserve system composed mainly of national parks. Ecological civilization is the result of reflection on the traditional industrial civilization as well as a practical and theoretical response to the ever-worsening ecological environment on the earth. Ecological civilization should be built on the basis of respecting and maintaining the nature. We should aim at paying equal attention to current development and the development of future generations so as to lead the transformation of the way of production, life, and consumption.

Compared with other industries, tourism is an energy-conserving and environment-friendly industry and an important handle for building ecological civilization. Moderate tourism development will contribute significantly to ecological conservation, ecological protection, and ecological civilization building. In recent years, the governments at all levels attached enormous importance to environmental protection while developing tourism. The *Tourism Law* adopted in 2013 defined the notion of environmental carrying capacity. China National Tourism Administration and the Ministry of Ecology and Environment are making standards on ecological tourism and evaluating and selecting demonstrative zones for ecological tourism. We have adopted many effective measures such as building functional zones, environment-friendly buildings, ecological toilets, and environment-friendly walkways and using ecological vehicles. Tourism has become the most effective way to carry out the idea that clean waters and green mountains are invaluable assets.

In the future, we should formulate regulations, rules, and relevant standard and certification systems to support sustainable tourism development in line with China's reality on the basis of the overall requirements of building ecological civilization. We should work hard to establish and improve the national park system according to the *Overall Plan for the Building of National Parks*. In addition, we should establish a supervision and early warning system for major tourist resorts, properly handle the traffic during peak hours and prevent risks. We should also work hard to raise people's awareness of ecological civilization.

15.3.2.8 Reflection of Modern Governance

A modern governance system and modern governance capability are major content in developing modern socialism. They represent the quality of institutions and their execution ability of a country. National governance system is a management system to run the country under the leadership of the Communist Party of China. It consists of the institutional mechanisms and the legal and regulatory arrangements in economic, political, cultural, social, ecological advancement, and the Party building. National governance capacity refers to the capacity to manage all types of social affairs through national institutions and systems. To build a modern governance system in line with economic and social development, political development, and cultural development is a major task in many socioeconomic fields.

Tourism is a comprehensive industry that covers many fields. To some extent, the governance capability and system in tourism can reflect comprehensively a country's governance capability and system. As our tourism develops rapidly, the mass tourism becomes more and more personalized and individualized. The tourism supply system will witness a general trend of integration of industries with blurring boundaries. Therefore, the coordination among different government departments and the joint governance by governments and businesses, trade associations, local residents, and tourists are increasingly important. In recent years, relevant authorities have proactively pushed forward reform of comprehensive tourism governance system and made many breakthroughs in the tourism law enforcement and market supervision.

In the future, we should further improve the organization system, institutional system, operation system, assessment system, and guarantee system of modern governance of tourism and encourage participation of diverse parties. We will fully leverage the role of governments, civil social organizations, trade associations, the general public, and tourists themselves and make comprehensive use of legal, administrative, economic, and social means to build a three-dimensional and efficient tourism governance system and improve our tourism governance capability, thus promoting the modernization of national governance system and capability.

The manufacturer's authorised representative in the EU is Springer Nature Customer Service Centre GmbH, Europaplatz 3, 69115 Heidelberg, Germany. If you have any concerns regarding our products, please contact ProductSafety@springernature.com

Printed and bound by CPI Group (UK) Ltd, Croydon, CR0 4YY

30/09/2026

02225326-0017